Handbook of
Preschool Religious Education

HANDBOOK OF PRESCHOOL RELIGIOUS EDUCATION

Edited by
Donald Ratcliff

Religious Education Press
Birmingham, Alabama

Library of Congress Cataloging-in-Publication Data
Handbook of preschool religious education/edited by Donald Ratcliff.
Includes bibliographies and index.
ISBN 0-89135-068-3
1. Christian education of preschool children. I. Ratcliff, Donald.
BV1475.2.H34 1988   88-30868
268′.432—dc19   CIP

Religious Education Press, Inc.
5316 Meadow Brook Road
Birmingham, Alabama 35243
10 9 8 7 6 5 4 3

Religious Education Press publishes books exclusively in religious education and in areas closely related to religious education. It is committed to enhancing and professionalizing religious education through the
publication of serious, significant, and scholarly works.

PUBLISHER TO THE PROFESSION

INTRODUCTION

The *Handbook of Preschool Religious Education* is a broad, comprehensive resource on the religious education of young children. As a handbook, it is a concise and informative summary of topics related to this area of study rather than an "idea book" or an "opinion book." While a number of idea books are available, they rarely have a firm theoretical or research foundation. Sometimes their suggestions are contrary to the best research available. Thus there is a need to "lay again the foundations" for quality religious education, foundations which may spawn new idea books that are thoroughly grounded rather than the result of armchair philosophy or one person's isolated experience.

Overview

The book is divided into three major sections. The first summarizes the general development of preschoolers, including their mental, social, and physical characteristics. General areas of child development most directly related to religious concerns are considered in the second section: preschool religious concepts, moral and faith development, and socialization. Section three concentrates upon methodology and evaluation of preschool religious education.

Chapter one considers the cognitive or mental development of the preschool child. A number of key topics are evaluated, including the ability of children to distinguish appearance and reality, their understanding of causal reasoning, intention, memory, time, number, language, their ability to empathize, and communication skills. Throughout the chapter applications are made to religious education. A concluding section considers how general developmental principles relate to biblical and religious content.

1

A number of other crucial areas of development are considered in chapter two. Physical development is outlined, including motor skills and perceptual characteristics. A subsequent overview of language abilities includes suggestions for encouraging language development. Parent-child relationships and relations to peers are also described. The authors then highlight the prominent emotions of preschoolers, including their fears, aggression, and feelings about death. The chapter concludes with the topics of positive social behavior, sex role development, and the play of young children.

An overview of the religious concepts of young children comprises the content of chapter three. The three European authors of this chapter have done a great deal of research of such concepts in their respective countries. They combine their efforts along with a summary of other significant research in this area to provide a comprehensive survey. The concepts considered include the child's understanding of God, prayer, denomination, and death. The methods used in conducting research, as well as the limitations of the work in this area, round out contents of the chapter.

The moral development of preschoolers is the topic of chapter four. The chapter opens with a description of several theories of moral development. The author then considers the factors that are related to moral behavior in preschoolers. A large section is given to suggestions for promoting moral growth in preschoolers, particularly in the home and church contexts.

Two associates of today's foremost faith development specialist, James Fowler, outline some components of preschoolers' faith in chapter five. Following an outline of Fowler's earliest stages, the authors concentrate their attention upon Mahler's theory of development as it expands upon Fowler's thoughts about the faith of young children. Several case studies from the authors' own research highlight both Fowler's theory and the contribution of Mahler's thought.

Chapter six considers the socialization of the preschooler, particularly socialization in the faith community. After an overview of the theories of Nelson, Westerhoff, and other writers in this area, several specific aspects of this topic are detailed. Socialization into faith is considered within the family, church, preschool, and other contexts. Family systems theory is given careful attention including the important question of whether children can adequately function within an institutionalized context. The chapter concludes with a discussion of how childhood is shortened in modern society and the role of friendships in early childhood.

In chapter seven James Michael Lee emphasizes key concepts and derivative teaching methods which flow from his well-known social-science approach to religious instruction. His chapter offers an abundance of key findings of social-science research that relate to the religious education of preschoolers. The author concentrates upon how an awareness of the teaching dynamic can assist early childhood religious education and make it more effective.

One of the world's foremost authorities on creativity, E. Paul Torrance, and his wife J. Pansy Torrance, summarize many of their thoughts on creativity in education in chapter eight. Creativity is seen as an outgrowth of the image of God and thus is an important component in religious education. In the second half of this chapter the Torrances describe a church curriculum they developed and field tested which combines their creative talents with religious instruction. Specific suggestions for creatively teaching youngsters concepts of God are included.

The ninth chapter considers the relationships between stories and play, as well as how the enactment of stories can aid the understanding and retention of story content by preschoolers. The current research in this area indicates that play is to be understood as a foundation for understanding stories. The structure and content of stories are related to preschoolers' abilities. Consideration is also given to the variation of story structure cross-culturally. Throughout the chapter applications to religious education contexts are suggested, and it concludes with a number of other applications of enactment in religious education contexts.

The final chapter details how religious educators can go about evaluating their programs for effectiveness. Specifying outcomes through objectives, evaluating outcomes, and other aspects of educational design are considered, with an emphasis upon practical applications for religious educators. A brief consideration of how to conduct research in religious education contexts is included.

Top scholars in preschool religious education or closely related fields have contributed their efforts to produce a handbook of superb caliber. Many of the writers have conducted their own significant religious education research with preschoolers. Areas of expertise represented include psychology, sociology, education, philosophy, child and family development, and theology.

What Is a "Preschooler"?

For this book, "preschooler" is defined as the child between three and six years of age. A number of developmental theories have found major changes in children at about five to seven years, although some of these have been challenged by more recent research (see chapter one). The

preschool period ends at age six, since most American children enter
first grade during their seventh year. Another evidence of six years being
a major transition point is the fact that most children begin reading at
about this time, although there is considerable variation in the age of
acquisition of this skill as well.

The beginning of the preschool period is more arbitrary than its end
point. Child developmentalists have often distinguished three age ranges
in early childhood: the infant, toddler, and preschooler, although the age
of each range varies from writer to writer. Many structured programs in
early education begin at the age of three. It is at this age that the child
has acquired sufficient language abilities to think about concepts that
are related to religion. Although important embryonic religious attitudes are being formed during the first three years, this book will
consider the preschool years to begin at age three.

While we have specifically delimited age ranges, authors will sometimes include descriptions of younger children for the purpose of illus-
trating preparatory or foundational processes. Older children are also
considered occasionally for the purpose of contrast in skills and abilities,
or when the performance of older children is likely to be similar to
preschoolers. When age is designated it generally refers to a typical child
or the majority of the children studied at that particular age, although it
should be noted that many children exceed or fall short of the average.

Why a Book on Preschoolers Now?

Recent demographic trends indicate that the number of preschoolers
in our society is increasing and will probably do so for some time. The
increase in births began about five years ago and, except for a downturn
in 1986, has generally continued to increase year by year. The "baby
boom" generation after World War II was followed by a rapid decline in
births during the 1960s and 1970s (the "baby bust"). The impact of this
"bust" can be seen in the current decline in college, high-school, and
elementary enrollments. However, as the baby boomers are now in their
thirties many of them are coming to realize that this is their last chance
for children. While the upturn in the number of babies is not yet
another baby boom, it is a definite change in direction.

A second demographic trend resulting in more preschoolers is the
influx of minorities, particularly from Hispanic countries to the south.
Within the next few decades Spanish-speaking groups (and their descen-
dants) will become the largest minority in the United States, and eventually constitute the majority in California and Texas. Characteristically
this minority has had a higher birth rate than other populations, and
thus many more babies can be expected to be born each year.

As a result of these trends there is a good possibility that a new "baby boom" is around the corner, perhaps one that will rival that of the late 1940s and 1950s. As a result the current increase in preschoolers may accelerate dramatically.

Many of these preschoolers will require day care. The large number of mothers entering the work force outside the home is hardly news to anyone, yet some provision must be made for their preschool children. A number of churches have provided facilities for the care and training of these children. This is a trend that will probably increase. Should government funding of "head start" and other programs for preschoolers be cut (or even remain the same), while the number of preschoolers increases, there will be more and more need for church preschools.

The recent trend toward Christian day schools has spilled over to the preschool population. In fact, churches are more likely to have a school for preschoolers than for school-aged children. The rise in religious preschools is a trend in education which has been overlooked by many who study education. Yet one only has to count the number of churches in any local community that have preschool day care to be impressed by this trend.

Is Preschool Religious Education Possible?

Unfortunately church preschools are often just copies of their secular counterparts. Perhaps the lack of interest in distinctively religious education is due to the mistaken notion that such education is unimportant for this age. The curriculum available is rarely backed by good research, and some researchers have even concluded that it is useless to attempt religious education with young children.

Churches often do little or nothing to influence the budding personality of the preschooler toward religious matters. There is considerable irony in this lack of attention since some psychologists conclude that the basic personality is shaped more during the early years than at any later point in life.

It is the thesis of the present book that religious education of the preschooler *is* possible. Indeed it cannot be avoided—the child will form some opinion of religion as a result of his or her experiences (or lack of experiences).

The present work is intended to give a solid research-based foundation for implementing religious education for preschoolers. Thus it will be helpful to churches with preschool programs that are interested in instilling religious values. In addition it will help Sunday school or catechism teachers and administrators be more effective in instilling religious values in young children. This book is also a resource to religious educators who wish to help parents instill Christian values; the most important religious education is obtained in the home. Educating parents in how to do this effectively should be a top priority. Finally, the book should become a standard work for curriculum developers as well as colleges and seminaries because of the wealth of research it details. Few if any other research-based works in this area exist at present, although it is hoped that others will follow.

Dedication

I am writing this introduction in the midst of a week when I am completely responsible for my own two preschool children, John Wesley (age five) and Stephen Earl (age three). Their mother is taking a much-deserved break by visiting her parents. Meanwhile I am punching keys on a computer, pausing occasionally to mop up spilled water paints. Even though I have completed my two chapters of this book, which involved analysis of a great many research studies by some of the finest psychologists, my children continue to fascinate and mystify me. Why, for example, does John want to see a videotape of a particular "Super-book" television Bible program a seventh time in two days, to the exclusion of a half dozen episodes he has never seen? And why does Stephen insist upon praying each night for our long-deceased cat?

This book may not completely answer either of these questions, but I believe it will help us build a general framework for quality religious education of preschoolers. If that goal is apprehended, the task of this book will be accomplished. To that goal, and my terrific kids, I dedicate this book.

Chapter One:

The Cognitive Development of Preschoolers

DONALD RATCLIFF

> Barbara was puzzled at the five-year-old's understanding of the simple, familiar song. Minutes earlier the class had sung "I will make you fishers of men" complete with the motions of casting out fishing lines and howls of laughter from the children. Afterward Jimmy told her he felt people shouldn't laugh at God and wondered why Jesus used a fishing pole to grab people. Barbara began to wonder what the children *really* did think as they sang the song— could they be visualizing Jesus throwing fishhooks in people's mouths?

There is evidence to suggest that the content of this song, so familiar to preschoolers, is beyond their understanding and may not be fully understandable until the adolescent years. While children are able to memorize the words and even parrot that fishing "stands for" people receiving the message of Christ, most will not understand the true nature of Jesus' statement. In spite of the best teaching, children— particularly preschoolers—will see the song as essentially absurd and ridiculous because of inability to understand the metaphorical language.

It may be that once children reach adolescence and develop the ability to understand such abstract reasoning, the substantive content will be considered childish and not worth their time. Sadder yet, the abstractions (and dozens of others that were beyond the child's ability to understand) may be hopelessly confused and distorted, a remnant of a religion to be discarded in adolescence.

Some have thus concluded that because of the mental limitations of preschoolers (and even older children) the church has nothing to offer youngsters. This is undoubtedly an exaggeration of the problem, and yet a central task remains for serious religious educators: determining what religious content a preschooler can and cannot learn. An important key to solving this problem is identifying the cognitive (mental) abilities of the preschooler; what are the mental assets and limitations in the thinking of young children?

Concepts of Preschoolers

Since the time of the ancient Greeks, people have attempted to describe the nature of concepts. The most accepted approach is to describe concepts in terms of their "properties," the characteristics that define them (Smith & Medin, 1981). For example the concept of "cup" can be described as having three properties: it is rounded, has a handle, and can hold hot as well as cold liquids. The person then tests a new object to see whether it has these three properties; if it does is it identified as a cup (Haber & Runyan, 1986).

While properties may sometimes be used by adults to identify concepts, do preschoolers use this approach? Recent research indicates that young children do not, but rather they rely upon examples in identifying an object as belonging to a conceptual category (Smith & Medin, 1981).

To use the cup example, the youngster first learns to label an object "cup" by seeing examples, and reasonably similar objects will also be called a cup. Rosch (1975) notes that the child compares the best or most typical example of "cup" with a new object. If the new object is closer to that example than the best example of other concepts (such as a bowl or dish), it is identified as a cup. Thus a cracked cup that cannot hold liquids and lacks a handle is still considered a cup.

The first concepts a child learns are called "basic" concepts. They tend to be simpler than other concepts and are more readily identified by children than broader or more specific concepts. Mervis and Crisafi (1982) found that while children as young as two can categorize using a basic concept (such as dog), it is not until they are four that they categorize using broader concepts ("animal") and by five they can use narrower concepts ("beagle"). However, it should be noted that four-year-olds can also use the more specific concepts, given experience and verbal prompting (Waxman, 1985). Thus basic concepts are a priority with younger preschoolers.

Mervis and Crisafi also found that the earlier basic concepts tend to be more differentiated from one another, a tendency confirmed by Gelman (1985b). He also found that inductive reasoning was more likely to be used by four-year-olds when examples were similar. Inference was more likely when less abstract categories and familiar characteristics were used (Gelman, 1985a).

Preschoolers are more skilled at working with certain kinds of concepts than others. This seems likely since first graders were more skilled at answering questions about social regularities (can you change the rules of the game "tag") than about physical or logical regularities (can pencils float in air) (Komatsu & Galotti, 1985). The children indicated that physical regularities such as seasons and gravity could not be altered in this world, but suggested that these might be different in another world.

The idea of using "best examples" indicates that the religious educator should make frequent use of examples in forming new concepts, rather than attempting to teach concepts by teaching features. For example, the story of the good Samaritan will teach sharing better than having children list three aspects of sharing. Practical examples of how *they* can share would help even more.

Existing best examples (or "prototypes") can sometimes be built upon, while at other times new prototypes need to be introduced. This may be why the Bible contains so many human examples of qualities to be admired (such as Hebrews 11); they are prototypes from which people are to understand concepts. Not only are people used as prototypes of qualities to be shunned and admired, but even the temple is used as a prototype for understanding heaven. These "best examples" are in vivid contrast to the more detached nature of theology, which fits the classical theory better which is less suitable for preschoolers' understanding.

Religious educators might take note of the more highly developed concepts of social regularities in preschoolers. Thus descriptions of miracles may not be as surprising to preschoolers as to adults, since regularities in the physical world are apparently not as well understood. Yet content which involves social regularities, particularly those which they have been previously exposed to, is more likely to be understood. To some extent they come to understand that social customs vary from context to context, and perhaps even that modern practices differ from biblical customs, but the abstract meanings of customs and traditions (logical regularities) are less likely to be understood. The understanding of physical variations in another world might indicate that some teaching of a future world or heaven is possible.

These findings indicate that religious educators would use concrete descriptions (as well as many examples) in developing basic concepts, and later in the preschool years begin considering broader and narrower conceptualizations. The tangible is always more accessible to preschoolers, and other kinds of concepts must be based upon previous experience with basic concepts related to concrete objects. We can only abstract what we have experienced.

Appearance and Reality

Child psychologists have sometimes suggested that perception is all-important in how preschoolers identify concepts; outward appearance rather than actual characteristics is given attention. While this is sometimes the case, there are exceptions. Gelman (1985a) cites research in which preschoolers did not associate blackbirds and bats, in spite of both being black, and instead associated flamingos and blackbirds as both being birds even though they are different colors. Yet when more ambiguous concepts are used, youngsters fall back on perceptual appearance rather than conceptual relationship. The latter is most likely when the child is less familiar with the concept (such as gender determined by hair length rather than actual differences).

The distinction between appearance and reality becomes better understood as the preschooler matures. Flavell, Flavell, and Green (1983) exposed three-, four-, and five-year-olds to several objects which had an appearance that was contrary to their actual identity. For example they showed the children a sponge that looked like a rock, and a red car that looked green when viewed through a filter. When asked about the appearance of the object and what the object really was, most four- and five-year-olds and a substantial number of three-year-olds answered correctly.

The small minority who made mistakes tended to report appearance when reality was requested if asked about the *properties* of an object (asked what the *real* color of the car was, they answered "green"). Yet they reported reality when appearance was requested if asked about the identity of objects (asked what an imitation rock *looked like,* they answered "a sponge"). Accuracy clearly improved with age.

Thus the distinction between appearance and reality is made as early as three years of age, yet it initially is unstable and precarious. When asked about appearance, children who answered incorrectly were more likely to report reality when they were asked about actions and identities of objects. In contrast, when asked about reality, children were more likely to describe appearances when asked about size, shape, and color. Such differences are more than cultural artifacts; replication in mainland China produced very similar results (Flavell, Zhang, Zou, Dong, & Qi, 1983). Yet it must be emphasized again that few four- or five-year-olds made *any* errors on these tasks.

A further replication by Taylor and Flavell (1984) yielded similar results. However, when transformations of the objects were used (milk being poured into a colored glass so it looks like Koolaid), three-year-old children who made mistakes were more influenced by the end state of the substance, not just the property or identity.

Clearly the distinction between appearance and reality is fragile during the early preschool years, while older preschoolers have less difficulty with the distinction. When mistakes were made, the most obvious characteristics determined the conclusions made. The poorer performance indicated by some of the earlier research by Jean Piaget apparently involved objects with which the children were unfamiliar.

Flavell, Flavell, and Green (1983) note that the appearance/reality distinction is a basis for religion as well as science, philosophy, and other areas. The concept of a phenomenal world (the world as we experience it) as distinct from a real world (the world as it really is) is foundational to the religious presupposition of a spiritual existence distinct from physical existence. A basic assumption inherent to religious belief is that life is not what it seems, and preschoolers are apparently beginning to understand this.

The appearance/reality distinction is important to the religious education of preschoolers since preschoolers may easily come to believe that these are equated. One thinks of many paintings and movies which are not accurate, yet they will be assumed to be realistic to preschoolers. A child may question this equivalence, but rarely do adults verify such doubts. One thinks of statements such as "the church is God's house." Again the youngster may have his doubts (rightly so theologically), yet adults continue to perpetuate the myth and thus the child does not distinguish reality from the statements.

Conservation

The distinction between appearance and reality relates closely to what Piaget described as "conservation." To illustrate, he poured liquid from one container to another one which was taller and thinner, and preschoolers would generally conclude the amount of liquid had changed since the water line was higher. He further illustrated conservation by lining up two rows of five pennies each, then separating the pennies in one row to make it longer. Preschoolers generally stated the long row of five pennies had more than the short row of five pennies. Thus he concluded that preschoolers (and some older children) do not "conserve," they pay attention to irrelevant features in a transformation and conclude that substantial change occurs when actually the amount or quantity only appeared to change.

Siegler (1981) has taken a more careful look at the Piagetian tasks described above and concluded that these involve far more than one skill (conservation). He has identified several rules which must be developed sequentially to achieve "conservation" in its final form.

In a series of experiments, Siegler found that about one-third of three-year-olds tested paid attention only to the height of the liquid in concluding which had more; the others just guessed. In contrast a large majority of four- and five-year-olds used the dominant dimension (height of the liquid) to determine which had the most. Four- and five-year-olds were far more adept at the pennies task, correctly stating that the longer row of pennies had the same number as the shorter row.

Siegler believes that the difference in preschooler performance between the two tasks is because children can use verification in the pennies task—the children can count the pennies to verify a belief or hunch that the number is unchanged. Such verification is not possible with the liquid containers task, and thus they decide on the basis of appearance rather than contrary hunch they may have.

Siegler concludes that these results imply two phases in children's thinking. At first preschoolers understand that transformations have some effect but are unsure of what that effect is (unless the situation allows verification of their hunch). At this point they decide in favor of appearance or perceptions rather than their suspicions. By the age of eight (when they complete the liquid containers experiment correctly) they are able to understand transformations to the extent that they no longer need outside verification. Other researchers note that minor changes in instructions can result in greater success in this experiment (Hall, Lamb, & Perlmutter, 1986).

These conclusions call into question Piaget's idea that preschoolers lack conservation. Instead, some and perhaps many of them have a notion of conservation, but it is fragile and is easily negated when outward appearance contradicts it and there is no means of verification. Siegler postulates the presence of a "general rule" in preschoolers' thinking in which the most obvious dimension is attended to. When the child has little information about a particular skill or concept, he or she tends to fall back on this general rule rather than use more advanced reasoning.

Sometimes we expect preschoolers to conserve the notion of "being a Christian" across contexts, even though the person's actions change according to context. Thus the child may conclude that being a Christian is only possible in the church building or with church people. Notions to the contrary may need to be confirmed by religious educators, a precursor to the child's eventual understanding of roles and context specific behavior.

The lack of abstract thinking may also be a factor in listening to stories and singing songs by the preschooler. Here the tendency will be to overlook subtle points and concentrate upon the major themes and most salient actions. To foster a more complete understanding, the religious educator will need to emphasize the more subtle elements of story and song, both to encourage conservation skills and to verify the need to attend to these less overt components.

The importance of the "general rule" in unfamiliar domains may be represented in an important observation David Elkind made in his survey of children's religious concepts (1971). He noted that preschoolers have very similar religious concepts, regardless of their denominational affiliation, but these concepts become more differentiated as they grow older. Apparently in their understanding of religion, preschoolers attend to the most salient features of their experiences in developing their religious concepts, since for many this is an unfamiliar area. As they have more experiences with religious concepts, they will take on denominational and theological nuances later in childhood and no longer concentrate solely on the most obvious content, which differs little across denominations: belief in God, Jesus, the Bible as important, and so on (see chapter three).

Causal Reasoning

Jean Piaget's early research concluded that young children understood effects as being due to magic rather than systematic causation (Schultz and Kestenbaum, 1985). More recent research, in contrast, indicates that even three- and four-year-olds understand causal chains to some extent. Even one- and two-year-olds indicate surprise when an expected causal law is violated (if objects fail to collapse when not supported). Although preschoolers may not fully understand causation, the research does not reflect a belief in "magic."

Schultz and Kestenbaum cite a study in which three- and four-year-olds correctly chose a missing illustration in a series of drawings, identifying a needed missing step in a cause and effect relationship. The description of the causal relationship was more complete for the four-year-olds, yet even the three-year-olds were able to identify the relationship. Furthermore, when asked to reverse the sequence, most of the four-year-olds and about half of the three-year-olds were able to do so. Contrary to Piaget's theory, this indicates some ability at thought reversal.

Time delays between cause and effect are more distracting to five-year-olds than older children, say Schultz and Kestenbaum. Yet even four-year-olds were able to attribute causation accurately when a plausible rationale for the delay was provided. The initial event in a sequence was often credited as causative by preschoolers (less so by three-year-olds), while the physical closeness of causal agents and effects influenced the choices of four- and five-year-olds.

By the age of six children were also able to use similarity of property in determining cause and effect (a loud sound being produced by a large lever rather than a small one). While two- and three-year-olds are less consistent in assigning cause and effect relationships, older preschoolers actively seek information by which to understand and explain a sequence of events, Schultz and Kestenbaum conclude.

Cowan (1978) points out that preschoolers involved in a spat often blame one another for beginning the fight, not because of accuracy in reconstructing the event (they may lack the cause/effect reasoning to do so adequately), but because of the most salient feature present: the poke or insult each received.

Religious educators should use the cause and effect reasoning abilities of preschoolers, even though they may be latent at times. "Just because" is a poor rationale for rules, even though teachers and parents quickly become weary from the persistent "why" of preschoolers. Stories need to emphasize likely effects from desirable and undesirable behavior; young children are capable of understanding causal linkages to some extent.

In contrast, two- and three-year-olds are less likely to profit from explanations. Perhaps the best indicator of readiness to gain from causal reasoning is the child's asking "why." Gradually children are more able to develop their own causal reasoning, which can be fostered by prompting the child to think through reasons, rather than immediately supplying the answers.

Immediacy of consequences is important in discipline as well as stories at this age. Short delays between action and consequence may be required in certain contexts, which is more acceptable with older preschoolers. Mentally reconstructing events may help children understand the cause/effect relationship between a behavior and subsequent reinforcement or punishment. The development of causal reasoning is an important aspect of religious education of preschoolers.

Intention

The understanding of intention in causal reasoning is another significant development in preschoolers' cognitive abilities. While some human behavior seems to require more mechanistic explanations, it is thought that most significant behavior is the product of intention.

Schultz and Kestenbaum (1985) cite research which indicates that by five or six, children clearly make moral judgments on the basis of intention. Yet these studies fail to distinguish moral responsibility and intention; cannot one reason about intentions without making moral conclusions?

Psycholinguistic studies indicate that even two-year-olds appear to have some understanding of intention, since they use verbs such as "gonna," "hafta," and "wanna" which signify intention. Other research mentioned by Schultz and Kestenbaum involved five-year-olds who were asked to judge the intentionality of actors in a film. While the children correctly judged intentional actions, these children also judged accidents to be intentional (unlike older children). When live acting was performed, three- and five-year-olds were able to discriminate mistakes from intentional actions in both themselves and others.

In a study of game playing by children three years and older, only those five and above were able to disguise their intentions from others. A "matching" rule appears to exist as young as age three: if an outcome and a stated intention match, the child concludes that the outcome was intended.

Other rules may also be used by children in judging intentionality. The "valiance" rule states that intended outcomes are those that are positive for the actor, whereas negative outcomes to the actor are not considered intentional. The "monitoring" rule states that if the actor monitors a relationship between outcome and action, the outcome is intentional. Children five years and older used both of these rules, whereas four-year-olds did not; younger children tended to see all of the observed behavior as intended (Schultz & Kestenbaum, 1985). Smiling was also used as a cue to intentionality by five- and six-year-olds, while neutral affect and frowning were not.

The intention of story characters is often a key component to understanding biblical and other stories. Clearly children are able to understand intentionality at this age to some extent, although religious educators will probably need to encourage the developing of causal rationales, perhaps by discussing intentions of characters.

Causal reasoning is apparently less developed when viewing films, probably due to the more detached nature of the medium. If videotapes and other passive media are used with preschoolers, these need to be supplemented by questions and perhaps enactment (see chapter nine) which will prompt involved thinking. This would also be the case in storytelling as well; the goal is not just to entertain but to involve and stimulate reasoning abilities.

In some biblical accounts, there may well be a lack of congruence with the rules preschoolers use in causal reasoning. In these cases either the religious educator will need to exclude those stories from the curriculum, or perhaps "simplify" the content by excluding details that are incongruent with the rules

Thinking, Behavior, and Reality

The preschooler's understanding of intention implies a distinction between the inner and outer worlds of the person. Studies by Johnson and Wellman (1982) indicate that first graders (and thus probably preschoolers) are able to think about the mind, including their own minds, and realize that mental activities are not always synonymous with behavior. Even kindergartners believed their real selves would be shifted if they received a brain or mind transplant (Wellman, 1980).

The ability to distinguish reality from mental activity was indicated in research conducted by Wellman and Estes (1985). Children were told to imagine a character *thinking* of a cookie and to imagine a second character actually having a cookie. They were then asked which character could see the cookie and eat it. Well over half of the three-year-olds were correct in their responses, while virtually all of the five-year-olds responded accurately. When asked to sort real from nonreal objects three-year-olds were correct most of the time, while four- and five-year-olds were almost always correct.

In a study involving dramatizations, Wellman (1985) notes that preschoolers used behavior as an indicator of the actor's mental experience; knowing was assumed when correct performance occurred, while children assumed the actor guessed when incorrect performance occurred. Likewise forgetting was inferred by the preschoolers when the actor performed incorrectly and remembering was inferred when the performance was correct. Four-year-olds were particularly likely to infer mental states using only the present behavior.

Yet other evidence points to a clear understanding of a private internal mental world apart from behavior. Wellman (1980) placed an object in one of two boxes which were presented to four-year-olds, then covered both boxes. Covertly the object was removed from the box, without the child realizing it. Upon questioning the child afterward, the preschooler clearly distinguished his or her *mental* representation of where the object was which contradicted the actual location of the object. Thus in situations where conditions allow they can make this important distinction, although they generally identify behavior with mental activity. This private mental representation is usually less salient to the preschooler and is thus obscured in most situations. Wellman also notes research evidence that preschoolers can distinguish ability from performance.

Wellman (1985) conducted experiments which indicate that preschoolers are able to distinguish several *kinds* of mental processes. While three-year-olds were unable to discriminate between remembering and forgetting, as well as thinking and knowing, four-year-olds were able to make such distinctions. Preschoolers could generally distinguish knowing from guessing and remembering from guessing, and guessing was understood to be independent of being correct. After age four children gradually became more consistent in their use of such mental verbs and in their definitions of mental processes.

The distinction between thinking and behavior is manifest in the preschooler more informally as well. One thinks of the child who, in obeying a parent's command to sit down, stated, "I may be sitting down on the outside, but I'm standing up on the inside." Religious educators should take note of this distinction and point out the difference between behavior and thinking in stories. One might even discuss the fact that you can sing a song yet not think about what you are singing. This might encourage children to discuss what they sing and hear, thus illuminating areas of confusion and misunderstanding (as in the opening illustration of this chapter).

To some extent, the religious educator might introduce the need to make thinking and behavior congruent, yet acknowledge that often they are less than that. Perhaps through such discussion the child will become more aware of his or her own mental activities.

Guessing, forgetting, and remembering are often included in the content of religious education, and these can be understood by the preschooler. They are certainly capable of understanding such mental constructs, both in themselves and others, although the educator should certainly refrain from criticizing the child excessively through accusations of guessing. Positive comments for desired responses are always preferred to shaming the child.

Egocentrism

Preschoolers can easily overlook subtle yet important features which are cues to the feelings and thoughts of others; the child may assume a person is happy when he or she sees a smile rather than realizing it is a forced smile. Piaget spoke of the preschooler being "egocentric" in that his or her own perspective is easily projected upon others. But is the preschooler as egocentric as Piaget thought?

Wellman (1985) describes the progression away from egocentrism by noting that older infants realize that what another person sees is not always what the infant sees. However this is a global, all or nothing understanding. By age four or five the child comes to realize that an-

other person can have another perspective; he or she comes to realize
that *how* something looks can vary from person to person as well. This
latter skill requires the child to infer another person's distinct visual
experience.

Many believe that children think they cannot be seen if they keep
their eyes shut. In initial tests of this idea reported by Flavell (1985)
two- to four-year-olds stated others could not see them, while five-year-
olds correctly stated that an adult could still see the child that closed his
or her eyes. Yet when questioned further, the younger preschoolers
stated that the adults *could* see their arms, back, and other body parts.
The apparently egocentric response to the question "Do I see you?" is a
misunderstanding of the question—perhaps the preschoolers were
thinking of their inner selves rather than their outward bodies!

The development of "metacognition," the ability to think about the
mind and its activities, can be facilitated by the religious educator. This
may be an important component of religious education which has been
neglected in favor of more academic matters, yet it is a key aspect of
development at this age. The religious educator is particularly able to
encourage metacognition related to the thinking of others in conflict
situations and thus move the child away from egocentrism.

For example, when the child demands candy the parent or teacher
might respond, "If you ask nice, I'm more likely to give it to you." Later
this communication may become internalized so the preschooler begins
to use such statements mentally. A second example would be that when
a conflict erupts over the use of a toy, the adult might say, "If you take
turns playing with it, the other child will like playing with you more."

Empathy and Understanding Personality

Egocentrism can be displaced by developing empathy, the ability to
infer the feelings of others. Flavell (1985) notes that during infancy the
child may imitate expressions that are observed, almost a reflexive
response, but apparently lacks an understanding of that response. In
contrast, preschoolers are able to infer feelings from facial expressions
and situational context, even when they do not feel those feelings. Early
in the preschool years the inferred feelings are global ("he feels good" or
"he feels bad") but later become more differentiated.

In one study cited by Flavell, three-year-olds were able to predict
what another person *saw* from a different perspective (as noted in
Wellman's study), but could not predict what the other person *thought*.
In contrast the five-year-old could predict thinking as well as perception
from another vantage point. Children three to five years of age often fail
to realize that people can have different thoughts and feelings about the
same situation.

Flavell notes that when asked to describe personality, preschoolers refer to appearance, identity, and externals rather than personal traits. When personal traits *were* mentioned, they tended to be either global ("he's very bad") or self-referenced ("she gives me things").

The limitation in empathizing and understanding personality has two principal areas of application to religious education. First, in interpersonal relationships between children each is often unable to understand the other child's thinking. Helping the child to reflect upon the other's viewpoint, using the golden rule for example, might be of some benefit when two children have had *different* experiences, (such as seeing an event from different angles). Yet conflicts between children may involve different conclusions about the *same* experience, which may be less understandable. The research to date would suggest that trying to explain the other child's thoughts about the situation would probably be fruitless.

A second application is in the understanding of biblical and story characters. Personality is not as well understood by preschoolers, and global traits are often assumed (a character being good or bad), thus the mixture of negative and positive traits is less likely to be comprehended. Again the religious educator may need to decide whether stories with a mixture of personality traits within a character (such as a vile person with some desirable qualities) may need to be deleted or simplified to include only dominant traits.

Memory and Cognition

The child's understanding of memory develops throughout the preschool years. By first grade children already realize that the longer a memory is retained the more uncertain it is and that recall is more difficult than recognition (Wellman, 1985). Even by age three the child realizes that a small number of items are easier to remember than many and that memory is adversely affected by distracting noise (sometimes this is forgotten by the college years!). By five years children realize that adults often remember better than young children and that having a friend share part of a memory task makes it easier. These older preschoolers realize that drawing something helps in recalling a memory, lengthy study aids recall, and retrieval is expedited by external cues. They also realize many factors are irrelevant to the ability to recall.

On the other hand, Wellman notes that preschoolers incorrectly assume that the delay between learning and recall is more important than the number of items to be recalled. Also the children considered effort at a memory task to be more crucial to memory than the length of the task.

As children grow older, attributing recall to effort alone decreases.

Mental variables in memory, such as using associations to increase recall or disinterest decreasing recall, are not appreciated until later in the elementary years.

Wellman notes that preschoolers tend to be unrealistic about their own memory limitations. Four- and five-year-olds consistently predicted that they could recall all items, regardless of how many were presented.

How many items can a child actually remember? To some extent this depends upon how familiar the child is with the content to be recalled. The more familiar the material, the more processes can be performed simultaneously. One estimate comes from a memory task cited by Flavell (1985) in which the average four-year-old is able to recall three or four digits, in contrast to the average adult who can recall five to nine digits. Processing *ideas* is more difficult than recalling digits; five- and six-year-olds can manipulate more than one idea simultaneously, while younger children can handle only one at a time (Hall, Lamb, & Perlmutter, 1986).

Memory tasks are an important component to many religious education activities. Parents and teachers believe themselves to be successful when a child is able to recount a story, song, or other experience accurately. Yet too often the limitations of preschoolers can be overlooked in this area, even by the children themselves. These youngsters can become quite frustrated when unable to perform a memory task which they believe themselves capable of; clearly they tend to overestimate their own memory abilities.

In the religious education of a young child, instructors should take care to provide tasks that are within the child's ability. Preschoolers often want to hear stories and songs over and over, but this is a means of learning for the child. As events are repeated, the child becomes able to grasp more and more until finally the major components are acquired.

One is tempted to place a limit on the number of conceptual items a child can process simultaneously, and to some extent this is possible at least with novel material. The most likely limit in this case would be the three or four items or chunks of information to be processed at one time. Applying this to memorizing a Bible passage, only three or four words would be presented, recited by children, then another three or four words would be learned, and so on (shaping a verbal response).

Yet behavioral shaping has its limitations; the religious educator must keep in mind the necessity of the child's *understanding* the content to be recalled. A child may be able to repeat three or four words, yet fail to comprehend the meaning of what he or she is saying. Such a practice may very well set a lifelong pattern for one's religious life in which words are stated that are devoid of meaning and understanding; the mind and spirituality become compartmentalized from one another. Indeed, how many adults sing hymns and read the Bible in church without thinking about what they are singing or reading? Perhaps this to some extent stems from unwise religious education experiences early in childhood.

While much of this chapter has called into question some of Piaget's conclusions, his most important contribution to cognitive development should also be underscored, the idea that for the child, *doing* is a requirement for *learning* (Cowan, 1978). Thus instead of emphasizing verbal fact learning, religious educators need to use strategies where children act upon the materials, preferably seeing, touching, and imitating (Wadsworth, 1978). Drawing may be a good start, but enacting a story or playing it out with dolls or puppets is even better (see chapter nine).

Animism

Piaget believed that preschoolers were "animistic" in their thinking; they supposedly attribute life to things that are nonliving. Research indicates that this is most likely to occur with objects that make autonomous movements, such as fire (Flavell, 1985).

Richards and Siegler (1984) tested the understanding of living and nonliving objects by four- to seven-year-olds. The children were asked to judge whether objects portrayed in pictures were alive or not. Nonliving objects were rarely believed to be alive by either group, although older children were more likely to affirm that trees and plants were living than were the preschoolers. Afterward the children were asked to name as many living objects as possible, and again nonliving things were almost never named. With this second approach, older children were again more likely to name plants and trees, and they were also more likely to mention *parts* of living things. No evidence was found to support Piaget's notion that young children associate life with motion.

The concept of animism is often seen in cartoons and stories for preschoolers (talking houses, a smiling sun, and so on). Preschoolers are not above speaking in such terms, but apparently they realize that these do not actually happen. Any animism that occurs may be due to the exposure to animism in the stories and television programs!

Religious educators need to be cautious in the use of animistic stories, though not avoid them completely. If a story with animistic features is used, it may be wise for the teacher or parent to comment parenthetically a disclaimer such as "we all know that the wind doesn't talk" and then go on with the story. Children may use animistic language in part because of their love for pretending and imagining.

Religious educators usually have a strong commitment to "the truth" particularly in matters of faith, yet the preschooler has an ability to fantasize which may lack such an allegiance. At this age it would be healthiest for the religious educator to encourage intellectual growth in relation to both reality and fantasy (Cowan, 1978).

Time and Number

The research of preschoolers' understanding of time has been surveyed by Hall, Lamb, and Perlmutter (1986). While Piaget's research indicated that children associate size with age (a larger tree is assumed to be older than a smaller one), other research using "sleeping" dolls indicates a genuine, though simple understanding of time. With additional complexity, however, the children had difficulty with the concept. If two dolls went to sleep at the same time, the first one to awaken was understood to have slept a shorter time, but if the dolls went to sleep at different times, the first to awaken was still thought to have slept less.

Distance can also be confused with time for preschoolers; regardless of whether they ran or walked, the time required for going to school was assumed to be the same. In another study cited by Hall, Lamb, and Perlmutter, five-year-olds indicated that a cat that ran only while a dog barked, would run farther if the dog barked five seconds than if it barked two seconds. Yet when a second speed/distance comparison was added to the task, the children failed to respond correctly. Research also indicates that measurement of time by the use of a clock might not be possible until age seven or eight (Bybee & Sund, 1982).

Flavell (1985) summarizes an extensive literature on the development of the concept of number. There is evidence that number abilities develop naturally during the preschool years in every culture and that children at this age realize that subtraction is a reversal of addition. Not only does the ability to count develop, but most five-year-olds can add or subtract as long as the problems begin with six items or less. By the end of the preschool years youngsters have learned that number is not affected by color, identity, or movement of the items.

With the apparently limited concepts of time and number, religious educators should be careful in their use of terminology related to these. "Long ago" to a preschooler might very well mean last week, while "thousands of soldiers" could be completely meaningless. Certainly the memorization of exact numbers (such as "How many people did Jesus feed?") is likely to be unproductive; religious educators should focus on relationships and major themes rather than numerical facts.

Communication Skills

Two kinds of communication are possible during the preschool years, Flavell (1985) concludes in his survey of the literature in this area. First, informative communications develop which involve facts and ideas. Initially the infant only absorbs communications directed to him or her, later the child is able to respond and thus receive correction for poorly understood information, and finally the preschooler is able to communicate with himself (internally by thinking or externally by talking to the self).

The second variety of communication is statements intended to control the activities of others. As with informative communications, this is at first control from others (complying with demands), then control of others, and finally self-control, one of the most significant developments in the preschool years. Self-control includes being able to plan and maintain that plan over time, and the ability to resist temptation which involves ability to wait and delay of gratification.

Self-control by delay of gratification increases between the ages of two and three, concludes Flavell, and control of self in this manner continues to develop into the school years. Research indicates that delay of rewards is most likely for preschoolers when the reward is not visible; younger preschoolers often focus on the immediate object, making delay of gratification more difficult.

While self-distraction by thinking about other things does not characteristically develop until about age nine, some four- or five-year-olds attempt to distract their own attention from the desired reward by singing, covering their eyes, pounding their feet, verbalizing the need for delay, and even praying to the ceiling!

Communication is central to the task of religious education, and is closely interwoven with language abilities (more on this later). The importance of delay of gratification is important to lifelong success, and the religious educator can help develop this ability by providing metacognitive knowledge in this area. For example, the educator might suggest distracting activities to help in delay of gratification, verbalizing to the child that "looking at it only makes you want it more." With such prompting the child may eventually begin to internalize these ideas in the form of self-statements. Prayer before a snack may inadvertently be a small step in this direction, although giving thanks should be the focus of the child's attention. Perhaps distraction from the treat at hand is a good reason for children to close their eyes when praying!

Language is an important aspect of evaluating preschoolers' learning, usually through speech since written tests require reading skills most preschoolers lack. For example preschoolers might be asked to retell a story or restate ideas, using their own words. This approach is far superior to recitation, since in the latter words are more likely to be repeated without understanding. In addition, the retelling is likely to uncover misconceptions the child may have that need correcting (see chapter ten on evaluation).

Verbalizing can also be used as a part of active learning. Hall, Lamb, and Perlmutter (1986) cite research that indicates that learning by preschoolers can be maximized by an adult describing an ongoing event as it is watched and the child repeating the adult's words. Thus religious educators might consider augmenting media presentations with adult description and the child echoing that description. Again, evaluation should follow in which the event is described by the child in his or her own words.

Language and Cognition

Language interrelates closely with the cognitive development of the child. In fact, a key reason that earlier developmentalists such as Piaget underestimated the cognitive abilities of preschoolers is because they relied heavily upon verbal report even in object manipulation tasks. The child who has a mental skill but is unable to verbalize some indication of that skill might be incorrectly thought to lack the mental ability. Likewise, if children were unable to understand what was required in a task, due to receptive language limitations, they are unlikely to use what cognitive skills they have in that area.

Many of the abilities recently discovered in preschoolers have been due to the development of nonverbal or less verbal measures (Wellman, 1985). In addition researchers note that some earlier researchers, after a child gave a correct response, would probe further until an erroneous response would be produced. In light of the need for verification of skills, noted earlier, the additional probing would be the opposite of verification, leading children to use earlier, less-advanced reasoning rather than their optimum cognitive skills. Schultz and Kestenbaum (1985) note that Piaget's probing for animistic responses was often in the form of leading questions.

Richards and Siegler (1984) performed an entire experiment which indicates that the phrasing of a question could produce completely different responses from a preschooler. The final phrase in the instructions, emphasizing one dimension of a task, resulted in preschoolers making inaccurate judgments, while children who did not receive that phrase made accurate judgments.

The preschooler is apparently limited in his or her use of abstract forms of language. While a child may be able to use, or at least parrot, simple metaphorical speech (Wellman & Estes, 1985) which is incorrectly attributed to animism, in general he or she is not able to understand satire, analogy, metaphor, or irony (Phillips, 1981, Elkind, 1971). These language abilities do not customarily surface until adolescence.

Religious educators should be careful in their use of abstractions in language. Too often young children are expected to understand the tone of voice that denotes sarcasm which implies the comprehension of two levels of speech, such as saying "that's a fast car" (level one) to describe a slow car (level two). Likewise the rich metaphors abundant in many parables and songs used with children (see the illustration that opens this chapter) are best reserved for later when the adolescent can understand them (Goldman, 1964). In a previous review (Ratcliff, 1987) it was noted that the research produces an unclear picture as to when the abstract content of parables can be understood by children, but even the earliest estimate is well beyond the preschool years.

Rote verbalizing without understanding could be possible with preschoolers, repeating phrases without genuine comprehension, but children would be separating cognition from the words they use. As has been mentioned before, this could carry over into adult life so that the person never does come to appreciate the richness of the metaphors and other abstract language. Unfortunately when the child reaches adolescence and can for the first time appreciate the symbolism, he or she may have lost interest ("I learned that as a kid") or worse yet reject the religion that did not make sense earlier (Goldman, 1964).

Can the religious educator use *any* of the parables or stories with multiple meanings (such as C. S. Lewis' *Chronicles of Narnia*)? It can be helpful to give preschoolers experiences that will help prepare them to understand the abstract content of parables later on. For example, the parable of the sower and the seed cannot be understood unless one has an understanding of farming. This can certainly be taught to preschoolers, even having the child grow plants in different kinds of soil, but the parent or teacher should refrain from discussing the spiritual meaning of the parable and probably leave out the section of the story where Jesus told what the seed, sower, and soil stood for. This can come later when the child is able to understand such abstractions.

Should Children Attend Church?

Considering the child's cognitive abilities and limitations, should preschoolers be present in adult church services? This a most controversial issue which has been considered by several authors previously (such as Benson & Stewart, 1979, and Postolos-Cappadora, 1983).

Adult worship generally presents unrealistic challenges for pre-schoolers. The advanced verbal content of most sermons and a majority of the music used in church would probably be incomprehensible to most preschoolers and many school-aged children. Preschoolers exposed to adult level content are probably going to be bored. Boredom usually translates into squirming, whispering preschoolers, which is at best distracting to adults.

Four options may be considered in attempting to resolve this issue. First, the church may totally separate parents and children by having developmentally appropriate content for each. This option should be seriously considered, particularly when the coping abilities of adults in a church are minimal—better separation than resentment by adults and/or children.

A second option, perhaps the least acceptable alternative, is meeting together for every service for the entire length of the service. The result of this approach is likely to be an unfortunate conditioning of children—the church context (and the concept of God) will be associated with boredom, confinement, and punishment. Such associations will produce avoidance of the unpleasant stimulus, behavioral psychology would suggest, an avoidance which is likely to bear fruit in adolescence by a rejection and avoidance of God and church (Dobbins, 1975, and Ratcliff, 1982). On the other hand, if church members are willing to change the service to fit the cognitive abilities of children, the content will necessarily need to be simplified to the point that adults will receive little. Boredom translates into avoidance for adults as well as children. I suspect most adults wish to have spiritually and cognitively challenging services, and it is most difficult to challenge both adults and small children simultaneously.

A third option, used by many churches, is for the morning worship to be divided roughly in half so that adults and children meet together for opening activities, singing, and perhaps a children's sermon. The youngsters would then be dismissed for their own alternative service during the sermon. This sometimes works out quite well, particularly if the pastor or priest has had coursework in child development so that he has some idea of what children can and cannot understand in the children's sermon. But what is often overlooked is the cognitive content of the music—words outside of children's vocabularies (and sometimes adult vocabularies!) are included in many great hymns of the faith. The messages of the music is likely to be outside the experience and cognitive abilities of children. Thus one must either omit many of the wonderful hymns (from which adults could benefit), producing an intellectual and spiritual barrenness, or conversely children will be exposed to and probably participate in singing words they cannot at present understand. As noted previously, this dichotimizes faith from understanding; people learn to mouth the words without thinking the thoughts.

A fourth possibility is to have a smaller section of the church service with adults and children present, in which cognitively simpler songs can be used and perhaps a children's sermon. After perhaps ten or fifteen minutes, the youngsters would be excused to attend their own service (which might include training the child to eventually participate in adult worship—see chapter nine) and adults could then sing adult-level hymns and hear an adult sermon. This would allow for family participation yet age-distinctive content as well. If the adults in church can tolerate some noise and disruption for a brief period of the service, this is a live option.

Rather than relying upon the church service for intergenerational ministry, family-based religious education is a far better alternative. Parents need to be trained in providing such education in the home (see Barber & Peatling, 1981, and Barber, 1984). Sunday school or special classes should be provided by churches to provide education of parents in child development and religious education of one's children.

This is not to say, however, that children should never be allowed to attend complete adult services. If children are curious or an occasional circumstance requires it, children can tolerate some of the ambiguity of adult worship. In such circumstances, it is wise for the parent to provide plenty of materials for children to occupy their time when the child is unable to comprehend what is happening, and the parent should be willing to take the child out, not for punishment but to relieve boredom (Dobbins, 1975).

Developmental Religious Education

Not only should preschoolers be understood in terms of cognitive development, but the Bible also should be considered within a developmental framework (Ratcliff, 1987). One needs to take the insights of cognitive development, and analyze the content of the Bible and other religious materials to be used with preschoolers. Not always do curriculum writers and publishers take into account the current research in cognitive development, thus materials sometimes imply that children can learn what they cannot, and vice versa. Thus the religious educator needs to study biblical and other content carefully before using it with preschoolers.

Sometimes the clues to whether material should be used, modified, or not used are in the language—as has been mentioned, parables and other kinds of language which require multiple levels of understanding are inappropriate for preschoolers and perhaps for older children as well. Yet one may also look to the general *type* of material as well. The Bible contains doctrine, miracles, laws, history, poetry, prophecy, history, letters, moral discourses, and other kinds of literature. Are all of these accessible to the preschooler? To an extent some of these will be considered in later chapters of this book, yet much is lacking in our knowledge of what preschoolers can and cannot understand of religion. The insights of cognitive development can at least give us hints of answers, and caution us not to underestimate the preschooler's abilities. Further research may give us clearer direction in understanding how cognitive development influences the religious education of preschoolers.

REFERENCES

Barber, L. W. (1984). *Teaching Christian values.* Birmingham, AL: Religious Education Press.

Barber, L. W., and Peatling, J. H. (1981). *Realistic parenting.* St. Meinrad, IN: Abbey Press.

Benson, D. C., & Stewart, S. J. (1979). *The ministry of the child.* Nashville: Abingdon.

Bybee, R. W., & Sund, R. B. (1982). *Piaget for educators* (2nd ed.). Columbus, OH: Charles E. Merrill Publishing Co.

Cowan, P. A. (1978). *Piaget with feeling.* New York: Holt, Rinehart and Winston.

Dobbins, R. D. (1975). Too much too soon. *Christianity Today,* October 24.

Elkind, D. (1974). *A sympathetic understanding of the child: Birth to sixteen.* Boston: Allyn and Bacon.

Elkind, D. (1971). The development of religious understanding in children and adolescents, in M. Strommen, (Ed.), *Research on religious development: A comprehensive handbook.* New York: Hawthorn Books.

Flavell, J. H. (1985). *Cognitive development* (2nd ed.). Englewood Cliffs, NJ: Prentice Hall.

Flavell, J. H., Flavell, E. R., & Green, F. (1983). Development of the appearance—reality distinction. *Cognitive Psychology, 15,* 95-120.

Flavell, J. H., Zhang, X. D., Zou, H., Dong, Q., & Qi, S. (1983). A comparison between the development of the appearance—reality distinction in the People's Republic of China and the United States. *Cognitive Psychology, 15,* 459-466.

Gelman, S. A. (1985a). Gender as a natural kind category. Paper presented at the Biennial Meeting of the Society for Research in Child Development, Toronto.

Gelman, S. A. (1985b). Children's inductive inferences from natural kind and artifact categories. Paper presented at the Biennial Meeting of the Society for Research in Child Development, Toronto.

Goldman, R. (1964). *Religious thinking from childhood to adolescence.* New York: Seabury.

Haber, A., & Runyan, R. P. (1986). *Fundamentals of psychology,* (4th ed.) New York: Random House.

Hall, E., Lamb, M. E., & Perlmutter, M. (1986). *Child psychology today* (2nd ed.). New York: Random House.

Johnson, C. N., & Wellman, H. M. (1982). Children's developing conceptions of the mind and brain. *Child Development, 53,* 222-234.

Komatsu, L. K., & Galotti, K. M. (1985). Children's reasoning about social, physical and logical regularities: A look at two worlds. Based on a presentation at the Society for Research in Child Development, Toronto.

Mervis, C. B., & Crisafi, M. A. (1982). The order of acquisition of subordinate, basic, and subordinate-level categories. *Child Development, 53,* 258-266.

Phillips, J. L. (1981). *Piaget's theory: A primer.* San Francisco: W. H. Freeman and Co.

Postolos-Cappadora, D. A. (1983). *The sacred play of children.* New York: Seabury.

Ratcliff, D. E. (1982). Behavioral discipline in the Sunday school. *Journal of the American Scientific Affiliation,* December.

Ratcliff, D. E. (1987). Teaching the Bible developmentally. *Christian Education Journal, 7,* 21-32.

Richards, D. D., & Siegler, R. S. (1984). The effects of task requirements on children's life judgments. *Child Development, 55,* 1687-1696.

Rosch, E. (1975). Cognitive representations of semantic categories. *Journal of Experimental Psychology, 104,* 192-233.

Schultz, T. R., & Kestenbaum, N. R. (1985). Causal reasoning in children. *Annals of Child Development, 2,* 195-249.

Siegler, R. S. (1981). Developmental sequences within and between concepts. *Monographs of the Society for Research in Child Development, 46.*

Smith, E. E., & Medin, D. L. (1981). *Categories and concepts.* Cambridge: Harvard University Press.

Taylor, M., & Flavell, J. H. (1984). Seeing and believing: Children's understanding of the distinction between appearance and reality. *Child Development, 55,* 1710-1720.

Wadsworth, B. J. (1978). *Piaget for the classroom teacher.* New York: Longman.

Waxman, S. (1985). Hierarchical structures in classification and language. Paper presented at the Biennial Meeting of the Society for Research in Child Development, Toronto.

Wellman, H. M. (1980). Mental self-concepts. A talk presented at the "Development of Self" conference, Mt. Kisco, NY.

Wellman, H. M. (1985). The child's theory of mind: The development of conceptions of cognition. In S. Yussen (Ed.), *The growth of reflection in children.* Orlando, FL: Academic Press.

Wellman, H. H., & Estes, D. (1985). Early understanding of mental entities: A reexamination of childhood realism. Paper presented at the Biennial Meeting of the Society for Research in Child Development, Toronto.

Chapter Two:

Physical, Language, and Social-Emotional Development

CHARLOTTE WALLINGA AND PATSY SKEEN

A number of important and exciting developmental changes occur during the early childhood years which include ages three to six. The areas of physical, language, social and emotional development will be considered in this chapter.

PHYSICAL DEVELOPMENT

Although important advances in physical development are made, the early childhood period can best be described as a smoothing out and consolidation of growth and development. Changes are also occurring in motor and perceptual development.

Physical Growth

Physical growth during the early childhood years is slower than during the first two years of life (Tanner, 1970). Parents and teachers may notice that preschool children eat less than they did when they were infants, but their growth rate has slowed since infancy, and thus preschool children do not need as many calories to maintain normal growth. Differences in growth rates between girls and boys are quite small during these early years (Lowrey, 1986), with girls tending to be slightly lighter and shorter than boys. Boys have more muscle tissue than girls, but girls tend to have more fat tissue. It must be noted, however, that considerable variation is common among young children.

The brain and nervous system continue to develop during the preschool years and by age five the brain has reached 90 percent of its adult weight (Tanner, 1978). Both the size of the nerve cells and the elaborate connections between the nerve cells in the cortex and other parts of brain and nervous system increase (Tanner, 1970). Myelinization, a process in which nerve cells become coated with an insulating substance which facilitates transmission of neural signals, also increases during early childhood allowing children to have more control over their motor abilities.

The brain is divided into two cerebral hemispheres—right and left, with each hemisphere often controlling different functions. In most people the right hemisphere controls visual-spatial abilities, emotions, music skills, and creativity. The left hemisphere controls language skills and motor activities. As the brain becomes more specialized, the child can perform increasingly complex intellectual and motor tasks. Hand preference is an indication of brain specialization. By age three or four most children are clearly right-handed, left-handed, or ambidextrous, with over 90 percent preferring their right hand (Coren, Porac, & Duncan, 1981). Since most people are right-handed, some teachers become concerned unnecessarily if children prefer to use their left hand. Children should be allowed to use whichever hand they prefer and never be forced to perform skills with their right hand. Provisions for left-handed children such as left-handed scissors should be made in every classroom. Contrary to a once popular belief, researchers have found no relationship between reading disabilities and handedness (Kinsbourne & Hiscock, 1983).

Since many physical changes are occurring and important attitudes developing during the preschool years, it is important for parents and teachers to provide an environment in which positive health concepts are practiced (Flake-Hobson, Robinson, & Skeen, 1983). Proper rest, including opportunities for naps and quiet times, regular exercise and good nutrition need to be emphasized every day. A healthy diet which avoids "junk foods" that are high in calories but low in nutritional value is vital for every child. Healthy nonsugared snacks during midmorning and midafternoon are helpful in preventing hunger and irritability throughout the day and children should be allowed to leave unwanted food on the plates. Small and attractive serving sizes at meal times, as well as cooking projects involving children, often entice them to try new foods. Such good health practices are necessary for proper growth and development including motor development.

Motor Development

A major reason why preschoolers have much better locomotor and manipulative abilities than toddlers is because of physical changes which allow them to refine their gross and fine motor skills (Gallahue, 1982; Wickstrom, 1983). Gross motor activities involve large muscles and tend to develop progressively from head-to-tail. Running, skipping, jumping, and climbing are examples of gross motor skills. Because children should practice these skills daily, they need access to a safe environment with plenty of space and appropriate equipment.

In contrast, fine motor activities which involve the small muscles of the hands and fingers develop from the center of the body toward the outer extremities. Examples of these skills include drawing, cutting with scissors, lacing shoes, zipping, buttoning, and teeth brushing. Fine motor skills are dependent on brain maturation and are more difficult to master than gross motor skills. Because fine motor activities are often frustrating to young children, toys and clothing must be chosen carefully to insure that they are appropriate for the child's developmental level. Preschool girls tend to have better-developed fine motor skills than boys (Tudor, 1981), but young children vary widely in fine motor skills and need a positive and adaptable environment in which to practice these skills.

Perceptual Development

As children get older many gains in perceptual development take place, but wide individual differences are still apparent (Gibson, 1969; Gibson & Spelke, 1983). Preschool children's eyesight improves (Pick & Pick, 1970) and allows them to see finer detail when cutting out a shape or identifying similarities and differences in forms and letters. Attention span increases (Miller & Zalenski, 1982) and enables children to sit and listen to a story or engage in an activity for longer periods of time. As discussed in the previous chapter on cognitive development, pre-schoolers refine their discrimination skills and learn that an object can change in some way but still be the same object. Eye-hand coordination improves and most five-year-olds are more successful in tracing figures and copying shapes on a piece of paper than are three-year-olds.

Perceptual skills develop best in a caring environment rich in stimulation. When children have a stimulating environment containing interesting and developmentally appropriate activities in which to participate, they generally have a longer attention span and are more cooperative than children in a less suitable environment. Additionally, perceptual skills, like all skills, follow a developmental progression and do not develop in isolation. Playing a board game or drawing a picture requires motor skills, a desire and motivation to try, as well as cognitive and language abilities.

LANGUAGE DEVELOPMENT

Important changes are occurring in language development during early childhood. Although they will continue to refine their language ability in later years, children typically emerge from this period with a good basic command of their language.

Vocabulary Growth

There is a language explosion during the preschool years, although estimates concerning the size of children's vocabulary vary greatly (Nagy & Anderson, 1984). A two-year-old child has a vocabulary of about 50 to 100 words or more (Capute, Palmer, Shapiro, Wachtel, & Accardo, 1981), while the average six-year-old knows between 8000 and 14,000 words (Carey, 1978). Young children learn the meanings of words gradually (Mezynski, 1983). They first learn concrete words which are meaningful to them personally such as table, milk, and puppy (Anglin, 1970). It is not until around age ten to twelve that they fully understand abstract words such as love, death, God, and faith.

Much to parents and teachers surprise, it is not unusual for preschool children suddenly to begin using profanity and other taboo words. Children may also enjoy whispering and using words that concern body parts and body functions, typically to elicit a reaction from adults or peers. The less reaction they receive when a taboo word is said, the less likely children are to continue to use such words, thus, it is generally best to ignore the word completely. Since the children receive no reaction from the teacher, there is no reinforcement for their behavior. The children soon tire of that particular behavior and join in the appropriate group activity. Another approach is for parents to discuss with the child why adults do not like to hear profanity or other taboo words.

At the same time children's vocabulary is growing, their sentence length is increasing (Brown & Hanlon, 1970). While a two or three-year-old child may have a sentence length of only three words, by age five or six years the child will be speaking in six to eight word sentences (deVilliers & deVilliers, 1978). Adults and peers will be able to communicate more easily since the older child is able to elaborate in more detail.

Grammar

Language is more than vocabulary and sentence length. To communicate effectively children must understand grammar, the rules of word order in their language. The understanding of grammar develops gradually and is often considered a better indicator of language development than is vocabulary (Brown, 1973).

Three-year-old children already demonstrate considerable grammatical knowledge. However, three- and four-year-olds are particularly sensitive to passive sentence structures as well as word order and sequence. For example, when children hear the sentence, "The dog bit the snake," it seems identical to the passive sentence, "The dog was bit by the snake."

The preschooler may also have difficulty constructing questions. At first children raise their voices at the end of a sentence to indicate they are asking a question, "Daddy gone?" Later in their development young children refine their question asking ability, "Daddy gone?" becomes "Where's my daddy?" Researchers have suggested that questions beginning with why, how, and when are more difficult for young children to understand than questions beginning with where, what, and who (deVilliers & deVilliers, 1979). As a result, when an adult asks a young child, "Why did you slap your sister?" the young child might respond, "On her arm." This illustration is an indication that the young child may not be deliberately avoiding answering the question, but may in fact not understand the question.

Learning exceptions to grammatical rules is difficult for preschoolers. Young children may say, "I see two sheeps," or "I eated the whole thing." These are examples of overgeneralization. The child learns one grammatical rule such as add an "s" to words to make plurals or an "ed" to make past tense and then must learn that there are many exceptions to these rules. By age four or five, however, children usually can use irregular verb and noun forms correctly (Kuczaj, 1978). Even though children make these errors of overgeneralization, it is a developmental sign that they are beginning to understand grammar and adults need not be alarmed by such grammatical errors. If children hear consistently good speech models, they will correct their own speech, which is far better than severely correcting children's errors or giving them long-winded explanations. If a child says, "Look at the two fishes," the teacher might respond by saying, "Oh, yes, I see the two fish. They really have a lot of bright colored speckles on them."

Preschool children also have difficulty with words which make comparisons such as more and less and near and far (deVilliers & deVilliers, 1978). Young children who have a very tall and old teacher might associate the tallness with being old. Children are also likely to make literal translations of sentences, which can confuse them. For example, one teacher saw several four-year-old boys hitting themselves as they rolled down the playground hill. When he asked what they were doing, one little boy said, "Don't you remember? You told us to roll with the punches of life." Even though preschoolers have developed amazing language abilities in such a few years, their language and cognitive abilities are still immature sometimes, making communication with adults and other children difficult. Adult-child relationships are more effective when adults are sensitive to how communications are perceived by young children.

While children are learning language and rules of grammar, it is not uncommon for them to make a variety of articulation errors, such as changing beginning consonants or omitting sounds from words. At some time in their preschool years most preschool children will hesitate or stammer when speaking, often distressing adults. Most preschoolers who have these problems will gradually outgrow them without professional help. It is estimated that there are two million people who stutter in the United States with four times as many males stutterers as females (Jonas, 1977).

Some children are slow in speaking their first words or have difficulty in understanding sentence structure. These language delays may be due to a variety of developmental reasons. If a parent or teacher suspects a language problem such as articulation, stuttering, language delays, or hearing problems, the younger the child is referred to a speech specialist the better the chances are for improvement (Leitch, 1977).

Language Environment

Language skills are important prerequisites for reaching readiness and future success in school and social situations. Most educators believe that, in order for language skills to develop and expand, children must hear the speech of others, have warm contacts with others and have opportunities to practice speech. Socio-economic class is an additional important factor in the linguistic environment which affects children's language development. Children raised in middle-class families use more complex sentences and have larger vocabularies than children raised in lower-class families (Hess, 1970).

Researchers have studied mothers' and toddlers' communications (Schachter, Marquis, Shore, Bundy, & McNair, 1979). In one study, thirty mother-toddler dyads were categorized into three groups: white advantaged, black advantaged, and black disadvantaged. The two groups of advantaged mothers averaged one year of graduate school while the group of disadvantaged mothers averaged somewhat below high-school graduation. No racial differences were found in the verbal environments of the mothers in the two advantaged groups. However, advantaged mothers tended to use less directives with their toddlers than disadvantaged mothers. Advantaged mothers also talked twice as much to their children and their speech was three times more likely to be responsive to their children's interests and desires than the disadvantaged mothers. No significant differences, however, were found among the three groups on the quantity of mothers' spontaneous speech. The researchers concluded that the social class differences produced different communication styles; advantaged mothers tended to adopt an active process and speak responsively "with" their toddlers while disadvantaged mothers spoke "to" their toddlers.

Other researchers have found that lower- and middle-class mothers use different speech patterns when interacting with their children (Bernstein, 1972). Lower-class mothers speak in short, grammatically simple sentences which refer mainly to concrete objects and events, while middle-class mothers use long, grammatically complex sentences that include abstract and social concepts (Hess & Shipman, 1965). The lower-class mother might say, "Be quiet," to her child as she is talking on the phone. In contrast, the middle-class mother might say, "Would you keep quiet a minute? I want to talk on the phone."

Researchers also have found that lower-class children often are actually more competent in producing elaborated sentences than their daily speech patterns would indicate (Tizard, Hughes, Carmichael, & Pinkerton, 1983). Bernstein (1972) suggests that, if given the opportunity, low income children can learn elaborated language. As low income children increase in the number and richness of verbal interactions, their verbal problem solving capabilities improve (Jay & Farran, 1981; Radin & Kamii, 1965).

Educators must be cautious when drawing conclusions about language differences which appear to be based on socio-economic status because of possible problems in research design. Such problems include research methods which focus only on vocabulary words and overlook language complexity, judge low income children by middle-class standards, and conduct research in settings which are so foreign to lower-class children and parents that they do not perform to their best ability and seem to be set up for failure.

Child-care arrangements also affect language development and are becoming increasingly complex for many families. Approximately half of the children under six have mothers in the workforce (Kahn & Kamerman, 1987). Many of these children are cared for in centers outside the home, and thus concern has risen about what happens to these children's language development. As a result of her examination of 146 preschoolers attending nine day care centers in Bermuda, McCartney (1984) believes that language development, as well as the amount of verbal interaction between children and caregivers, depends upon the overall quality of the day care center. She suggests that teachers who overcontrol and give many commands hamper children's development of language skills. In contrast, caregivers can encourage children's linguistic abilities by providing activities in an organized environment and creating an atmosphere in which children feel free to initiate conversations.

Fostering Language Development in the Preschool Child

There are many ways both parents and educators can encourage and foster children's language development. Children need to be given a chance to communicate with others (Cazden, 1981). Since mothers and fathers tend to use different styles of interaction, the importance of verbal interactions with both parents cannot be underestimated (Masur & Gleason, 1980). An environment in which the child feels secure, objects are labeled, and everyday experiences discussed will also encourage language. Caregivers who take the time to really listen to children by providing eye contact and giving positive feedback will find that their children want to communicate with them. On the other hand, forcing children to speak or nagging and criticizing them about mispronunciations or speech errors usually has an adverse affect on language development.

Caregivers who ask questions and use the technique of expansion (elaborating on the child's speech) help encourage language development (Barnes, Gutfreund, Satterly, & Wells, 1983). If the child says "Up Mommy," the parent can expand this sentence by saying, "You want Mommy to pick you up and set you on the counter." Modeling appropriate speech and vocabulary is helpful also. Children who hear adults say "please" and "thank you," are likely to use these words as well.

Language skills grow when parents play and read with their children on a regular basis (Irwin, 1960; Karnes, Teska, Hodgins, & Badger, 1970). Children who are read to regularly are better able to comprehend stories when they become readers (Chomsky, 1972). In addition, reading to children helps expand vocabulary development. Allowing children to participate in the reading experience in ways such as pointing out the brown horse, answering questions about what happens next in the sequence of events or labeling pictures will make the interaction both learning oriented and enjoyable (also see chapter nine on story enactment).

Provision for appropriate play materials in the child's environment also is related to language development (Elardo, Bradley, & Caldwell, 1977). Children learn through active, hands-on exploration of their surroundings. A suitable play environment and appropriate adult-child interactions are important to social development as well as language development.

SOCIAL-EMOTIONAL DEVELOPMENT

Although influences and experiences outside the home increasingly impact on the social development of the older preschool child, the family is still the core socialization agency (Maccoby & Martin, 1983). Parents work to help their children develop desirable values and learn to behave according to appropriate limits. On the other hand, although children have more control over their world than ever before, their abundant energy and curiosity often get them into difficulty as they try to adhere to the rules of parents and society. The needs and increasing abilities of children, the type of relationship parents and children establish, and the guidance techniques parents employ play important roles in determining how children behave during this period as well as in the future. Additionally, at this age peers and societal factors are becoming more influential, sex roles are developing, and play becomes an increasingly important avenue for all areas of development including psychosocial development.

Psychosocial Development

The theory of psychoanalyst Erik Erikson (1963, 1982) is particularly concerned with psychosocial development and is helpful in understanding children's behavior and the parent-child relationship. According to Erikson, once children have successfully resolved the autonomy versus shame and doubt conflict characteristic of toddlerhood, they realize that they are separate persons with separate wills and feel a positive sense of self or self concept. This new independence—combined with gains in locomotor abilities and cognitive, language, and social-emotional development—gives children a feeling of power, and they show great initiative and boundless energy in exploring all aspects of their world. At the same time, adults and sometimes peers insist that children must behave according to the rules of parents and society. For example, hitting other children is forbidden and children are expected to share their toys and take more responsibility for their actions. Such rules are internalized in the child's conscience. Problems typically occur as curious, energetic children must learn to initiate and control their own behavior according to the rules of their society. According to Erikson (1963), this conflict is central to the initiative versus guilt stage. That is, children's new abilities enable them to think about and initiate behavior which they may not be able to control or is not allowed by parents and society. When children interfere with the rights of others (as they do frequently) and do not live up to what they think their parents' expectations are, they feel guilty and fearful.

If children resolve the initiative versus guilt stage successfully they will gradually develop self-control, assume responsibility for their behavior, continue to build a positive self concept, find ways to use their energy and power constructively, and be better able to cooperate with others. Unsuccessful resolution of this stage results in children who overcontrol themselves to avoid guilt. Often these children are fearful, unhappy, and may grow up to be fearful adults who also overcontrol themselves. The behavior of caregivers is important if the initiative versus guilt stage is to be appropriately resolved and other positive behaviors developed by the child. Such caregiving behavior is discussed in the following section.

Parent-Child Relationships

The parent-child relationship remains at the center of the older preschool child's life. There are many ways for parents to interact with their children and the approach parents adopt in guiding their children's behavior varies greatly. It might be noted that Diana Baumrind (1967, 1971, 1980) studied parenting practices and their effects on preschool children, identifying three different styles of parenting—authoritarian, permissive, and authoritative (see chapter six).

As parents and caregivers are likely to discover, guiding children's behavior is not an easy task; most parents at some time wish they could improve their skills. There is no one best approach for all parents to use to raise all children (Jackson, 1983), but there are some general guidelines which are helpful. An important goal of all guidance approaches is to help the child exercise self-control or self-regulation (Marion, 1981). One helpful way to examine guidance approaches is to divide the information into two areas: positive guidance and punishment. Positive guidance is intended to prevent negative behavior, encourage positive behavior, and promote self-controlling behaviors. This approach is especially useful in helping children resolve the initiative versus guilt stage discussed in the previous section concerning psychosocial development. On the other hand, punishment is intended to reduce negative behavior.

Positive guidance. There are several helpful guidelines to remember when using this approach (Flake-Hobson, Robinson, & Skeen, 1983). Setting firm, consistent, and reasonable limits which encourage children to control their own behavior is beneficial. When setting a limit, it is helpful to tell the child what is expected in words the child can understand and also explain the reasons for the limit. Adults can then firmly, but kindly, enforce the limits. When adults speak calmly and directly to children, make eye contact, place their bodies on the child's physical level, and give short concise explanations versus long-winded tirades, they are more likely to be successful.

Sometimes, however, adults do not feel calm and are in fact angry. While such feelings are acceptable and usual, the child should not receive the brunt of the anger. Instead, parents can take time to "cool down" after telling the child, "I am angry and need to be alone for a few minutes." When parents and child are calmer, they can discuss how everyone feels, why they feel as they do, and decide what to do to solve the problem. In fact, it is very important to help children become aware of their feelings and express them in ways that help them feel better, but also show respect for other people and property. For example, it is acceptable for an angry child to say, "I'm angry," pound on the ground, or run around the yard, while it is not acceptable to hit or call someone names. Be honest, but not hurtful, when expressing feelings, as well as in all forms of communication between parent and child. Adults who say to a child, "Beth didn't mean to kick your block building down" when the child saw Beth deliberately kick the building, send a dishonest and confusing message. A more appropriate response for the adult to say is, "I'm sorry Beth kicked your building. She is feeling very angry because her balloon popped when she came in the house. I will talk to Beth about what she did."

Fortunately, there are many positives in the parent-child relationship. It is important to point out these positive behaviors and focus on what children can do instead of what they cannot do. For example, saying things such as "I like how you are sharing" or "Thanks for helping me set the table, it really saves me time" requires little effort and is likely to result in an increase in the desired behavior. In contrast, children who are belittled, frequently criticized and threatened, made to feel guilty, and receive harsh and regular punishment are not likely to resolve the initiative versus guilt stage successfully. Additionally, overusing the word "no" or "don't" may eventually cause children to tune the parent out. Instead of saying, "Don't bump your tricycle into Susie," the parent can say, "Please ride your tricycle around Susie. If you bump into her, Susie can get hurt. You might wreck your trike and get hurt too."

When using the positive guidance approach it is helpful if adults give children only appropriate choices, involve them in solving problems, and answer their questions. While a five-year-old might want to know all the choices and be able to consider them all, a younger child is better able to make a choice from only a few alternatives. In addition, it is helpful to maintain consistent routines and a safe environment, provide toys and stimulating materials which are appropriate to the child's developmental abilities, and schedule the day to alternate between active and quiet periods.

Punishment. Punishment occurs when an unpleasant behavior is administered to decrease a behavior (Flake-Hobson, Robinson, & Skeen, 1983). That is, an unpleasant behavior or punishment is administered by the parent after the child has behaved in an undesirable way. As with positive verbal guidance, there are a variety of ways to give punishment. For instance, a five-year-old child takes everything out of her sisters' closet and spreads it around the room. When mother enters the room and sees the mess, she sternly tells her daughter how unhappy she is with this situation and demands that she clean up the room immediately. Another example is yelling at or spanking a child who pinches her baby sister. While spanking may stop the immediate behavior, there are some problems with this approach. The child has not learned alternate positive behaviors and is probably feeling very angry without knowing what to do about the anger. The spanking usually does not improve the child's relationship with the sister and may in fact tend to contribute to future trouble in the relationship. Also, spanking provides an aggressive model of "might makes right." Additionally, children who are spanked may begin to avoid the punisher and become sneaky and devious in their misbehavior to avoid getting caught. Another problem with spanking is that the parent can get carried away and physically harm the child without really meaning to do so. Children who are harshly punished at home may be temporarily obedient, but in the long run they tend to store up frustration and anger. In later years these children may take out their anger on parents or at school (Martin, 1975).

An additional way to administer punishment is to take something pleasant away from the child when an undesirable behavior has occurred. For example, a father might take away the game his son is quarreling over or he may call for a "time out period" in which the child is temporarily removed from the room or activity which he is enjoying. The use of "time out periods" with young children can be very effective, but their duration must be closely monitored. These need to be only long enough for children to calm down, get their behavior under control, and think about the situation. When the child can behave in a positive manner, the child can return to the previous or a new activity.

Parent-Child Partnership

It may sound at this point like the parent-child relationship is all one direction, that is, parents do certain things and children behave in certain ways as a result. Although parents are clearly a strong and

guiding influence, they are not the only important influence in this
relationship. Instead, children are also important influences in shaping
the child-rearing practices used by their parents (Buss, 1981; Grusec &
Kuczynski, 1980). In actuality, the parent-child relationship is a reciprocal process and can best be described as bi-directional. For instance, a
child who is a skilled athlete and not very scholarly would have different
relationships with parents who place high value on excelling at sports
than the child would with parents who are quite scholarly themselves
and want a child who loves to pursue intellectual activities rather than
sports. Also, parents who expect and value a quiet, obedient child would
be likely to have quite different relationships with a child who actually
behaved this way than they would if their child was active and fiercely
independent.

Another example of how children themselves impact on the parent-
child relationship is the change in children's dependency behavior during early childhood. After age three, as children's cognitive and other
abilities mature, separation becomes less upsetting to them as they get
older (Marvin, 1977). Instead of clinging and needing to be physically
close to their mothers as they did in infancy, they are now more adven-
turesome. Children can play with peers for longer periods of time without checking on the whereabouts of their parents. Typically, parents and
preschoolers form a partnership that is based upon greater cooperation
and sensitivity for others' feelings and plans (Bowlby, 1969; Marvin,
1977). At the same time the parent-child relationship is changing, children are more influenced by peers.

Development of Peer Relationships

Preschoolers spend increasing amounts of time interacting socially
with their peers (Rubin, Fein, & Vandenberg, 1983). Learning to get
along with peers is an important developmental process during the
preschool years. Often the first social experiences with other children
occur through relationships with siblings. Since their relationships are
long lasting, a great amount of playing, interacting, and modeling of
behavior occurs. For example, Lamb (1978) found that younger siblings
imitate the behavior of older siblings including prosocial or helping
behavior and older siblings sometimes comfort a younger sibling when
their mother leaves (Stewart, 1983). In fact, siblings demonstrate many
positive behaviors toward one another (Lamb & Sutton-Smith, 1982)
and often help each other (Brody, Stoneman, MacKinnon, & MacKinnon, 1985).

In addition to positive interactions among siblings, there are often
quarrels, fights, feelings of jealousy, and sibling rivalry. Sibling rivalry
may occur when a new baby is born because the older sibling gets less

attention from the mother (Dunn & Kendrick, 1980). Sibling rivalry appears to be most prominent among children who are the same sex and close in age. When parents and caregivers compare siblings, show favoritism, and do not carefully meet each individual child's needs, sibling rivalry is likely to escalate.

Besides their relationships with siblings, preschoolers also interact socially with peers outside the home. Such peer interactions increase during the early childhood years (Hartup, 1983). Even at a young age peers reinforce each other and model behaviors. Teachers are well aware of how a prestigious peer model can encourage preschoolers to exhibit either desirable or undesirable behavior. Peer interactions also help children learn much-needed social skills (Hartup, 1983). Because of their egocentric nature, preschool children tend to select friends who are the same sex and close in age.

Societal Influences

In addition to parents and peers, societal influences from inside and outside the family become increasingly important as children get older. Family forms, needs, and problem solving approaches vary as families strive to function effectively in their society. Situations such as divorce, single-parent families, blended families, child abuse, hurried children, latchkey children, and working parents affect every family member. Also, influences such as technology, the knowledge explosion, educational practices, religion, governmental policy, and economic conditions all impact on the family and children's development. Television is a particularly pervasive societal influence which affects children's development in both negative and positive ways.

It has been estimated that preschoolers watch approximately four hours of television each day (Osborn & Osborn, 1977). The average child will have viewed 15,000 hours of television by the time high-school graduation occurs (Kaye, 1979) and will have viewed more than 13,000 violent deaths (Gerbner & Gross, 1980). Since violence, racism, ageism, sexism, and explicit sexuality are frequently portrayed on television, it is understandable that parents and caregivers are concerned about what effects television has on their children.

Most researchers agree that there is a relationship between watching violence on television and the occurrence of aggressive behavior (Rubinstein, 1980), but violence is not the only concern. Children who watch large amounts of television are likely to have lower school grades (Gadberry, 1980), and spend less time playing and interacting with their peers (Winn, 1977). In addition, these children are spending many hours in a lethargic activity instead of running, exercising, and playing. Cultural stereotypes can also be transmitted by television, such as, only women wash clothes, it is best to be young and sexy, and all men must be excellent athletes. A particular problem for preschool children is that, because of their level of cognitive development, they are not able to understand the implied subtleties in much of the television advertising. They think that the toys and food advertised on television are desirable and they pressure their parents to buy these items (Stoneman & Brody, 1981) only to find that the products do not always live up to their expectations. Young children also have difficulty understanding the difference between real and pretend and are likely to be scared that frightening fictional events or people such as criminals or monsters can harm them.

Even though television can be a negative influence in many ways, it also has a positive value. Television programs such as "Sesame Street" can provide good information for children and expose them to people, animals, and places they would not ordinarily have the opportunity to see. Watching shows like "Mr. Roger's Neighborhood" can help children build prosocial skills (Friedrich & Stein, 1975). Also, prosocial television shows appear to have at least a short-term effect of reducing aggression during preschoolers' free play time (Bankart & Anderson, 1979).

What can parents and teachers do about the television dilemma? Alice Honig (1983) urges parents and teachers to be in charge of the television and to help children develop good viewing habits early. The television is not a good babysitter nor an appropriate substitute for time spent interacting with parents and teachers. Instead, adults can limit the amount of television viewed and select programs which are appropriate for preschool-age children. Also, watching television with children is very important and helpful in that the adults can explain what is happening in the program and answer any questions children might have. Sharing views about the television program such as what you liked and what you did not like is also appropriate. Television programs, even inappropriate ones, can serve as the starting point for educational discussions about morals, values, and emotions.

EMOTIONS

Emotions play an important role in preschoolers' development. In this section the focus will be on fears, aggression, prosocial behaviors, and how to help children cope with death.

Fears

Preschoolers may develop a variety of fears; what is scary to one child may be another child's fun. Most preschoolers tend to have unrealistic fears. Young children fear imaginary creatures, animals, being left alone in the dark, and frightening dreams (Bauer, 1976). Because of their vivid imagination and immature cognitive abilities, which hinder clear differentiation between reality and fantasy, it is not uncommon for preschoolers to insist that there are lions and tigers under their beds or witches behind their curtains. They may demand that lights be left on and nightly inspections made to see whether there are creatures lurking nearby.

Children also can remember vividly a particularly frightening experience such as getting stitches in their hand at the doctor's office or being scratched by a cat. They are likely to become frightened when they are in a similar situation. Furthermore, events seen on television newscasts and other shows can be frightening to children, while new people and unfamiliar social situations can also cause alarm. Sometimes children react to strangers and new situations by hiding, crying, or becoming excessively shy.

Children observe others in order to find cues for their own behavior. For example, if a father becomes nervous and agitated during thunderstorms, children quickly learn that thunderstorms are to be feared. Siblings and peers also model fearful behavior which preschoolers may readily acquire. Six-year-old Ann was terrified of army worms and insisted if she was anywhere near them she would get a rash. Laura, Ann's two-and-one-half-year-old sister, heard Ann screeching about army worms. Soon after that Laura saw some army worms and ran into the house yelling, "Mommy, Mommy, worms, rash, rash, rash, red rash!"

Given encouragement and understanding most children will outgrow their early fears. Fears will also become more realistic and reasonable with time as children's cognitive abilities mature (Bauer, 1976). Parents and siblings must be careful not to make fun of the preschool child's fears because to the child the fear is very real. In fact, when parents become angry or impatient with a child's fear, the child may feel rejected and the fears may become even worse (Wolman, 1978). Parents need to be supportive of each child's needs. If a child is afraid of the dark, a small light or flashlight next to the bed can give comfort and reassurance to the child.

Just as modeling can help children acquire fearful behavior, modeling also can help children learn to cope with fears. Having a peer exhibit calm behaviors near the feared situation can be helpful to preschool children (Bandura, Grusec, & Menlov, 1967; Bandura & Menlov, 1968). Reading books and stories about the child's fears, discussing the fears with the child in a nonjudgmental and sensitive manner and allowing the child to act out fears with puppets or dolls in play situations can be useful in helping preschool children overcome their fears. Children with phobias or extreme fears, however, should have professional help.

Aggression

Physical aggression typically peaks during the preschool years (Parke & Slaby, 1983). Parents are shocked to see their young preschooler knock another child off a tricycle or snatch a sandwich from a friend's hand. Parents often do not realize that such behavior is quite common. As children get older, physical aggression lessens, but verbal aggression, such as name calling and character assassinations, escalates (Parke & Slaby, 1983).

There are different viewpoints concerning why children are aggressive. Aggression is thought to have either a biological or learning basis or to be a combination of both these factors. Freud (1961) regarded aggression as a biological instinct, while Lorenz (1966) suggested that aggression was an innate response to a specific situation. Others believe aggression is the result of frustration or a blocked goal (Dollard, Doob, Miller, Mowrer, & Sears, 1939). Still others suggest that aggression is learned by observation (Bandura 1973; Bandura, Ross, & Ross, 1961). That is, preschool children can model aggressiveness displayed by their parents, peers, or television and movie characters.

According to Feshbach (1964) there are two types of aggression: instrumental aggression and hostile aggression. The purpose of instrumental aggression is to accomplish a goal such as recovering an object, territory, or privilege. Three-year-old John grabs the scissors away from Bill so that he can cut his own paper. In contrast, the goal of hostile aggression is to harm or attack another person. Four-year-old Mary slaps Susan for calling her a "doodle brain." In a study of aggressive behavior in children ages four to seven years, Hartup (1974) found that older children exhibited more hostile aggression while younger children exhibited more instrumental aggression. Boys used more hostile aggression than girls, but there was no difference in boys' and girls' expression of instrumental aggression. Even though studies have indicated that boys tend to be more physically aggressive than girls, Hyde (1984) believes that gender differences in aggression are not as large as previous studies have indicated. After a meta-analysis of reviewing 143 studies, Hyde concluded that approximately 5 percent of the variation in aggression is due to gender differences while 95 percent of the variation in aggression is due to within-gender variation and error in measurement.

Not all aggression in preschool children is undesirable, but caregivers must help children learn to curb their destructive aggression and find acceptable ways to express anger. Caregivers are more successful in helping children control their aggressive behavior when they show restraint themselves, use positive guidance such as encouraging children to take the other person's point of view, learn to express feelings in satisfying and acceptable ways, use nonaggressive methods to solve conflict, and teach children positive social skills and prosocial behaviors.

Prosocial Behaviors

Even though young children tend to be aggressive toward each other, friendly behavior and interactions typically outweigh negative ones (Moore, 1977). Prosocial behaviors such as helping, comforting, sharing, cooperating, and showing empathy increase during the preschool years. In fact, when prosocial behaviors are encouraged, aggressive behaviors often lessen. Contrary to popular opinion, most research studies find no differences between boys and girls in prosocial behaviors (Radke-Yarrow, Zahn-Waxler, & Chapman, 1983).

Parents and caregivers can foster prosocial behavior by encouraging the behavior they would like to see in their children. A father was helping his eight-year-old daughter Casey and her friend build a birdfeeder. While they were working on the birdfeeder, the father made statements such as, "I like how you are both cooperating, taking turns, and sticking to the project. It will be so nice that the birds won't have to go hungry this winter." Soon Casey's three-year-old brother carried nails from the basement and proudly announced, "I want to help. I don't want the birds to be hungry."

Children whose parents utilize guidance techniques based on induction, which help the child understand the other person's feelings and desires, tend to use more prosocial behaviors (Maccoby & Martin, 1983). For example, five-year-old Sally would not share her book with her friend Paul. When the teacher talked with Sally about how Paul must be feeling, Sally was given the opportunity to examine the situation from Paul's vantage point. When Sally finally put herself in Paul's shoes she said, "I would be really mad if no one shared with me. No, I would probably be very very sad."

Helping Children Cope with Death

One area of life in which emotions play a large role is in how children and adults cope with death. Unlike earlier years, in today's society death is seldom openly discussed or even seen as it often happens in a hospital or other place outside the home. Whether death is a comfortable topic or not, it is a part of life and the topic needs to be discussed with preschoolers. Children's level of cognitive development is an important

determiner of how much they can grasp about the meaning of death
(White, Elsom, & Prawat, 1978). Since death is an abstract concept and
preschool children are concrete thinkers, they have trouble understanding what death means, particularly the irreversibility of death and that it
happens to everyone (Koocher, 1973).

Children react to death of a person or pet in a variety of ways. They
are often eager to talk about death (Koocher, 1974). Most children are
very curious and ask many question. "Does Grandma still eat? Why did
she die? You are old; are you going to die? Will she be floating up there
with Jesus?" They may want to touch the body and ask about the
physical functions of the dead person or pet. Some children may reenact
the death and funeral many times in their play as they try to make sense
out of this experience. Other children may react with anger because
Grandma left them or insist Grandma will come back and take them to
the farm as promised. Still others may react with great sadness, cry and
become depressed.

Children benefit when sensitive and appropriate death education begins at an early age. Books and stories for young children which discuss
death are a good avenue to encourage discussions. Children can learn
that a squashed bug and the goldfish floating at the top of the bowl are
dead and no longer breathe or eat and will never come back. Children
will be more ready to cope with the death of a person if they have
previously been exposed to the death of animals and plants.

Open and honest discussions and explanations of death are a necessity. If at all possible, the adult closest to the children should tell them
about the death (Jewett, 1982). Explanations should draw on the child's
experiences as much as is feasible (Koocher, 1974). Allowing children to
express feelings and ask questions is helpful. Sometimes it is good for
parents to have children repeat explanations so that misconceptions can
be corrected. Children should be reassured they are not to blame for the
death. Euphemisms should be carefully avoided. Statements like
"Grandma is only asleep" or "Grandma has been carried away on the
wings of angels" can, in fact, be very frightening to children. Children
might fear sleeping or that angels will come down and snatch them
away from their homes. Parents must also make sure children do not
feel abandoned. Children need to be reassured that they will still be
taken care of by their families.

It is appropriate for children to know that adults are very sad about
the death. Parents must remember that children need to share their
feelings of grief and happy memories of the dead person or pet just as
adults need to do. Children also need to be involved in the family's
mourning process. Children's exposure to the mourning process, howev-

er, should be planned according to the individual child's needs and abilities. Parents must use their own judgment as to what exposure is most appropriate for each of their children. (Chapter three describes preschoolers' concepts of death in more detail.)

SEX ROLE DEVELOPMENT

Sex roles are shaped as early as birth. Parents and adults treat boys and girls differently beginning in infancy (Etaugh, 1983). Are the behavioral differences in boys and girls based on learned factors such as differential treatment by parents and caregivers or biological factors? Many researchers agree that biological factors make some contribution to sex differences in some behaviors, such as aggression, but socialization seems to account for most of the differences and include such factors as the influence of parents (Huston, 1983), preschool teachers (Robinson, Skeen, & Flake-Hobson, 1980), peers (Lamb & Roopnarine, 1979), siblings, picture books (St. Peter, 1979), and television (Downs, 1981).

By about three years of age, children develop gender understanding (Thompson, 1975). It is not uncommon for children to engage in stereotypic sex role behavior even before age three, with some children as young as twenty-six months having definite views about what men and women can do (Weinraub, Clemens, Sockloff, Etheridge, Gracely, & Meyers, 1984). Most, but not all, young children also prefer to play with sex-typed toys and assume sex-typed roles (Huston, 1983). Preschool children may, in fact, criticize each other for not playing with traditional sex-appropriate toys (Roopnarine, 1984).

Sex role stereotyping is considered by some to be a necessary stage of sex role development (Rebecca, Hefner, & Oleshansky, 1976). Maccoby (1980) suggests that preschool children exaggerate their sex-typed behaviors so that they can better understand who they are. Sex role stereotyping also may be related to the preschool child's cognitive development stage (Kohlberg, 1966; Ullian, 1976). Since preoperational children are not flexible and abstract in their thinking, they see sex role behaviors in terms of either boy behaviors or girl behaviors. It is only as children get older when their thinking becomes less concrete and more abstract and their gender identity more stable, that they are capable of being more flexible in their view of appropriate sex role behaviors. Only at this point can they understand the concept of androgyny.

Instead of forcing children and people to accept stereotypical sex role behaviors, Bem and Lenney (1976) advocate that it is more humane and better for mental health if people adopt androgynous roles when they so choose. Androgyny's purpose is to allow people to adopt the masculine and feminine roles that best meet their own individual needs. For example, both boys and girls can choose to be nurturant to children and spouses as well as assertive at work. Such flexibility is thought to be beneficial to healthy functioning in a complex world.

In contrast to this positive view, some psychologists criticize the concept (Baumrind, 1982; Locksley & Colten, 1979). Baumrind (1982) examined competency in children raised by either sex-typed or androgynous parents. She found that children of sex-typed parents tended to be more competent than children who had androgynous parents. Additionally, sex-typed parents tended to be more firm and authoritative with their children whereas androgynous parents tended to be more permissive and child-centered in their child rearing. However, since the concept of androgyny is relatively new, more research needs to be conducted to find what effects it has on the developing child.

CHILDREN'S PLAY

The study of children's play has increased since the 1970s (Pepler & Rubin, 1982). While it is difficult to define play precisely, it is clear that play serves many valuable functions. Play is a tool for communication and learning, and it helps children develop fine motor and gross motor skills. Children also use language to communicate with others during play. Social development is promoted through play as children learn the importance of sharing and cooperation. In addition, play helps children experience joy and release anger and frustration. Through play children are able to practice adult roles and cope with their feelings of being small in comparison to adults and their physical world. Children also frequently use cognitive skills to solve problems inherent in play situations, while the enhancement of creative and imaginary skills is fostered through play as well. In fact, play greatly contributes to all aspects of the child's physical, language, social, emotional, sex role, and cognitive development.

Mildred Parten (1932) studied preschool children's play. As a result of her classic study, she identified six types of preschool play which are considered still to be applicable today. In *unoccupied* play the child does not play as we generally think about play, but is occupied with anything that happens to be of fleeting interest. *Solitary* play occurs when a child plays alone or independently with toys. In *onlooker* play the child does not participate directly and only watches others play. In *parallel* play children play with toys beside other children but do not interact.

Associative play occurs when children interact with each other, including sharing materials, but do not have the same goal. An illustration of associative play is when three children are playing zoo next to each other in the following way. They are sharing animals, cages, and food supplies, but each child is participating in his own individual play experience. The children carry on separate conversations and do not interact with each other concerning the zoo play.

Cooperative play occurs when children are all playing together, sharing, taking turns, and are trying to achieve the same goal. An example of cooperative play is three children playing zoo together in another way. Not only do they share the necessary toys, but they also talk to one another, cooperate with each other and organize who will be the zookeeper, the visitor, the zoo veterinarian, and various other roles. As preschool children get older they spend more time in associative and cooperative play and less time in the other play forms which characterize younger children's play (Rubin, Watson, & Jambor, 1978).

Dramatic Play

As they age, children tend to engage in more complex, pretend play concerning social situations called dramatic or sociodramatic play. Researchers suggest that dramatic play has many benefits for children (Fein, 1981). In dramatic play children are able to try out many different roles—they may pretend to be an astronaut, a police officer, a teacher, or a superhero. At times they may even confuse reality and fantasy. Four-year-old Mark was pretending to be a police officer with a group of his peers. When the teacher asked him to come inside for lunch, he began yelling at the teacher, "I'm a cop. I tell you what to do! I make the rules around here." The teacher then helped Mark clarify that even though he was a pretend police officer, in reality he was a boy who needed to eat his lunch with his classmates.

Through participation in dramatic play children build on cognitive skills, practice taking another person's point of view and participate in peer negotiation. Children also begin to learn what effects their actions have on others. Since dramatic play is important for children's development, Griffing (1983) urges teachers of young children to do the following: Observe their play; be creative in fostering play; make time for play; provide the needed space, resources, and props for play; make play fun and exciting; and encourage children to actively participate in dramatic play. (Also see chapter nine on play and stories.)

Sometimes children's play may surprise parents. It is quite common for young children to "play doctor" with their friends or peers. Parents who happen to observe such an episode often react with shock. The first thing parents need to keep in mind is that children's sexual curiosity is a normal part of childhood and is no different from their abundant curiosity about everything in their world. Since children do not have the experiences, values, and cognitive maturity of the adult, they do not view sexuality in the same way adults do. To them sexuality is like everything else in their world, just one more thing to "figure out."

It is typical for preschool children to want to watch the other sex go to the bathroom or look at each other's bodies. One three-and-one-half-year-old girl saw one of her friends changing into his swimsuit. The little girl said to her father, "Look Daddy, Jimmy has got his tail on backwards." Parents and caregivers who react with horror to preschooler's natural sexual curiosity only make children feel that there is something wrong with or dirty about the human body. Instead of acting shocked with finding children "playing doctor," parents can gently and matter of factly suggest an alternate activity. Parents must also feel comfortable enough with their own sexuality so that they can answer children's questions openly and honestly. Parents who are overly modest and do not allow their children to dress in front of other children may find that instead of decreasing sexual curiosity they may in fact be increasing sexual curiosity. Additionally, such parents encourage children to develop the attitude that sex is evil or dirty instead of helping children satisfy their sexual curiosity in ways that eventually lead to healthy and responsible adult sexual behavior.

CONCLUSION

During the early childhood years, important developmental changes continue to occur. Physical development during this period can be characterized more as a refining and smoothing out process when compared to the rapid and dramatically changing prenatal, infant, and toddler periods. By the end of the preschool years, children have fairly good control of their bodies and an excellent command of their language. Although preschoolers remain quite egocentric and still need the middle childhood and adolescent years to develop social and emotional maturity, they emerge from this period as social beings quite capable of social interaction with peers and adults and in better control of their emotions than toddlers. Although the areas of children's development have been discussed separately in this chapter, it must be remembered that in actuality all areas of development are interrelated. Changes in any one area of development affect and are related to changes in all areas of development during early-childhood.

REFERENCES

Anglin, J. M. (1970). *The growth of word meaning.* Cambridge, MA: MIT Press.

Bandura, A. (1973). *Aggression: A social learning analysis.* New York: Holt.

Bandura, A., Grusec, J. E., & Menlov, F. L. (1967). Vicarious extinction of avoidance behavior. *Journal of Personality and Social Psychology, 5,* 16-23.

Bandura, A., & Menlov, F. L. (1968). Factors determining vicarious extinction of avoidance behavior through symbolic modeling. *Journal of Personality and Social Psychology, 8,* 99-108.

Bandura, A., & Ross, D., & Ross, S. A. (1961). Transmission of aggression through imitation of aggressive models. *Journal of Abnormal and Social Psychology, 63,* 575-582.

Bankart, C. P., & Anderson, C. C. (1979). Short-term effects of prosocial television viewing on play of preschool boys and girls. *Psychological Reports, 44,* 935-941.

Barnes, S., Gutfreund, M., Satterly, D., & Wells, G. (1983). Characteristics of adult speech which predict children's language development. *Journal of Child Language, 10,* 65-84.

Bauer, D. H. (1976). An exploratory study of developmental changes in children's fears. *Journal of Child Psychology and Psychiatry and Allied Disciplines, 17,* 69-74.

Baumrind, D. (1967). Child care practices anteceding three patterns of preschool behavior. *Genetic Psychology Monographs, 75,* 43-88.

Baumrind, D. (1971). Current patterns of parental authority. *Developmental Psychology Monographs, 1,* 1-103.

Baumrind, D. (1980). New directions in socialization research. *American Psychologist, 35,* 639-652.

Baumrind, D. (1982). Are androgynous individuals more effective persons and parents? *Child Development, 53,* 44-75.

Bem, S. L., & Lenney, E. (1976). Sex-typing and the avoidance of cross-sex behavior. *Journal of Personality and Social Psychology, 33,* 48-54.

Bernstein, B. (1972). A sociolinguistic approach to socialization; with some references to educability. In J. J. Gumperz & D. Hymes (Eds.), *Directions in sociolinguistics* (pp. 465-497). New York: Holt, Rinehart and Winston.

Bowlby, J. (1969). *Attachment and loss: Attachment Vol. 1.* New York: Basic Books.

Brody, G. H., Stoneman, Z., MacKinnon, C. E., & MacKinnon, R. (1985). Role relationships and behavior between preschool-aged and school-aged sibling pairs. *Developmental Psychology, 21,* 124-129.

Brown, R. (1973). *A first language; the early stages.* Cambridge, MA: Harvard University Press.

Brown, R., & Hanlon, C. (1970). Derivational complexity and order of acquisition in child speech. In J. Hayes (Ed.), *Cognition and the development of language* (pp. 11-53). New York: Wiley.

Buss, D. M. (1981). Predicting parent-child interactions from children's activity level. *Developmental Psychology, 17,* 59-65.

Capute, A. J., Palmer, F. P., Shapiro, B. K., Wachtel, R. C., & Accardo, P. Q. (1981). Early language development: Clinical application of the language and auditory milestone scale. In R. E. Stark (Ed.), *Language behavior in infancy and early childhood* (pp. 429-436). New York: Elsevier/North Holland.

Carey, S. (1978). The child as a word learner. In M. Halle, J. Bresnan, & G. Miller (Eds.), *Linguistic theory and psychological reality* (pp. 264-293). Cambridge, MA: MIT Press.

Cazden, C. B. (1981). Language development and the preschool environment.

In C. B. Cazden (Ed.), *Language in early childhood education* (pp. 3-15). Washington, D.C.: National Association for the Education of Young Children.

Chomsky, C. (1972). Stages in language development and reading exposure. *Harvard Educational Review, 42,* 1-33.

Coren, S., Porac, C., & Duncan, P. (1981). Lateral preference behaviors in preschool children and young adults. *Child Development, 52,* 443-450.

deVilliers, J. G., & deVilliers, P. A. (1978). *Language acquisition.* Cambridge, MA: Harvard University Press.

deVilliers, P. A., & deVilliers, J. G. (1979). *Early language.* Cambridge, MA: Harvard University Press.

Dollard, J., Doob, L. W., Miller, N. E., Mowrer, O. H., & Sears, R. R. (1939). *Frustration and aggression.* New Haven, CT: Yale University.

Downs, A. C. (1981). Sex-role stereotyping on prime-time television. *Journal of Genetic Psychology, 138,* 253-258.

Dunn, J., & Kendrick, C. (1980). The arrival of a sibling: Changes in patterns of interaction between mother and first born child. *Journal of Child Psychology and Psychiatry and Allied Disciplines, 21,* 119-132.

Elardo, R., Bradley, R., & Caldwell, B. M. (1977). A longitudinal study of the relation of infants' home environments to language development at age three. *Child Development, 48,* 595-603.

Erikson, E. H. (1963). *Childhood and society* (2nd ed.). New York: Norton.

Erikson, E. H. (1982). *The lifecycle completed: A review.* New York: Norton.

Etaugh, C. (1983). Introduction: The influence of environmental factors on sex differences in children's play. In M. B. Liss (Ed.), *Social and cognitive skills: Sex roles and children's play* (pp. 1-19). New York: Academic Press.

Fein, G. (1981). Pretend play in childhood: An integrative review. *Child Development, 52,* 1095-1118.

Feshbach, S. (1964). The function of aggression and the regulation of aggressive drive. *Psychological Review, 71,* 257-272.

Flake-Hobson, C., Robinson, B. E., & Skeen, P. (1983). *Child development and relationships.* New York: Random House.

Freud, S. (1961). *Civilization and its discontents.* New York: Norton.

Friedrich, L. K., & Stein, A. H. (1975). Prosocial television and young children: The effects of verbal labeling and role playing on learning and behavior. *Child Development, 46,* 27-38.

Gadberry, S. (1980). Effects of restricting first grader's TV-viewing on leisure time use, IQ change, and cognitive style. *Journal of Allied Developmental Psychology, 1,* 45-57.

Gallahue, D. L. (1982). *Understanding motor development in children.* New York: Wiley.

Gerbner, G., & Gross, L. (1980). The violent face of television and its lessons. In E. L. Palmer & A. Dorr (Eds.), *Children and the faces of television: Teaching, violence, selling* (pp. 149-162). New York: Academic Press.

Gibson, E. J., (1969). *Principles of perceptual learning and development.* Englewood Cliffs, NJ: Prentice-Hall.

Gibson, E. J., & Spelke, E. S. (1983). The development of perception. In P. H. Mussen (Ed.), *Handbook of child psychology Vol. 3. Cognitive Development* (4th ed., pp. 1-76). New York: Wiley.

Griffing, P. (1983). Encouraging dramatic play in early childhood. *Young Children, 38*(2), 13-22.

Grusec, J. E., & Kuczynski, L. (1980). Direction of effect in socialization: A comparison of the parent's versus the child's behavior as determinants of disciplinary techniques. *Developmental Psychology, 16*, 1-9.

Hartup, W. W. (1974). Aggression in childhood: Developmental perspectives. *American Psychologist, 29*, 336-341.

Hartup, W. W. (1983). Peer relations. In P. H. Mussen (Ed.), *Handbook of child psychology Vol. 4 Socialization, personality, and social development* (4th ed., pp. 103-196). New York: Wiley.

Hess, R. D. (1970). Social class and ethnic influences upon socialization. In P. H. Mussen (Ed.), *Carmichael's manual of child psychology Vol. 2*(3rd ed., pp. 457-557). New York: Riley.

Hess, R. D., & Shipman, V. C. (1965). Early experience and the socialization of cognitive modes in children. *Child Development, 36*, 869-886.

Honig, A. S. (1983). Television and young children. *Young Children, 38*(4), 63-76.

Huston, A. C. (1983). Sex-typing. In P. H. Mussen (Ed.), *Handbook of child psychology Vol. 4. Socialization, personality, and social development* (4th ed., pp. 387-467). New York: Wiley.

Hyde, J. S. (1984). How large are gender differences in aggression? A developmental meta-analysis. *Developmental Psychology, 20*, 722-736.

Irwin, O. C. (1960). Infant speech: Effect of systematic reading of stories. *Journal of Speech and Hearing Research, 3*, 187-190.

Jackson, R. H. (1983). Parenting: The child in the context of the family. In C. E. Walker & M. C. Roberts (Eds.), *Handbook of clinical psychology* (pp. 905-936). New York: Wiley.

Jay, S., & Farran, D. (1981, August). *Socioeconomic differences in mother-child interaction.* Paper presented at the American Psychological Association, Los Angeles, CA.

Jewett, C. L. (1982). *Helping children cope with separation and loss.* Harvard, MA: Harvard Common Press.

Jonas, G. (1977). *Stuttering, the disorder of many theories.* New York: Farrar, Straus & Giroux.

Kahn, A. J., & Kamerman, S. B. (1987). *Childcare: Facing the hard choices.* Dover, MA: Auburn House.

Karnes, M. B., Teska, J. A., Hodgins, A. S., & Badger, E. D. (1970). Educational intervention at home by mothers of disadvantaged infants. *Child Development, 41*, 925-935.

Kaye, E. (1979). *The ACT guide to children's television or . . . How to treat TV with TLC.* Boston: Beacon Press.

Kinsbourne, M., & Hiscock, M. (1983). The normal and deviant development of functional lateralization of the brain. In P. H. Mussen (Ed.), *Handbook of child psychology Vol. 2. Infancy and developmental psychology* (4th ed., pp. 157-280). New York: Wiley.

Kohlberg, L. (1966). A cognitive-developmental analysis of children's sex-role concepts and attitudes. In E. E. Maccoby (Ed.), *The development of sex differences* (pp. 82 173). Stanford, CA: Stanford University Press.

Koocher, G. P. (1973). Childhood, death and cognitive development. *Development Psychology, 9*, 369-375.

Koocher, G. P. (1974). Talking with children about death. *American Journal of Orthopsychiatry, 44*, 404-411.

Kuczaj, S. A. (1978). Children's judgments of grammatical and ungrammatical irregular past-tense verbs. *Child Development, 49,* 319-326.

Lamb, M. E. (1978). The development of sibling relationships in infancy: A short-term longitudinal study. *Child Development, 49,* 1189-1196.

Lamb, M. E., & Roopnarine, J. L. (1979). Peer influences on sex-role development in preschoolers. *Child Development, 50,* 1219-1222.

Lamb, M. E., & Sutton-Smith, B. (Eds.). (1982). *Sibling relationships: Their nature and significance across the lifespan.* Hildsdale, NJ: Erlbaum.

Leitch, S. M. (1977). *A child learns to speak: A guide for parents and teachers of preschool children.* Springfield, IL: Thomas.

Locksley, A., & Colten, M. E. (1979). Psychological androgyny: A case of mistaken identity. *Journal of Personality and Social Psychology,* 37, 1017-1031.

Lorenz, K. (1966). *On aggression.* New York: Harcourt Brace.

Lowery, G. H. (1986). *Growth and development of children* (8th ed.). Chicago, Year Book Medical Publishers.

Maccoby, E. E., (1980). *Social development: Psychological growth and the parent-child relationship.* New York: Harcourt Brace Jovanovich.

Maccoby, E. E., & Martin, A. (1983). Socialization in the context of the family: Parent-child interaction. In P.H. Mussen (Ed.), *Handbook of child psychology Vol. 4. Socialization, personality, and social development.* (4th ed., pp. 1-101). New York: Wiley.

Marion, M. (1981). *Guidance of young children.* St. Louis: Mosby.

Martin, B. (1975). Parent-child relations. In F. D. Horowitz (Ed.), *Review of child development research. Vol. 4* (pp. 463-540). Chicago: University of Chicago Press.

Marvin, R. S. (1977). An ethological-cognitive model for the attenuation of mother-child attachment behavior. In T. Alloway, P. Pliner, & L. Krames (Eds.)., *Attachment behavior* (pp. 25-60). New York: Plenum Press.

Masur, E. F., & Gleason, J. B. (1980). Parent-child interaction and the acquisition of lexical information during play. *Developmental Psychology, 16,* 404-409.

McCartney, K. (1984). Effect of quality of day care environment on children's language development. *Developmental Psychology, 20,* 244-260.

Mezynski, K. (1983). Issues concerning the acquisition of knowledge: Effects of vocabulary training on reading comprehension. *Review of Educational Research, 53 ,* 253-279.

Miller, P. H., & Zalenski, R. (1982). Preschoolers' knowledge about attention. *Developmental Psychology, 18,* 871-875.

Moore, S. G. (1977). Considerations and helpfulness in young children. *Young children, 32*(4), 73-76.

Nagy, W. E., & Anderson, R. C. (1984). How many words are there in printed school English? *Reading Research Quarterly, 19,* 304-330.

Osborn, D. K., & Osborn, J. D. (1977). Television violence revisited. *Childhood Education, 53,* 309-311.

Parke, R. D., & Slaby, R. G. (1983). The development of aggression. In P. H. Mussen (Ed.), *Handbook of child psychology Vol. 4. Socialization and personality development* (4th ed., pp. 547-641). New York: Wiley.

Parton, M.B. (1932). Social participation among preschool children. *Journal of Abnormal and Social Psychology, 27,* 243-269.

Pepler, D. J., & Rubin, K. H. (1982). Current issues in the study of children's play. *Human Development, 25,* 443 447.

Pick, H. L., & Pick, A. D. (1970). Sensory and perceptual development. In P. H.

Mussen (Ed.), *Carmichael's manual of child psychology Vol. 1.* (3rd ed., pp. 773-848). New York: Wiley.

Radin, N., & Kamii, C. K. (1965). The child rearing attitudes of disadvantaged negro mothers and some educational implications. *Journal of Negro Education, 34,* 138-146.

Radke-Yarrow, M., Zahn-Waxler, C., & Chapman, M. (1983). Children's prosocial dispositions and behavior. In P. H. Mussen (Ed.), *Handbook of child psychology: Vol. 4. Socialization, personality, and social development* (4th ed., pp. 469-545). New York: Wiley.

Rebecca, M., Hefner, R., & Oleshansky, B. (1976). A model of sex-role transcendence. *Journal of Social Issues, 32,* 197-206.

Robinson, B. E., Skeen, P., & Flake-Hobson, C. (1980). Sex-stereotyped attitudes of male and female child-care workers: Support for androgynous child care. *Child Care Quarterly, 9,* 233-242.

Roopnarine, J. L. (1984). Sex-typed socialization in mixed-age preschool classrooms. *Child Development, 55,* 1078-1084.

Rubin, K. H., Fein, G. G., & Vandenberg, B. (1983). Play. In P. H. Mussen (Ed.), *Handbook of child psychology: Vol. 4. Socialization, personality, and social development* (4th ed., pp. 693-774). New York: Wiley.

Rubin, K. H., Watson, K. S., & Jambor, T. W. (1978). Free play behaviors in preschool and kindergarten children. *Child Development, 49,* 534-536.

Rubinstein, E. A. (1980). Television violence: A historical perspective. In E. L. Palmer & A. Dorr (Eds.), *Children and the faces of television: Teaching, violence, selling* (pp. 113-127). New York: Academic Press.

St. Peter, S. (1979). Jack went up the hill . . . but where was Jill? *Psychology of Women Quarterly, 4,* 256-260.

Schachter, F. F., Marquis, R. E., Shore, E., Bundy, C. L., & McNair, J. H. (1979). *Everyday mother talk to toddlers—early intervention.* New York: Academic Press.

Stewart, R. B. (1983). Sibling attachment relationships: Child-infant interactions in the strange situation. *Developmental Psychology, 19,* 192-199.

Stoneman, Z., & Brody, G. H. (1981). The indirect impact of child oriented advertisements on mother-child interactions. *Journal of Applied Developmental Psychology, 2,* 369-376.

Tanner, J. M. (1970). Physical growth. In P. H. Mussen (Ed.), *Carmichael's manual of child psychology: Vol. 1* (3rd ed., pp. 71-155). New York: Wiley.

Tanner, J. M. (1978). *Foetus into man: Physical growth from conception to maturity.* Cambridge, MA: Harvard University Press.

Thompson, S. K. (1975). Gender labels and early sex role development. *Child Development, 46,* 339-347.

Tizard, B., Hughes, M., Carmichael, H., & Pinkerton, G. (1983). Language and social class: Is verbal deprivation a myth? *Journal of Child Psychology and Psychiatry and Allied Disciplines, 24,* 533-542.

Tudor, M. (1981). *Child development.* New York: McGraw Hill.

Ullian, D. Z. (1976). The development of conception of masculinity and femininity. In B. Lloyd & J. Archer (Eds.), *Exploring sex differences* (pp. 25-47). New York: Academic Press.

Weintraub, M., Clemens, L. P., Sockloff, A., Ethridge, T., Gracely, E., & Myers, B. (1984). The development of sex role stereotypes in the third year: Relationships to gender labeling, gender identity, sex-typed toy preference, and family characteristics. *Child Development, 55,* 1493-1503.

White, E., Elsom, B., & Prawat, R. (1978). Children's conceptions of death. *Child Development, 49,* 307-310.

Wickstrom, R. L. (1983). *Fundamental motor patterns* (3rd ed.). Philadelphia: Lea & Febiger.

Winn, M. (1977). *The plug-in-drug.* New York: Viking.

Wolman, B. B. (1978). *Children's fears.* New York: Grosset & Dunlap.

Chapter Three:

The Religious Concepts
of Preschoolers

KALEVI TAMMINEN, RENZO VIANELLO,
JEAN-MARIE JASPARD,
AND DONALD RATCLIFF

The religious concepts of children have been considered in a large number of studies, and several major reviews of the literature have been published (such as Elkind, 1971; Torrance, Goldman, & Torrance, 1975; Ratcliff, 1985, 1987; and Riccards, 1978). Most of the research, however, excludes preschool-aged children, and the few studies that include them almost always describe their lack of understanding in contrast with the accomplishments of older children. Systematic studies concentrating upon the abilities of preschoolers are virtually unknown.

The three European researchers who are the primary authors of this chapter have systematically studied the religious concepts of hundreds of preschoolers over the last two decades. Nearly all of this work has only been available in the original languages and is collected here in English for the first time. In addition, this chapter will summarize most of the other studies that include preschoolers (tangentially or otherwise) at the beginning of each section.

Methodologies of Research

A wide variety of methods have been employed in studying the religious concepts of children. Both quantitative and qualitative approaches have been used, and specific techniques include questionnaires, interviews, picture drawing and interpretation, storytelling, and other methodologies.

Likewise the three primary authors of this chapter have also used a variety of approaches, lending greater depth and comparative value. Tamminen and his fellow researchers, in their studies of Finnish chil-

dren, made use of personal interviews of children with the aid of drawings or photographs in a semiprojective manner, supplemented by religious background information provided by parents. Longitudinal findings from over 600 children are analyzed, supplemented by Swedish and
Norwegian studies of additional children.

Vianello, who studied a large number of Italian children over a twen-
ty-year period, made use of clinical interviews similar to those of Jean
Piaget, as well as stories which preschoolers completed or discussed. In
his Belgium study, Jaspard used an observational method (inspired by
Gesell) over a three-year period, where parents recorded the religious
questions and reflections of their children using a standardized protocol.
Parents were trained in the procedure and regularly supervised in their
observations of the ninety children.

CONCEPTS OF GOD

The study of children's concepts of God is by far the most researched
area of religious understanding, and the earliest studies extend back to
the last century (Barnes, 1892, and Brown, 1892). Piaget briefly described the four- to seven-year-old as attributing all origins to human or
divine activity (for example, clouds come from God smoking a pipe).

A landmark study of religious concepts was conducted by Goldman
(1964) in which six-year-olds were considered to belong to the "intuitive
religious" stage. Goldman found that the young children in his British
study were extremely literalistic, oversimplifying biblical accounts, and
tended to focus upon irrelevancies. Such was indicative of egocentric,
fragmented, and unsystematic thinking, claimed Goldman.

In studying letters written to God, Ludwig, Weber, and Iben (1974)
found that six-year-olds pictured God as primarily concerned with providing for physical needs. More recently Shelly (1982) and her associates
found that when preschoolers were asked to draw a picture of God, 12
percent of them produced drawings related to death.

In his study of Michigan children of Catholic, Jewish, Baptist, and
Hindu faiths, Heller (1986) found a general absence of information
about religion in four- to six-year-olds. Children were much more likely
to recognize than recall religious concepts. God was associated with fun
and play, a permissive deity who was concerned with children's welfare
and who performed certain functions for them. God was sometimes
described as good, at other times bad, and occasionally as a moral
mixture. Heller concluded that good and bad parental images were
projected upon God.

At this writing, Wilcox (1987) is conducting ongoing research of preschoolers, though present findings are only suggestive and not yet definitive. Her preliminary study indicates that children can understand religious concepts in virtually any biblical account, as long as the story has action and interesting characters and figures or props are available that correspond to the story line. She believes that children may grasp fairly sophisticated theological concepts because they are not as concrete and literalistic as older children, and that preschoolers can profit from religious content when allowed to make their own meanings from religious symbols and relate them to their lives.

Scandinavian Research

For the young child the image of God is generally considered to be anthropomorphic (Goldman, 1964); the child conceives God as being manlike, with human actions and physical limitations. He lives in a definite, though usually distant, place called heaven.

This concept is not merely the result of concrete thinking, the child's image of God is clearly related to his closest and earliest human relations at home. The child's first impressions of God reflect the experiences he or she has had with other humans, particularly the mother and father, a tendency accentuated by references to God such as "heavenly father." Biblical pictures and drawings in religious books also transmit an image of God that is often anthropomorphic. Yet, within the Christian perspective, even a developed image of God has certain anthropomorphic features; God is not "faceless," but rather a person with whom one can have a close relationship. Anthropomorphism becomes a problem when it becomes an obstacle to a person's religious growth and faith.

The picture provided by Scandinavian studies about the preschooler's images of God are not unambiguous concerning anthropomorphicity. All studies have brought out many expressions which are clearly anthropomorphic, such as the six-year-old girl's reply to a question on what God is like, "A fellow with some beard and a white gown," or as a five-year-old girl stated, "It has clothes on and a tie." Many children, especially at the age of four, conceive of many gods and multiple Christs, such as the four-year-old girl who said, "Because there are so many children there must also be many Jesuses, so that there would be enough of them for all of us."

Yet there is considerable variation in the degree to which researchers report anthropomorphism. Almost all the drawings by the twelve children in Kjellgren's (1987) study revealed an anthropomorphic image of God, with only one response that was diffuse. In Horberg's (1967) research as many as 95 percent pictured God in an anthropomorphic manner. Yet only a few children (aged four to six) in Hakomaa's (1981) study described God as clearly manlike. The majority of children in this study, as well as that of Vaatainen (1974) who considered seven- and eight-year-old children, described God as helpful, good, kind, invisible, and/or spirit. These children may have had clearly anthropomorphic features in their concepts of God that were not elicited. Massinen (1981) concluded that anthropomorphic features were neither found in isolation or even very emphatically in the image of God.

The *development* of the God concept also varies in the studies of preschoolers. In Haavisto's (1969) research, four-year-olds found it difficult to answer the question "What does God look like?" Most of them reported that he was bright, fine, kind, and some described him as invisible. Not until the age of six did about half describe God with clearly anthropomorphic features, sometimes referring to a picture they had seen. In contrast, Keskitalo (1987) discovered that almost all of the four-year-olds in his study gave exclusively anthropomorphic descriptions of God, while five- and six-year-olds gave both anthropomorphic and superhuman features. A few five-year-olds did not conceptualize God in human terms. It should be noted that Keskitalo formed these conclusions by analyzing answers given to several different questions, and the same child often reflected different levels of understanding to the different questions.

Kjellgren (1987), who made use of the drawings of children, elicited fairytale-like features in some drawings, as did Harms' (1944) earlier study. Other studies produced expressions such as "God lives far, far away in a castle, and the witch lives there too." Usually, however, children distinguish fairytale figures from God, as evidenced by Massinen's (1981) study. When comparing belief in God to belief in such figures, about 90 percent of his six-year-old subjects expressed a belief in God, an equal percentage believed in Jesus, more than half believed in the Holy Spirit, while only one-third considered Santa Claus as real and very few believed in the sandman.

A few studies indicate that some small children have a frightening image of God. From his Swedish research, Ottersen (1962) claimed that children from homes that are antireligious or neutral to religion do not receive positive input for the image of God, and thus the God concept is usually frightening or gloomy. Likewise some of the drawings and interpretations of their drawings given by children included fear imagery related to the divine in Kjellgren's (1987) study. Tamm (1986) considers the God concept typically to include both punishing and loving elements during the preschool years.

When six- and seven-year-olds were asked, "When you hear talk about God or when you think about him, do you feel frightened or good and safe?" almost all responded with the latter conclusion, although some answered "both" and only one child reported feeling frightened (Tamminen, 1979). Helohonka (1973), Hakomaa (1981), and Vaatainen (1974) obtained similar results. Keskitalo (1987) asked children, "How does it feel to think about the Heavenly Father?" and 75 percent answered with a positive expression such as "nice," "good," or "happy," about 10 percent gave a neutral response, and about 10 percent responded negatively. Some of the latter group considered it sad that God was so far away in heaven or that they never see God. Equivalent responses ensued when preschoolers were asked about Jesus. Four-year-olds found it difficult to answer these questions, and expressions clearly became more positive as children grew older, perhaps because the God concept is more familiar to them. Other studies bear out this general increasingly positive concept of God (Horberg, 1967; Helohonka, 1973; Helve, 1977; Hakomaa, 1981; Massinen, 1981).

In the Finnish studies, children were nearly unanimous in believing that God loves them and all children and that God is good, loving, and safe, although some children saw God's love as conditional upon being nice or believing in God. Older children used positive attributes to describe God when asked to complete the sentence "When I think of God . . ." Very few spoke of God as being frightening (Tamminen, 1983a).

Several studies describe the preschooler concept of God as a Being who is distant, somewhere far away, a Creator who functions in nature (Harms, 1944; Tamm, 1986). Yet the Finnish studies of six- to eight-year-olds describe him as someone who is at times "very close." Many of them could tell about situations in which God felt close, experiences often associated with evening or night, being alone, or praying in the evening. In addition, difficult situations in life, such as being rescued from danger or being in a hospital, were often mentioned. Quite often these youngsters also mention moral situations when they had done something wrong and had been forgiven. Very few say they have experienced God's closeness in nature (Tamminen, 1979, 1983b).

Preschoolers are almost unanimous in stating that God is in heaven, often explaining that his location is why some find him difficult to get in touch with. Yet Keskitalo (1987) found that 80 percent of preschoolers believe that God is close to them and close to other children and adults as well. When asked how God can be both close and distant, children offered a variety of explanations. Some think God is in heaven and his closeness is limited to his watching from there. Other children think that God is not restricted to being in heaven but can come down in a real form. Still others think God uses angels as helpers. About one-third speak of God's supernatural abilities in attempting to explain this apparent contradiction. Often children's answers include very strange explanations as they try to resolve the dilemma.

When Hakomaa (1981) and Keskitalo (1987) asked how the world or animals or flowers came about, most of the children who answered gave a religious explanation: God is the creator of everything. As in Helohonka's (1973) study, God as creator was most commonly emphasized by six-year-olds.

When asked, "What does God do?" his activity as a creator did not predominate until children were six years old. In Massinen's (1981) study, more than half of six-year-olds described God as the creator, although in other studies the children described God more in terms of a helper, guardian, or protector.

The concept of God, even for a small child, is an entity with many levels and dimensions, and contradictory features often appear together. It seems that preschool children have a readiness to understand God in ways that are not anthropomorphic, and some features of the divine image are clarified or otherwise change between the ages of four and six. God's omniscience and omnipotence may be in part understood. Children at this age have a generally positive emotional attitude toward God, particularly as God becomes more familiar, which in turn increases children's trusting attitude toward God and feelings of safety.

Italian Research

As noted in the Scandinavian research and other studies (Mailhiot, 1964; Nye & Carlson, 1984), Italian preschoolers also manifested an anthropomorphic perception of divinity. At this age God is a man, although a rather special one. For three- and four-year-olds, God and Jesus are often two names for the same person. In one Italian study of 137 Catholic children (Vianello, 1980), only 8 percent of children age four and 33 percent of children age five attributed some kind of omnipotence to God. Most of these children thought of God as a person who, as a four and one-half-year-old girl stated, "is like us": he has no beard but possesses long hair: he can save a drowning man because he is able to swim, yet he is unable to help airplane passengers in danger because the aircraft is too heavy, Jesus is good and knows a great deal, but a kindergarten teacher (a nun) is even better than Jesus.

Until five or six years, God is only a man to children, perhaps more knowledgeable and powerful than others, but he lacks omniscience, omnipotence, and omnipresence. For children from three to six, Jesus is fundamentally the hero of a sad and moving story of events of long ago—they are particularly struck by how Jesus died. They may ask adults why Jesus died by crucifixion yet, regardless of the explanation offered, will maintain that it was because "there were bad men around." At the same time these preschoolers may be convinced that Jesus is still alive, in heaven.

At about six or seven years of age, children begin to develop less anthropomorphic ideas, as God becomes a giant, a magician, or an invisible man: He can "pass through doors even when they are closed" and "he is enormous and, for example, when he is here, he may also be at school." As they progress through middle childhood, their concepts become even less anthropomorphic.

This research confirms Piaget's (1926) concept that the preschooler believes the universe was created by God, who is considered to be a special man. Since preschoolers attribute godlike characteristics to adults, such as believing that people cause snow, rain, clouds, mountains, and so on, they easily assimilate creative abilities to God, who is also human. However, as Deconchy (1964) notes, when they speak of creation, young children (in his research, seven-year-olds) do not mean creation from nothing, but use this term as meaning "building" or "making."

Werner (1948) and Piaget (1926) have emphasized the existence of magical thinking in youngsters' mental abilities. Magical thinking may be described as the perception of two phenomena as having a direct influence upon one another, although no causal link exists between them, and that the supposed relationship can be controlled by a person to modify reality (Piaget, 1926). More recent research (Vianello & Marin-Zanovello, 1980) indicates that magical thinking is not only due to precausal thinking limitations, but also due to a partially covert cultural process. In other words, adults may actually be promoting magical thinking instead of discouraging it in preschoolers.

While a number of authors (Arago-Mitjans, 1965; Gruehn, 1956; Terstenjak, 1955; Vergote, 1966) consider the child's religion to be magical, the present research suggests that there is a reciprocal influence between magical thinking and religious instruction. Children easily assimilate certain concepts, such as God is omnipotent, but at the same time religious instruction may reinforce magical thinking. The more preschoolers feel surrounded by an atmosphere of mystery (Vergote, 1983), the more influential that magical component becomes. If God is magical, this is because in some way everyone is magical to a lesser extent.

Piaget's (1932) Swiss research of immanent justice and divine providence has been replicated in a number of Italian studies which have included children younger than those in the original studies. Children were told three stories, including one about two children who stole apples and then ran away—one was caught while the other fell into the water as he crossed the bridge. The children were then asked if the latter child would have fallen into the water if he had *not* stolen the apples. Piaget's original research found that children decreasingly attributed the fall to the theft as they grow older, thus Piaget concluded that children decreasingly believe that all bad actions must be followed by punishment (immanent justice). The five Italian studies and Piaget's original study results are summarized below:

Research Study	n	age					
		4	5	6	7-8	9-10	11-12
Piaget	?	—	—	86	73	54	34
Tettamanzi-Vianello	202	63	55	17	32	57	50
Pizzo-Vianello	139	—	52	14	58	62	64
Gambarian-Vianello	168	25	45	55	48	49	—
Marin-Vianello	1408	12	40	49	48	39	41
Bozzolo-Vianello	369	23	35	16	19	37	—

As can be seen, the Italian studies definitely conflict with Piaget's, particularly with six-year-olds. In contrast to the 86 percent reported by Piaget, Italian children scored between 14 percent and 55 percent. Even more perplexing is the finding that belief in immanent justice apparently *increases* between seven and ten years.

How can this contradiction be explained? Piaget apparently overestimated the influence of the child's preoperational limitation while he underestimated environmental influences. From the age of four to five and particularly by six years children show a strong capacity for causal reasoning, which leads them to deny the link between the theft and the fall from the bridge. The belief in immanent justice tends to increase at about age seven due to environmental influences, particularly religious instruction. The belief in immanent justice is abandoned at about six years unless adults intervene by asking children to believe that God guarantees justice in the world.

Belgian Research

Children of practicing Catholic families were studied to consider how children increasingly differentiate God as "Other" in contrast to God as being anthropomorphic. Three successive stages in the preschooler's concept of God were found as a result of the study of children in Louvain, Belgium.

The first stage may be described as "God as Object/God as Human" (up to three years). Arago-Mitjans (1965) found that the one-year-old child is able to differentiate objects if they have a name that can be repeated and they are interesting and attractive. From eighteen months some children are interested in objects that represent the cross and call them "Jesus" (as do their parents). They enjoy handling such objects and may configure cubes to make a cross. They may express concern about this "Jesus" being present or absent in homes they visit. Arago also notes that religious behavior, such as making the sign of the cross or prayers, are imitated by children by the age of two.

By two-and-a-half this "Jesus" (or "Lord" or "God," whichever term is most used by the family) is differentiated from the cross, since the name for God has also been used to refer to the crucifix and statues. Often two- and three-year-olds have heard that God lives in church, and thus may ask, "Is that where he sleeps?" Children at this age wondered about God's occupation (ringing the church bell, singing), his work in his house (eating, cooking, knitting), and his sensations and feelings (he feels cold, cries, is sad, is friendly; his eyes are sore, he is ill). Occasionally the child confuses the priest with God. By age three Jesus is identified as a human character and linked to certain objects, places, and behavior.

A second stage can be termed "God as Superhuman" (three- and four-year-olds). At about three, the child comes to acquire additional features which are more selectively associated with God. Thus Jesus is represented by a crucifix, yet he lives in the church and one can go to say "hello" to him while one cannot see him. Natural events, such as rain and sunshine, are associated with his activities. The child also begins to use the term "God" more often. Contrary to the previous stage, he is not believed to participate in household tasks, but instead is sometimes associated with deceased family members or neighbors.

As the God concept becomes more differentiated, the child becomes increasingly interested in the divine, eventually asking to see God. When told that God is in heaven, that he is invisible and cannot be directly perceived, the child finds this hard to accept and sometimes expresses his or her resistance to this new revelation adamantly. Often the child asks questions regarding how far away heaven is and how one may get there and return. Eventually the child realizes that this is not possible or even desirable at the present time. The preschooler learns that certain religious story characters (Mary, Joseph, Santa Claus, the saints) and the deceased have access to heaven and see God. These people are understood to live in heaven and occasionally come to earth to satisfy people's demands and bring blessings through more or less personal forms (statues, Santa Claus). They believe that Jesus or God comes down from heaven to accomplish specific actions, such as being in church, at home with the child and parents, creating the weather, and so on. God is understood to bring all that is needed as well as things the child requests in prayers.

Arago-Mitjans (1965) reports similar findings among Spanish children, although he did not use a longitudinal approach as did the present study. He reports that the child's religion is inherently selfish; God is believed to be completely concerned with serving the child. God was found to be less anthropomorphic than some maintain; the child's wondering and desire to get in touch with God imply an understanding that God is powerful but different from humans, yet this understanding is syncretistic and, from an adult perspective, full of contradictions.

Arago-Mitjans notes that certain aspects of religion are more acceptable than others to the child, and thus a three- or four-year-old may refuse to participate in certain religious activities, particularly when they are compelled. The present research confirms this observation, and it should be noted that the child's interest in God is proportional to the mother's religious interest, particularly for boys. Males take great pains to repeat their mothers' religious gestures and attitudes faithfully, and their concern for praying is clearly related to the pleasure they give their mothers through such activity. If Jesus is the mother's friend, then he is also the boy's friend. Yet the boy also believes that he could provoke his mother by refusing to say his prayers or by saying that he does not love Jesus.

Little girls are also sensitive to their mothers' opinion at this age, but they are apparently more independent. They often take the initiative in spontaneous gestures or personal ceremonies (with candles, for example). Girls are also observed to have Jesus as an invisible companion in their solitary games, often developing a casual attitude toward him. The differences between boys' and girls' attitudes toward God become even more pronounced during the next stage, apparently because of God's male status. Girls are very sensitive to Jesus' friendship, although the father-God aspect may be problematic—one three-year-old girl reacted to her mother's attempt to teach the Lord's prayer by stating, "I have one father, not two. I don't want two."

The third stage can be identified as "God as Divinity," from age four-and-a-half to six years. At this time the child understands God to be transcendent (beyond space and time as well as omnipotent) and immanent (including omnipresent and omniscient). The child conceptualizes the divine as located in two spheres: 1) before and after life; prior to birth or conception and after death in heaven, and 2) in the present, maintaining the order of nature and concurrently supervising family life, alternately serving as the parent's partner and being the child's ally, a friend as well as an absolute model.

The child seeks to verify his or her conceptualization of God through questions about God's age, his size, the number of places he resides simultaneously, his ability to see everywhere ("even dark corners?"), and his ability to move through obstacles. The child comes to imagine God as acting upon phenomena unattainable to people, such as providing sunshine, controlling the weather, overcoming illness, giving life to plants and animals, and placing babies within mothers. The child assigns God the possibility of knowing everything and granting every wish.

The present research, as well as that of Arago-Mitjans (1965) in Spain, Klink (1970) in the Netherlands, and Wurth (1961) in Austria indicate that God's omnipotence takes on a socialization function—rewards from religious characters (Jesus, the saints, etc.) are related to the child's behavior (being polite, friendly and thoughtful, and treating God as one would adults) or at least to the quality of the child's prayers. Conversely, disappointments that take place, including unanswered prayers, are interpreted as the consequence of God's bad will or to some extent the deficient behavior of the child; the child before age six does not see negative events as disconfirming of the deity's omnipotence. Thus if it rains, it is because God does not want sunshine, or if a sick little brother does not improve, the cause is lack of adequate prayer.

Disappointments sometimes produce momentary guilt or promises to be good. It may also produce other emotional reaction, such as one girl who was asked to say "hello" to Jesus when entering a church. When she received no response from God, she refused to practice any further religious activity for five months, saying "I am waiting for him to say hello to me first." This kind of disappointment is particularly present in girls, yet rarely found in boys; girls expect to perceive God directly and an invisible Jesus is problematic.

Between four and five many girls compensate for the latter disappointment through an almost hallucinatory imagination. They see God appearing in a cloud, one girl "feels God's sun in my heart," another slightly ill girl sees Jesus above her (a crucifix) watching and healing her. Blessings that occur to the family or to the girl are the result of prayer with the Friend, who never refuses her anything. Girls show their gratitude to God by affectionately giving him flowers or putting on a pretty dress in his honor.

The girl's understanding of God may be sexualized, such as one four-year-old who wondered how Jesus could come into the host during Mass complete with his sex organs. Some believe Jesus could impregnate them. But these sensitive perceptions decrease after age five and the relationship to Jesus comes to be expressed through liturgy. Communion becomes an object of particular interest and potential source of conflict, such as one five-year-old girl who wanted to participate in communion because "the teacher said so, Jesus comes into our hearts. And if I can't go to communion, Jesus won't come into me."

For boys, God's omnipotence seems to nourish the self-image and identification. They are fascinated by spectacular performances of Jesus, including driving a car at high speeds, walking on water, or going down all of the steps in one jump without falling. As God comes to be attributed with unlimited power, the omnipotence previously attributed to parents is decreased: "Jesus is stronger than Daddy and Daddy is stronger than Mummy. Mummy, do you know everything? What about Daddy? So God knows everything." "God is the strongest, the kindest, he decides everything" and "he is the chief of everything."

Boys also are sensitive to absolute power for evil, which is just as fascinating as God's power for good. They will quickly pick up on religious discussions of beings with such power and are relieved to learn of the devil. If adults do not teach the child about the devil, some boys transfer this absolute power to "the villains who killed Jesus" and often ask for stories about these men (apparently to show they do not belong to this group and even that they would have avenged Jesus). Five- and six-year-old boys form an alliance with Jesus or God, which allows them to give God's blessing upon others, seen in forecasting the next day's weather, for example.

Some boys express overt oedipal concerns during this stage. In the previous stage boys were interested in God to please the mother, but now they join forces with him hoping to supplant the father in her eyes. Others more modestly content themselves with moral promises: "Today I'll be like Jesus when he was small."

By age six the mother-God interference fades, producing a faith crisis related to God's omnipotence. Bad weather, stinging wasps, big bad wolves, dust that irritates the eyes, nasty people, unhappiness, and the handicapped all seem to contradict such omnipotence. Doubt is produced not by failure of divine goodwill, but because of the affirmation of God's ability to do everything with perfection. As noted long ago by Clavier (1913), the problem of evil at this age becomes a splinter in the belief in omnipotence. Religious education can now help broaden the understanding of divine presence and revive faith, omnipotence can now be understood in terms of more universal needs. In the process the former image of a protecting and kindly God becomes a more remote God, who keeps his secrets to himself and acts as a judge.

CONCEPTS OF DENOMINATION AND PRAYER

Elkind (1978) conducted a series of interviews, using Piaget's semi-clinical approach, in which he studied the concepts of denomination and prayer with Protestant, Catholic, and Jewish children. For the purpose of this chapter, only the results of children aged five to seven years will be summarized, although the original study also included older children.

Denomination concepts were described as global and undifferentiated with preschoolers; they often identified their denominational category and related it to the God concept, but were unable to specify its meaning further. When pressed to give specific details, they randomly drew from ethnic, racial, and national concepts. While this implied confusion about the concept of denomination, they realize it did not refer to all people or to any animals.

While children associated denomination with God and believed he had made the denomination, they spoke as if the denomination were a physically existing object. They also considered denomination to be exclusive of other groups, for example one could not be an American *and* a Catholic. Catholic and Jewish children were more familiar with their designations than were Protestant children, probably because the latter were more familiar with their specific designation (e.g., "Baptist") than the broader and less-used term "Protestant." Elkind also noted that the Catholic and Jewish preschoolers in this study were more knowledgeable of religious concepts.

Elkind (1978) also summarized his research findings on the subject of prayer among preschoolers. Five-year-olds gave responses that were global and undifferentiated, while six- and seven-year-olds were in transition to the next stage in which prayer was considered a behavior (they failed to consider its affective and mental aspects, central to the concept for older children and adults).

Children between five and seven years have a vague understanding of prayer. Elkind noted that prayers are linked to God by these children but are often recited as formulas without genuine understanding of the concept. For example, preschoolers were uncertain whether animals could pray, although they believed children everywhere prayed.

Prayers were oriented toward personal gratification and associated with fixed times (e.g., bedtime), and prayers were believed to originate

from heaven, God, or fairyland. Many believed God magically trans-
ported prayers to heaven or that they were self-propelled. Thus prayer,
like denomination, was considered to be an object.

Scandinavian Studies

In Scandinavian countries, as in many parts of the world, prayer is
the most powerful expression of a child's religious life. Evening prayer is
the part of religious tradition which is most often transmitted in the
home context. Commonly it is the mother who teaches the evening
prayer.

As noted above and by Long, Elkind, and Spilka (1967), preschoolers
have little real comprehension of the meaning of prayer. Thus the evening prayer or grace at meals has a firm structure, but little attention is
paid to its detailed contents. Yet at this age prayer is also spontaneous in
situations such as when the child becomes ill, and often the prayer is
accompanied by strong emotions in such contexts. Usually the tone of
that emotion is positive, and several researchers, such as Parviainen
(1987) note that most children conceive evening prayer as safe, fun, and
nice.

Children of this age often associate external behavior (folding the
hands) with prayer. They also have a good comprehension of the basic
purpose of prayer—Keskitalo (1987) found that about half of the four-to
six-year-old children knew that one can talk to God in prayer, a trend
that increased with age. These children believed you could talk to God
about anything, including both happy or sad subjects, and prayer for
others increased between four and six (Parviainen, 1987).

Parviainen found that prayers were an activity directed either to God
or Jesus, depending upon the child's training. One third of the children
prayed both to God/Heavenly Father, and Jesus, although such results
vary slightly from study to study. The person to whom prayers are
addressed can vary according to situation: Sick children are more likely
to pray to Jesus, perhaps due to hearing Bible stories about Jesus
healing the sick.

While some researchers have considered magical thinking to be typical in preschoolers' prayers (see the Italian studies in the previous section), this characterization may not do full justice to the young child's
praying. The result generally depends upon the criteria used in determining whether a given prayer is magical. It is indeed difficult to draw a
line between the magical and the religious in prayers at this age. There
is a tendency toward persuading God to provide services through prayer
at this age, and prayer tends to take on elements of a rite, since prayers
tend to be said in the same manner each time (Virkkunen, 1975). Yet

one must notice that the scanty verbal expressions of preschoolers make the distinction difficult.

Goldman (1964), in his study of British children, noted that six- and seven-year-olds think that all prayers will come true, and if they do not it is the child's fault; either he prayed too quietly or he has been naughty. The Finnish research produces a somewhat different picture; most pre- schoolers do have an implicit confidence in God hearing prayers, but that does not necessarily mean they will come true (Parviainen, 1987). At least six-year-olds understand that some things come true when they are prayed for, but not all of them (Massinen, 1981). Trust in prayers being fulfilled decreases between four and six, and the decline continues into the school years (Tamminen, 1983b). Meanwhile trusting that God hears prayers remains constant throughout this age range (Parviainen, 1987).

Parviainen pursued the magical nature of prayer further by asking children two questions: "Why do you say your evening prayer?" and "Why do you always pray the same prayer at night?" Only half of the children could give an explanation, and of these about half spoke of the comfort and security produced by prayer, while the others gave either a religious argument (e.g., trust in God's help and protection) or a magical reason (e.g., prayer guaranteeing a good night's sleep). Six-year-olds tended to give more magical answers than younger children.

Thus only a few of the reasons offered for repeated prayers were genuinely magical, while the most common arguments were that it was the only prayer they knew or that they particularly liked that prayer. Magical features were also absent in studies of older children, both in their own definitions of prayer and in examples of prayers (Tamminen, 1983a).Magical thinking is not necessarily implied by repetition of pray- ers; the same affection for repetition is found in the preschooler's daily routine. Magical thinking is most likely when the evening prayer is taught apart from the context of warmth and safety with a kindly adult.

Boys and girls are clearly different in their manner of praying. Boys tend to pray more irregularly and less frequently. Girls are more likely to say that they have experienced God's answers to their prayers, while boys are less likely to have positive emotional experiences in prayer. Sex differences in the motives for prayer were insignificant.

CONCEPTS OF DEATH AND AFTERLIFE

Death and life after death have been subject to more research than either denomination or prayer, yet the number of studies still falls short of those considering children's concepts of God. Note that concepts of death held by preschoolers were also briefly considered in chapter two, while their understanding of living versus nonliving objects was emphasized in chapter one.

In their review of the literature regarding concepts of death, Speece and Brent (1984) found three components in the concepts among preschoolers. First, children learn that death is irreversible; a dead body cannot become alive again. Second, they come to understand that the functions that define life cease upon death, and third, that all things that live eventually die. The age of acquisition of each of these components varied widely from study to study, with the average being five to seven years of age. The reviewers noted methodological difficulties often existed in the research.

Prior to acquisition of the above components of the concept, the preschooler understands death to be more like a trip, or sleep, or possibly like being ill, rather than being permanent. Children first associate death with more observable indications, such as the cessation of speaking and eating, rather than relying on a more comprehensive definition such as the end of all life functions. They also believe that certain people do not die or certain actions can cause a person to avoid death completely, rather than seeing death as universal.

The reviewers also noted that these descriptions are not conclusive since most researchers assumed children saw death as the opposite of, and thus incompatible with, life. Should this not be the case, the conclusions reached might require reconceptualization. It should also be noted that children might have confused the concept of irreversibility of death with the theological concept of life after death.

Research indicates that children often think of death (Grollman, 1967), indeed 80 percent of children's fears concern death (Reed, 1970). Questions about death are most likely to occur at bathtime (Hendin, 1973).

Nagy (1948), in her Hungarian study, has proposed three phases in the child's understanding of death. The first phase occurs between birth and age five, when the child sees death as impermanent and thus tends not to show intense sorrow; grief shown at this age is more likely to be imitative rather than the result of cognitive reflection. Until age three, death is only conceptualized as separation (Hendin, 1973). The death concept has its genesis in disappearance/reappearance games ("peek-a-boo") during infancy, as well as sleep.

Between five and nine or ten years of age a second phase in understanding develops in which permanence is understood, although death as a reality for everyone including the self is not accepted until late in this phase. Affective changes in the child's understanding of death are implied by the increased sweating in response to death-related words, when comparing children under five with others more than five years old. Yet the older preschooler continues to hold to the impermanence of death in free play.

The interest in death generally peaks at about age seven. Yet the child generally does not express strong fears of dying, or even his own death, at this time (Schoenberg, 1972). Nonsuburban children were more likely to cite violence as the cause of death, while suburban children were more likely to blame disease, old age, or "because they are bad" (Grollman, 1967, and "How Kids," 1972). Fear of hospitals, sleep, or darkness may in part be due to fear of death during the preschool and school years (Rosenblum, 1963), while Grollman notes that one four-year-old girl associated all broken bones with death.

Scandinavian Research

While preschoolers' conceptualization of death is concrete, it is also influenced by their religious education. Children speak concretely about putting a dead person into a grave, how the body rots, and so on, but they also include religious thoughts about death. The specific content of those religious thoughts varies from study to study, in part due to the approach of the study. In Helohonka's (1973) study, only a small number spoke of people going to heaven, yet in Haavisto's (1969) study more than half of the five- and six-year-olds mentioned this destination. Such differences were probably due to differences in the questions asked: Helohonka's "What happens to man *when he* dies?" contrasted with Haavisto's "What happens to man *after* death?" Helohonka also used a photograph of children in a cemetery, which may have produced more concrete thinking. Both studies indicated that religious thought about death increased between ages four and six. Most of the six-year-olds in Massinen's (1981) study thought that man or spirit or soul goes to heaven or elsewhere. Ninety percent of these children believed that children, not just adults, die.

Eternal life in heaven is usually associated with something above, such as the sky or space, an association that persists for many well into youth and adulthood (Tamminen, 1983b). This may partially be accounted for by the fact that the English words "heaven" and "sky" have only one synonym in some languages, such as "taivas" in Finnish.

Italian Research

Research involving several hundred hours of observation over more than a ten-year period, as well as maintaining diaries at home, have revealed that children's understanding of death is more highly developed than often thought (Vianello and Marin, 1985). Even by two to three years of age children experience death in a complex and organized manner. Two-year-old children, for example, show surprise and pity at the death of an insect or other animal. They gradually come to recognize death as different from simple sleep or illness, increasingly understanding it as a state opposite that of life. Preschoolers also recognize some of its causes as well as some of its effects (e.g., lack of movement).

While children at age three do not yet understand death to be irreversible, universal, and involving the cessation of vital functions, they no longer consider hospitals as places where the dead may return to life. They also do not consider death as something which only happens to others, but they realize it could happen to their parents and themselves. In describing death of self and others they may reveal separation anxiety and fear of being attacked. By the age of five most of the children studied understood that death is irreversible and universal.

This research indicates that religious instruction, particularly the belief that people go to heaven when they die, probably allows children to face the problem of death with less anxiety. However, religious beliefs tend to conflict with daily experience; dead people are put into caskets and buried (death is irreversible) yet they still go to heaven (death is reversible). This contradiction comes through in children's statements that vital functions cease upon death, yet they also describe playing games in heaven. Although the concept of "soul" may help overcome these contradictions, at the age of five or six children mentally tend to transform immaterial concepts into concrete material fact and thus teaching the idea of "soul" is not very helpful.

Preschoolers apparently accept but do not resolve these contradictions, since they believe anything related to religion is true, even though it may be incomprehensible and mysterious. It is precisely at this point of contradiction that there develops a fracture between the world and God, a fracture that seems to characterize nearly all preschooler conceptualizations of religion. At the same time, the problem of death is so important for children that they are strongly motivated to solve the contradiction. This may explain why children are more likely to speak spontaneously of God guaranteeing immortality than they are to speak of God as the Creator, God guaranteeing justice, or any other divine power, even when prompted by adults with statements of a religious nature, as research has indicated.

LIMITATIONS OF THE RESEARCH

It should be noted that a number of difficulties exist in making firm conclusions about preschoolers' religious concepts. Many of these result from young children's language limitations (see chapter one) while others are due to methodological difficulties. A number of these problems are noted by the primary authors of this chapter as well as Murphy (1977, 1978).

Interview techniques are very difficult or even impossible to use prior to the age of four or five. Even then it is very difficult for children to express verbally their religious concepts or experiences. The interviewer's personality influences the results to a great extent, as does the context of the interview.

One must also ask to what extent verbal expression reveals actual experiences or conceptualizations, a difficulty which also exists with older children but is particularly acute with preschoolers. A child often understands, experiences, and feels more than can be expressed during the preschool years. Are the age-related differences in religious concepts only the result of limitations in expressive abilities in small children? On the other hand, is it not possible that small children will use expressions that have been learned only as words, without actual understanding or internalizing?

Part of these limitations may perhaps be compensated for by use of drawings or pictures which can projectively bring out features that a child cannot express verbally. Yet the reliability of projective measures has often been rather poor (Mischel, 1968) and may force a child into a concrete mode of thinking, prematurely delimiting the child's perception of the task or subject matter. Thus the data and conclusions may reflect an understanding that is less advanced than the actual concepts of the child.

The specific formulation of questions can also influence the research results. Thus in Horberg's (1967) study, children were asked, "What do you think God is like? Do you believe God *looks* like something? What do you think God *looks* like?" while Helohonka (1973), Vaatainen (1974), and Hokomaa (1981) asked, "What is God/Heavenly Father like?" The former sort of questions are more directive to God's appearance and thus can be considered leading (they assume a physical appearance that can be described), while the latter is more general and may *not* elicit a physical description that the child has conceptualized.

One must also question whether the responses given indicate concepts that existed prior to the researcher's evaluation, or whether children may make up their responses as the examination occurs. Concepts which have been reflected upon are likely to be more developed than spontaneous comments made on the spur of the moment; one wonders if some of the supposedly distorted understandings are not merely the result of the child's attempting some response to researchers' probings into strange and unfamiliar topics.

In some of the studies reported in this chapter, children were found to give particular kinds of responses when they realized that the adult researcher was interested in religious topics. For example four- and five-year-olds usually responded affirmatively when asked whether God is the Creator or whether he is capable of doing miracles. Yet one must also ask whether their concepts have been organically linked with the events of daily life or whether conversely they have been assimilated separately (perhaps only verbally) apart from everyday events. As noted in the Italian research, a world/God fracture was found in preschoolers' understanding of death and afterlife, while concepts of God were more likely to be integrated with daily life.

A final limitation to the research may be the theoretical models used, particularly the anthropomorphism hypothesis. As noted in chapter one, Piagetian theory concentrates upon the limits of preschoolers' concepts, rather than their capabilities, and likewise the anthropomorphic theory may be inadequate because of its implicit negativism. The theoretical frame may be a limiting aspect in field observation in that it may truncate the analysis by bringing into consideration only the data which verify or contradict a specific hypothesis. Indeed, is a moral level of conceptualizing God necessarily more advanced than conceptualizing him as a physical creature? Perhaps one could posit an alternative framework contrasting an egocentric view of God (God for me) with a theocentric view (God for himself). A second axis could be considered as well: the realistic perception of God (God seen as a human image) versus a symbolic perception (God is other than purely human).

CONCLUSION

Considering the results of the above studies, the religious concepts of the preschooler appear to be limited, yet the precise nature of those limitations is sometimes unclear. The different nationalities of children may account for some of the differences, as may the differing denominations (e.g., the predominantly Lutheran orientation of Scandinavians versus the Roman Catholic population in the Italian studies). But even within a more homogeneous group, the family background and precise geographical location, as well as the methodology and precise nature of the study, also produce important variations.

Additional study of the religious concepts of preschoolers is needed, particularly research which includes a diversity of methods and instruments, so that the effects of differing approaches may be compared. Once these effects are better understood, we will be better able to separate the influence of denomination and other environmental influences on the result.

REFERENCES

Arago-Mitjans, J. M. (1965). .Psicologia religiosa del nino. Barcelona: Herder.

Barnes, E. (1892). Theological life of a California child. *Pedagogical seminary,* 2, 442-448.

Brown, A. W. (1892). Some records of the thoughts and reasonings of children, *Pedagogical seminary,* 2, 358-396.

Clavier, H. (1913). *L'idee de Dieu chez l'enfant.* Paris: Fischbacher.

Deconchy, J. P. (1964). L'idee de Dieu entre 7 et 16 ans; base semantique et resonance psychologique. *Lumen Vitae, 19,* 277-290.

Elkind, D. (1971). The development of religious understanding in children and adolescents. In M. Strommen (Ed.), *Research on religious development: A comprehensive handbook.* New York: Hawthorn Books.

Elkind, D. (1978). *The child's reality: Three developmental themes.* New York: Lawrence Erlbaum Pub.

Goldman, R. (1964). *Religious thinking from childhood to adolescence.* New York: Seabury.

Grollman, E. A. (1967). *Explaining death to children.* Boston: Beacon Press.

Gruehn, W. (1956). *Die Frommigkeit der Gegenwart.* Munster: Axendorf.

Haavisto, L. (1969). Lasten uskonnolliset kasitykset. *Tampereen yliopiston psykologian laitoksen tutkimuksia 20/1969.* Institute of Psychology of the University of Tampere.

Hakomaa, R. S. (1981). Nelja-kuusivuotiaiden lasten kasitys Jumalasta. Unpubl. Master in Theol. thesis in Religious Education. The Library of the Faculty of Theology, University of Helsinki.

Harms, E. (1944). The development of religious experience in children. *American Journal of Sociology, 50,* 112-122.

Heller, D. (1986). *The children's God.* Chicago: University of Chicago Press.

Helohonka, S. (1973). Esikouluikaisten lasten uskonnollisuus. Unpubl. Master in Theol. thesis in Religious Education. The Library of the Faculty of Theology, University of Helsinki.

Helve, H. (1977). Ala-asteen oppilaiden maailmankuva ja uskonnollisuus. Unpubl. M.A. thesis. Institute of Comparative Religion, University of Helsinki.

Hendin, D. (1973). *Death as a fact of life.* New York: Norton.

Horberg, U. (1967). Barn och religion. Unpubl., Pedagogiska institutionen av Uppsala universitet (Institute of Psychology of the University of Uppsala).

How kids look at death (1972, Sept.) *Science Digest, 72, 24.*

Keskitalo, M. (1987). 4-6 vuotiaiden uskonnollinen ajattelu ja jumalakuva. Unpub. Master of Theology thesis in Religious Education. The Library of the Faculty of Theology, Institute of Practical Theology, University of Helsinki.

Kjellgren, M. (1987). Om brans gudsbild. Unpubl. Institutionene for socialt arbete. Socialhogskolan. Stockholms Universitet (University of Stockholm).

Klink, J. L. (1970). *Kind en geloof.* Bilthoven: Ambo Boeken.

Long, D.,Elkind, D., & Spilka, B. (1967). The child's conception of prayer. *Journal for the Scientific Study of Religion, 6,* 101-109.

Ludwig, D. L., Weber, T., & Iben, D. (1974). Letters to God: A study of children's religious concepts. *Journal of psychology and theology, 2,* 31-35.

Mailhiot, B. (1964). E Dio si fece fanciullo. It. translation of Godin, A. (Ed.) (1961), *Adulte et enfant devant Dieu.* Bruxelles: Lumen Vitae.

Massinen, V. (1981). Esikouluikaisten uskonnollisuus ja sen liittyminen maailmankuvaan. Unpubl. M.A. thesis. Institute of Comparative Religion, University of Helsinki.

Mischel, W. (1968). *Personality and assessment.* New York: Wiley.
Murphy, R. (1977). The development of religious thinking in children in three easy stages? *Learning for Living, 17,* 16-19.
Murphy, R. (1978). *The development of religious thinking in children: A review of psychological theories.* Leicester, England: UCCF Religious Studies Committee.
Nagy, M. (1948). The child's view of death. *Journal of Genetic Psychology, 73,* 3-27.
Nye, C. W. & Carlson, J. S. (1984). The development of the concept of God in children. *The Journal of Genetic Psychology, 14,* 137-142.
Ottersen, O. (1962). *De viktigaste aren.* Stockholm: Diakonistyreleseys boktorlay.
Parviainen, K. (1987). Lasten rukouskasitys ja rukoileminen esikasvatusiassa. Master in Theology thesis, The Library of the Faculty of Theology, University of Helsinki.
Piaget, J. (1926). *La representation du monde chez l'enfant.* Paris: Alcan.
Piaget, J. (1932). *Le jugement moral chez l'enfant.* Paris: Alcan.
Ratcliff, D. E. (1985). The development of children's religious concepts: Research review. *Journal of Psychology and Christianity, 4,* 35-43.
Ratcliff, D. E. (1987). Teaching the Bible developmentally. *Christian Education Journal, 7,* 21-32.
Reed, E. (1970). *Helping children with the mystery of death.* Nashville: Abingdon.
Riccards, M. (1978). The structure of religious development. *Lumen Vitae, 33,* 97-123.
Rosenblum, J. (1963). *How to explain death to a child.* Lansing, MI: International Order of the Golden Rule.
Schoenberg, B. (1972). *Psychosocial aspects of terminal care.* New York: Columbia University Press.
Shelly, J. A. (1982). *The spiritual needs of children.* Downers Grove, IL: InterVarsity Press.
Speece, M. S., & Brent, S. B. (1984). Children's understanding of death: A review of three components of the death concept. *Child Development, 55,* 1671-1686.
Tamm, M. (1986). Barnens religiosa forestallningsvarld. Alvsjo: Verbum.
Tamminen, K. (1979). Koulutulokkaat ja uskonnonopetus. *Helsingin yliopiston kasvatustieteen laitos.* Institute of Pedagogy, University of Helsinki.
Tamminen, K. (1983a). Uskonnollinen ajattelu ja uskonnolliset kasitteet kouluiassa 2: jumalakuva, rukouskasitys ja kasitys kuolemasta. *Uskonnonepedagogiikan julkaisuja B 11/1983. Helsingin yliopiston kaytannollisen teologian laitos.* Institute of Practical Theology, University of Helsinki.
Tamminen, K. (1983b). Religious experiences of children and young people. *Research Reports on Religious Education C2/1983.* Institute of Practical Theology, University of Helsinki.
Terstenjak, A. (1955). Psicologia e pedagogia nell'insegnamento religioso. Milano: Vita e Pensiero.
Torrance, E. P., Goldman, R. J., & Torrance, J. P. (1975). The meaning and relevance of learning readiness for curriculum construction in Christian education. *Character Potential, 7,* 118-142.
Vaatainen, R. L. (1974). 7 ja 8 vuotiaiden uskonnolliset kasitykset. *Uskonnon-*

pedasgogiikan julkaisuja A 10/1974. Helsingin yliopiston kaytannollisen teologian laitos (Institute of Practical Theology, University of Helsinki).

Vergote, A. (1966). *Psychologie religieuse.* Bruxelles: Dessart.

Vergote, A. (1983). *Religion, fei, incroyance.* Bruxelles: Mardaga.

Vianello, R. (1980). *Ricerche psicologiche sulla religiosita infantile.* Firenze: Giunti.

Vianello, R. & Marin-Zanovello, M. L. (1980). Ricerca di sondaggio sull'atteggiamento magico infantile. *Eta Evolutiva, 7,* 24-39.

Vianello, R. & Marin, M. L. (1985). *La comprensione della morte nel bambino.* Firenze: Guinti.

Virkkunen, T. P. (1975). Yksilon uskonnollinen kehitys. *Suomalaisen teologisen kirjallisuuseuran julkaisuja 94.* Helsinki.

Werner, H. (1948). *Comparative psychology of mental development.* New York: Int. Un. Press.

Wilcox, M. (1987). [Personal correspondence and telephone conversation]. Also see her cassette tape and chart "Understanding faith development" (1986), Living the Good News, P.O. Box 18345, Denver, CO 80218.

Wurth, E. (1961). *Die religiose erziehung des kleinkinder.* Vienne.

Chapter Four:

Preschooler Moral Development

CLAITY P. MASSEY

Religious education, whether it is in the church, school, or home, must provide for the moral development of the child. Moral development includes the ability to understand the difference between right and wrong and moral action and the ability to choose to do the right thing. The developmental process of morality will be the focus of this chapter, clarifying how it occurs and ways that it may be enhanced.

One of the most difficult tasks in studying moral development is establishing reliable criteria for measuring the level of growth and development. A common approach in determining moral judgment has been to interview children and have them tell you what they would do in a situation or to explain why the choice someone else made was good or bad. Evaluations of moral actions have been conducted in naturalistic as well as contrived/research settings. Such evaluation is a difficult process for adults, but even more complex with preschoolers. What does it mean for a preschooler to act morally? Isolated behaviors may come to mind, but we must understand the context before we can be sure they are moral.

The question of understanding right and wrong is sometimes limited by the child's perspective during the early years. Frequently adults assume that children have chosen to do wrong when in fact they have chosen to do what they perceive to be right. The verbal limitations that inhibit the young child's ability to express thoughts and feelings compound the difficulty of moral evaluation.

One of the earliest studies focusing on children's moral thinking and behavior was reported by Hartshorne and May (1928-1930). This landmark study included thousands of children and their moral conduct in a variety of contexts. The moral code was found to change depending on whether or not the setting was a game, test, or contest. The moral behavior was generally inconsistent; for example, cheating seemed to depend on expediency. The moral behavior also changed in different settings (home, church, or playground). Because of the inconsistency of the response from the children, Hartshorne and May were convinced that it was impossible to categorize children as moral or immoral. Church leaders were particularly alarmed with their report that children who attended Sunday school regularly were only slightly more honest and helpful than children who did not.

More recently Sears, Rau, and Alpert (1965) studied children's ability to resist temptation in play settings. Using six different tests, the researchers came to the conclusion that resisting temptation in one situation was not predictive of resisting temptation in another situation. As in previous studies, they concluded that moral inconsistency was a problem in evaluating development.

THEORIES OF MORAL DEVELOPMENT

Moral development theory describes the way children are thought to progress from simple to more complex reasoning about right and wrong. Two major stage theorists, Jean Piaget and Lawrence Kohlberg, are primary theoretical references for moral development. The following considers the stages most applicable to preschoolers.

Piaget's Theory

Piaget studied children's responses to rules used in playing with marbles, the concommitant consciousness of rules, and children's responses to short stories that centered on a moral issue. Based on the age differences in the responses to these rules and stories, Piaget developed a two-stage theory of moral development.

An essential part of moving into the first stage of moral development, the "heteronomous stage," is developing a sense of obligation or obedience. This occurs within a relationship between at least two individuals. As soon as a ritual is imposed (either by adults or as the result of the collaboration of two children) it acquires, in the child's mind, the status of a rule. The feeling of obligation appears between the ages of four and eight when the child accepts a command from someone whom he respects or when the child—either through imitation or as the result of verbal exchange—wants to play in conformity with rules.

This stage is characterized by respect for adult authority and unquestioned obedience. During this time children regard rules as unquestionable, unchanging absolutes handed down by adult authority. Evaluation of whether or not an act is morally wrong or how wrong focuses on the amount of damage done. The child's suggested severity of punishment correlates with the consequences of the action, rather than the intent.

For example, Piaget told two stories, one in which a child broke one cup and one in which a child broke fifteen cups. Regardless of the reason for breaking the cups, the younger children focused on the consequences of the behavior, perceiving the child who broke fifteen cups as being the worst. During this stage children perceive their moral responsibility as one of obedience to adult authority.

Piaget called his second stage of morality the "autonomous" stage, characteristically beginning at eight years or older. During this stage children see morality as a matter of strict fairness among equals. They move away from the perception of adult authority and develop mutual respect with peers. A rule is considered a law only if everyone agrees, and rules may be altered if everyone agrees. Punishment, during this stage, is guided by intent. During this stage children perceive their moral responsibility to be one of mutual respect and cooperation.

Kohlberg's Theory

Kohlberg has defined six stages and three levels of moral development. An individual at a given level reasons consistently regardless of the situation and regardless of the particular aspect of morality being tapped. At each stage there is a single concept of the good, which only approaches a principled morality at the higher levels (Kohlberg, 1970).

Kohlberg characterized the first level as premoral. The first two stages within this level can be briefly summarized as follows:

Stage 1: Punishment orientation: "Right" action consists in obedience to authority for its own sake, avoiding physical damage of people and property, and not breaking rules, under threat of punishment. An act is considered wrong because it results in punishment.

Stage 2: Rewards orientation: "Right" action consists of acting fairly, but for concrete, pragmatic reasons. Conformity to rules is motivated by a desire to obtain rewards. The goal is to serve one's own needs and interests in a world where one recognizes that other people also have needs and interests.

Does the Research Support Kohlberg and Piaget?

Kohlberg's Stage 1 and Piaget's heteronomous morality both identify children as being concerned about the consequences of an action rather than the intent or motive behind the action. They also agree that the child's definition of right focused on obedience to authority. Kohlberg's Stage 2 and Piaget's autonomous morality both identify children as considering intent. Children at this stage are no longer responding to adult authority but are more democratic in their thinking.

Some recent studies of moral development have focused on the preschool child in an effort to identify the various stages of development evidenced in their *behavior*. An evaluation of fifty-eight three- four- and five-year-old children from middle- and lower-income groups enrolled in nursery schools revealed that the five-year-old children correctly understood more moral criteria than did the younger children. This supports the theory of developmentally ordered progression in moral judgment (Wellman, Larkey, & Somerville, 1979).

A few studies challenge the age guidelines suggested by the stage theories of Piaget or Kohlberg. Eisenberg-Berg and Neal (1981) studied forty-seven preschool children who responded to stories in which they were portrayed as characters. During this task they predominantly verbalized hedonistic reasoning. When the preschool children were asked to respond to stories about others in the third person ("they"), the youngsters reasoned with an orientation toward others' needs and were more likely to say they should help those in need. This indicated that when helping required personal risk the preschoolers reasoned in a more hedonistic way than when they were making judgments for others.

However, in a follow-up study with forty-five preschoolers no significant differences were found. The average age for the first group was fifty-seven months and the average age for the second group was fifty-three months. Following Piaget's or Kohlberg's stage theories, preschoolers should not be capable of reasoning in more than a hedonistic way. Flynn (1984) reported that fifty-eight preschool children made moral judgments in both restitution/apology and guilt/innocence dilemmas. The age and sex were significantly related to both moral judgment measures: The older children made more moral judgments and boys developed moral judgments earlier than girls. Intelligence and parent's occupation were also tested but proved to be insignificant.

Intent vs. consequence. Piaget's theory of consequences versus intent of action is supported by two studies which found children to be more influenced by consequences during the preschool years, and as they grow older they become more aware of intent. Moran's study indicated that before children move into the heteronomous stage of focusing on consequence, they concentrate upon negative events. According to Suls, Gutkin, and Kalle (1979), social consequence cues decrease with age while intent cues increase. Through the preschool years the influence of the amount of damage remains the same. Parental reactions had more impact on judgments than did peer reactions. Moran and O'Brien (1983b) conducted a study with a group of twenty-four three- and four-year-old children. They were exposed to eight moral judgment stories, with either positive or negative intentions and either positive or negative consequences. When the stories depicted a positive intent with negative consequence, both groups judged on the basis of consequence. When the stories indicated a negative intent with a positive consequence the four-year-olds made consequence-based decisions when it involved property damage while the three-year-olds did not make consequence-based decisions. The three-year-olds appeared to respond to any negative event, regardless of intent or consequence. The four-year-olds conformed to traditional Piaget theory when property damage was involved.

Several recent studies call into question the age at which the child emphasizes intent rather than consequence. Nelson-LeGall (1985) designed an intervention to help forty-six preschoolers, mostly three-year-olds, respond clearly to moral judgment literature. Intention was stated to be the reason for an action and then repeated to clarify whether the behavior was intentional or accidental. When such clarification was used judgments were influenced by intent and no differences by sex were found. Nelson (1980), in a similar study, told stories either with pictures and an implied motive or with pictures and an explicitly portrayed motive. She discovered that children as young as three use motive information when the information is available.

With a group of sixty-three children ages two, three, four, and five, Allen (1982) used an alternative measure of moral reasoning. The researchers examined the degree of complexity of the story pairs and descriptions of intent and consequence. Children as young as two and three made moral judgments based on intent information, with no gender or age differences. An earlier study by Gruen, Doherty, and Cohen (1979) confuses the issue. Thirty preschoolers were presented with the moral judgment stories. Four- and five-year-olds responded reliably to the consequences while three-year-olds responded to intent, punishing the bad intent and doing nothing to the good or neutral.

Several studies indicate that preschool children act and reason beyond the hedonistic stage of moral development. Eisenberg-Berg and Hand (1979) used four simple moral reasoning stories with thirty-five children focusing on altruistic moral conflicts relating to sharing, helping, and comforting. The preschoolers did not use Kohlberg's Stage 1 punishment/authority reasoning in response to the helping and sharing conflicts but instead used needs-oriented reasoning.

Eisenberg-Berg and Neal (1979) observed twenty-two preschoolers over a twelve week period and recorded acts of helping, sharing, and comforting. When the children were asked why they did those things, they justified their behaviors primarily with reference to others' needs. The children used little punishment- and authority-oriented, hedonistic reasoning.

Smetana (1981) designed a study of the child's ability to discriminate between more and less serious behaviors in the absence of rules. A list of conventional transgressions, such as not putting toys away, were mixed with more serious moral transgressions, such as hitting, and the children were asked to determine the degree of punishment that would be appropriate for each. Consistently the children evaluated moral transgressions as more serious offenses than the conventional events. This reflects a greater ability to distinguish between moral and conventional behaviors than would be possible for a purely heteronomous individual.

Siegal and Storey (1985) looked at two different groups of preschoolers, twenty that had been enrolled in a day care center for a minimum of eighteen months and twenty that had been enrolled less than three months. The newly enrolled children judged social rule transgressions as naughtier and more worthy of punishment than did the children that had been a part of the "system" for at least eighteen months. However, the groups regarded moral transgressions with equal seriousness. This indicates that those children that have been a part of a social setting are more capable of distinguishing between moral and conventional behaviors.

Children's distinction between right and wrong based solely on adult authority can be compared with their intuitive ability to interpret right and wrong. Turiel (1983) and Smetana (1981) theorize that children intuitively appreciate distinctions between rule domains from an early age. They suggest that young children do not see all rules as true and important simply because they come from authorities, as Piaget and Kohlberg had claimed. Children seem to be aware of some of the main ways that rules vary. Adults and children agree that some rules are more important than others. The adults communicate to children in each society a sense of what rules are most important.

Nucci (1982) summarizes a series of studies in which children were asked to comment on transgressions they had witnessed in the classroom or on playgrounds. When questioned about these transgressions, over 85 percent of preschool and school-aged children said that the act would not be right even if there were no school rule about it. In contrast, when questioned about other transgressions against school regulations, over 80 percent of children in each grade said the act would be right.

Reciprocity. A group of sixty-six preschoolers were asked to interpret moral judgement stories depicting reciprocal and nonreciprocal behavior. The children attended to more situational reasons for the reciprocal behavior (retaliation or returning favors) and asked for more information about the actor and the cause of his behavior. This may signal a beginning awareness of reciprocity, although the children did not use reciprocity reasoning to a significant extent. Reciprocity appears to develop shortly after school entrance, within the time frame suggested by Kohlberg and Piaget.

More recent interpretations of the moral development of the young child have been attempted by using both Piaget's and Kohlberg's theories as a basis. The following theories effectively fill out the critical areas of moral development that are taking place during these years.

Lickona's Theory

Lickona (1983) states that most three-year-old children are moving into "egocentric reasoning." Most four-year-old children function within that level as well. During this time children only recognize their own point of view, an egocentric reasoning that surfaces when their desires conflict with those of others. If their own interests are not at stake they are more likely to be open to the needs and feelings of others. Lickona has referred to this as Stage 0 of moral reasoning.

Between four-and-one-half and five-and-one-half years of age, the child enters Stage 1, that of unquestioning obedience. The Stage 1 child is capable of taking another person's viewpoint. They do not always use this ability, but they do possess it. These children tend to believe that the views of adult authority are the only truly correct perspectives. Their reasoning is that what is right is what adults tell you, and you do what you are told or you could get into trouble. However, the reason for obeying is because of the consequences if caught. Therefore, these children tend not to be obedient unless there is a strong possibility that they will be caught.

Some children will begin to produce characteristics of Stage 2 as early as five-and-one-half and others may not produce them until age seven or eight. The Stage 2 child believes that everyone has his or her own point of view and that each person has the right to follow his or her own viewpoint. You are also entitled to look out for yourself. Reciprocity, or being fair to those who are fair to you, is a motivating factor in behavior during this stage of development.

Damon's Theory

Damon (1977) criticized Kohlberg's stories/dilemmas as not being appropriate for children. Because his stories are beyond the realm of youngsters' experiences, the children's actual thoughts about their own moral judgment and behavior is rarely obtained. Damon proposed that it would be more appropriate to focus on moral reasoning about one's own general behavior rather than focusing on isolated behaviors such as cheating, lying, and helping. Damon developed a practical context for children, asking them to decide how to distribute rewards among other children. The children's justification for their behavior provided information about their moral reasoning. Damon also discovered that the correlation between judgment and behavior was highest among children at more advanced levels.

Damon (1983) has outlined six authority levels for children aged four to twelve years. Four of these levels are necessary for understanding how the three- to six-year-old child develops morally.

During levels 0-A and 0-B, the children focus on the perspective of only one person in the conflict. They justify giving the resources to someone by saying, "He wants it," or "He needs it," or "He's my friend." Damon's first two levels actually precede Kohlberg's and Piaget's first stages. They are helpful in explaining why preschool children's awe of adults does not translate into consistent obedience.

Level 0-A (Ages 3-4). Choices are based on self-interest. Because children feel that adults exist to fulfill their needs, they think that the authority's desire is the same as their own. They transform their own wishes to fit with the authority's or transform the authority's commands into their own wishes. This is most normally seen in the four-year-old child.

Level 0-B (Ages 4-5). Choices are based upon external realities such as size, sex, or perceived attractiveness. Children see authority from their own perspective but now perceive it as being an obstacle obstructing the child's desire. This is normally seen in the five-year-old child.

During levels 1-A and 1-B, strict equality enters children's reasoning about justice. They can now simultaneously see more than one person's perspective.

Level 1-A (Ages 5-6). Choices are based on strict equality; everyone gets the same. Children consider authorities to have an inherent right to be obeyed because of their general power, superiority, and position.

Level 1-B (Ages 7-8). Compromises are made between competing claims (for example, hardest workers versus most effective workers) and special needs (such as poverty) are taken into consideration. Children think that they obey in return for the concrete help, care, and material goods that adults give them.

Damon's research has shown that developmental progress in authority concepts is slow but steady throughout childhood. Most children show an upward change of one level or less per year. Development is gradual, and children usually show a mixture of levels at any one time.

Other Views of Moral Development

Some theorists have emphasized social/emotional development and its relationship to moral development. Rest (1982) proposes a theory of developing morality that includes three components:

Recognition and sensitivity. This refers to the affective and cognitive components of empathy.

Moral Judgment. Consideration of ideals and norms related to the situation are included in this component.

Execution and implementation of moral action. The child considers the personal costs, decides to act, and is responsible enough to carry through.

Hoffman (1975) proposes a model for the development of altruistic behavior. The theory proposes that empathic responses are present from birth and affective motivation leads to altruistic behavior. Empathy may increase or decrease as the child grows and develops cognitive skills that sensitize or desensitize the child to the needs of others. If sensitized, the child improves in moral judgment. Hoffman also believes that the child's sense of empathic guilt may be used to reinforce good moral values. Empathic guilt is a feeling of distress when one causes someone else discomfort. Radke-Yarrow and Zahn-Waxler (1984) report observing two-and-one-half-year-old children respond to others in distress by initiating contact, embracing the victim, giving gifts, and seeking help from a third party.

Spiritual Development

Kohlberg's stage theory is built around the issue of justice that advances with each stage. However some important questions dealing with the meaning of life are not included in the process until the sixth stage. In an effort to more effectively deal with religious questions, Kohlberg added a seventh stage which focuses on ultimate questions about the meaning of life. Joy (1979) suggests that the addition of the seventh stage is inadequate and that indeed Kohlberg's work is incomplete at every stage, not just Stage 6. If the theory is truly developmental, any construction about the meaning of life, God and faith, should be accepted at every stage as long as openness to growth is evident. Joy suggests that the following considerations are appropriate for committed Christians or "faith" people when dealing with moral development stages:

1. God's unconditional love and prevenient grace provide the basis for our inclination toward justice and righteousness.

2. Immature understandings of God's role in life and the meaning of life are to be expected as a part of the developmental process.

3. God may be expected to represent himself faithfully to any person at an appropriate structural level.

4. A faith response which presupposes that life is larger than disease and death must be more appropriately analyzed.

Moral Development Theory

Theorist	Age					
	3-year-old	4-year-old	5-year-old	6-year-old	7-year-old	8-year-old
Piaget	heteronomous stage: developing a sense of obligation unquestioned obedience					autonomous stage: fairness among equals
Kohlberg	premoral: stage one punishment orientation					stage 2 rewards orientation
Likona	stage 0 egocentric reasoning		stage 1 obedience		stage 1, stage 2 reciprocity	stage 2 reciprocity
Damon	stage 0-A self-interest	stage 0-A stage 0-B external realities	stage 0-B stage 1-A equality	stage 1-A equality	stage 1-A stage 1-B compromise	stage 1-B
Rest	component 1: sensitivity		component 2: moral judgment		component 3: execution	
Hoffman	empathy: increase decrease		sensitize—improves moral judgment desensitize—the opposite			
Joy	All have an inclination toward justice and righteousness based on God's unconditional love and prevenient grace.					

CHARACTERISTICS THAT CORRELATE WITH MORAL ACTION

Social, Emotional, and Intellectual Development

Matsumoto, Haan, Yabrove, Theodorou, and Carney (1986) worked with nineteen pairs of four-year-old children to examine the moral actions and emotions in moral development. Emotions were related to concurrent acts and predicted subsequent acts even though no one talked about morality. The degree of friendship between pairs, positive emotional tone, and active involvement positively related to sensitive moral action. The search for practical morality must include the emotional dimension. Several observations were particularly interesting. The four-year-old children acted morally in cognitively simplified moral conflict situations even though it threatened their self-interest. The pairs worked toward mutual moral solutions and increasingly coordinated their actions across sessions. Good friends resolved differences and reached moral mutuality more efficiently. The moral solution was associated with active problem solving and positive feelings. The nonverbal emotional processes related to concurrent moral behaviors, and the emotional reactions predicted future actions.

Benninga (1976) evaluated forty preschoolers in the areas of self-concept, sex, intelligence, and moral judgment. He could find no correlation of significance between any of the variables and moral judgment, although he found that all factors of moral judgment were correlated significantly with at least one factor of self-concept. In contrast, Ratcliff (1987) found intelligence and moral development to be related when comparing the mentally retarded and those with normal IQ scores.

Religious Training and Gender

Eisenberg-Berg and Roth (1980) interviewed thirty-four preschoolers they had evaluated eighteen months earlier to determine the rate of moral reasoning, comparing moral development, role-taking ability, and religious training. The role-taking ability was unrelated to moral reasoning. The religious training was rated as "little," "some" or "much" and the "much" category was positively related to the use of needs-oriented reasoning and negatively related to hedonistic reasoning.

Eisenberg-Berg and Roth also found that the number of years in day care, maternal affection, vocabulary ability, and role-taking abilities were all positively related to expressions of concern for others in boys. Role-taking ability was negatively related to choices of the moral concepts in boys. Among girls, age, parental education, and vocabulary ability were positively related to moral concept choices.

Group Care/Social Interaction

Moran and O'Brien (1983a) devised a study to compare the moral judgment of children in group settings with children at home. The social interaction seemed to positively influence the process of moral development. The group care children focused more on intention in contexts involving injury to another person and consequences in contexts involving personal property damage. The social experience appeared to be more important to moral development than did age.

Sociometric measures were gathered based on observations and reports from teachers and parents. There was a positive relationship between children's moral reasoning scores, the amount of time they spent in interaction with peers, and the proportion of time spent in positive interaction with peers. There was no significant relationship between moral reasoning and negative interaction (Allen, 1982).

SUGGESTIONS FOR HELPING CHILDREN GROW MORALLY

The biblical injunction states, "Train up a child in the way he should go and when he is old he will not depart from it" (Prov. 22:6). This verse no doubt includes moral development but leaves us with the question of how to "train" the child. Several have attempted to teach children moral responses, but such attempts have met with mixed results.

Discussion and Exposure to Other Viewpoints

Several studies have indicated the importance of experiencing other viewpoints and discussion. Jensen and Hughston (1971) introduced a two-week moral training program to a group of preschoolers. The children heard five stories which included good acts followed by punishment and bad acts followed by punishment. Groups of children then discussed why the act was good or bad. The children were tested three to eight days after the training and had achieved large gains while a control group evidenced no change.

In another effort to increase the ability to make moral judgments, Rotenburg (1980) provided reflectivity instruction to a group of preschoolers. Prior to the presentation of the story the children were instructed to "think about all the reasons why the child might be bad or might not be bad." Those children who received reflectivity instruction made greater use of intention information in moral judgment than did the children that did not receive the instruction. The children with the training also tended to use information about consequences to a greater extent than did the control group. The usual association between moral maturity and age was not found under these conditions.

Moran and O'Brien (1984) evaluated parental child-rearing attitudes on the development of moral judgment. The maternal democratic control model was related to more intention-based moral judgments by preschool children. They determined that when the child was becoming sensitive to intentions, the parental explanation and display of patience encouraged the child in that developmental process.

Piaget and Kohlberg agree on the importance of interaction/discussion and exposure to other viewpoints in facilitating moral development. Adults stimulate the development of autonomy by exchanging points of view with children (Piaget, 1932). Kohlberg (1970) felt strongly that the first step in teaching virtue was to create dissatisfaction in the child about his or her present knowledge of the good. This is done by exposing the student to moral conflict situations for which the child's present principles have no ready solution. Second, one should expose the youngsters to disagreement and argument about these situations with his or her peers. Our responsibility is to help the child see issues from the next stage of moral development.

In an effort to evaluate the impact social interactions have on the development of moral judgment, Ruffy (1981) gathered information on 390 children ages four through nine from two different countries, Sweden and the United States. The conclusion was that dynamic exchanges, including discussion and opposition, foster higher level responses in children. The same sequence in the development of moral judgment was observed in the two countries. The beginning of autonomy was observed at a younger age than had been suggested by Piaget.

Autonomy, Discipline, and Internal Control

Piaget (1932) discussed the importance of morality and autonomy in his book, *The Moral Judgment of the Child*. Autonomy means being governed by oneself as opposed to being governed by someone else. Ideally, the child becomes increasingly more autonomous as he or she grows older and becomes more self-governing. Autonomy is not equivalent to complete freedom; autonomy means taking relevant factors into account in deciding what the best course of action might be for all concerned.

Parents and teachers often reinforce children's heteronomy and unwittingly prevent them from developing autonomy. There is an enormous difference between "good" behavior autonomously chosen and "good" behavior as a result of blind conformity. We need to shift thinking from what WE do to how CHILDREN develop and thus begin to view moral education from the standpoint of how children learn (Kamii, 1982).

Piaget (1932) suggests that parents reinforce children's natural heteronomy when they use reward and punishment. Krebs (1980) stresses the importance of setting limits that are clear, fair, and reasonable followed by explanations as to why a specific behavior is being rewarded or punished. Kamii (1982) warns that punishment alone can lead to 1) the child trying to avoid being caught the next time, 2) blind conformity, or 3) rebellion. While rewards are nicer than punishment they also reinforce heteronomy (Kamii, 1982).

One of the greatest challenges for adults is to help children internalize control. Siegal and Francis (1982) tested eighteen preschoolers on a cognitive development test of concrete operations and then observed rule-following behavior with an adult either present or absent. They found that the rule-following behavior correlated with the performance on the test of concrete operations when the adult was present. When the adult was absent the children violated rules regardless of their cognitive stage.

Ward (1979) suggests that one of the most important factors in moral development is having parents around who are consistent. As long as the parent is gentle, almost anything done consistently to help children distinguish good and bad behavior will be useful.

Krebs (1980) suggests that adults clarify goals for premoral children. The most important thing the adult (parent) needs to do is care for the child in a loving manner. A second task is to set limits for the children. Initially the limits must be imposed by outsiders. Be sure the limits are clear, fair, and reasonable. The third task is to impose sanctions. Reward the child for obeying the established limits and punish the child for breaking the rules. These must be done consistently to be effective. The adult should take time to explain why behavior is being rewarded or punished.

The religious educator might consider four specific sanctions:

1. *Temporary or permanent exclusion from the group.* When a group is listening to a story and a child disrupts the group, the teacher might say, "You can either stay here without bothering the rest of us, or I must ask you to go to the book corner and read by yourself." Whenever possible the child must be given the responsibility of deciding when he or she can behave well enough to return to the group. Mechanical time limits serve only as punishment, and children who have served the required time often feel perfectly free to commit the same misdeed again (Kamii, 1982)

2. *Deprive the child of the thing he has misused.* Strictly enforced, the rule states that children cannot play in the block area if they knock anything over. Later, the teacher negotiates with individual children the right to go in that area when they know that this right is earned (Kamii, 1982).

3. *Describe consequences.* It is possible to encourage the child to think about the consequences of dishonesty, such as other people not believing or trusting him. An appeal to consequences may help the child develop morally. For example, when a child disturbs adults at the dinner table,

parents often say, "You can either stay here without bothering us or go to your room and be noisy" (Kamii, 1982).

4. *Restitution.* Give children an opportunity to make right a wrong or correct a mistake, which encourages the development of sensitivity and moral action. If a young child spills paint on the floor, the reaction would be, "Would you like me to help you clean it up?" until children understand the routine for cleaning up after various accidents.

Modeling, Role Play, and Prosocial Behavior

A study carried out in the Soviet Union would lead us to believe that children need positive self-concepts and positive fictional heros. A child's determination to retain a positive self-image may motivate him to defer immediate desires, thus providing moral regulation of conduct. This was tested by encouraging preschoolers to compare one isolated act with categories of good and bad. This only made an impact on three children. When the children were challenged to compare themselves with the description of a "bad" child it influenced eighteen children. The most effective method was comparing themselves with a negative hero of a story. This changed the behavior of the remaining six children. Thus we may conclude that bad behavior is best modified through models of fictional heros who enter into a situation of conflict which leads to the triumph of the good (Yakobson & Pocherevina, 1982).

Eisenberg, Pasternack, Cameron, and Tryon (1984) used videotapes over a nine-week period to record preschoolers behavior in a naturalistic setting. The tapes were coded for the behaviors of sharing, helping, sociability, asking for help or assistance, and making a verbal or physical defense of objects, noting whether the act was spontaneous or a requested behavior. The conclusion was that the different types of prosocial behaviors, whether requested or spontaneous, were not associated with moral judgments.

Ward (1979) suggests that people need opportunities for role playing so that other perspectives may be developed. Edwards and Ramsey (1987) suggest that teachers plan games that challenge the children to think about issues in an open-ended manner. Adults may plan skits, using adult actors to communicate with the youngsters, and allow the children to decide how the story should end. Such dramas might be based on themes such as fair distribution, justice, punishment, and rules (see Edwards for additional suggestions).

Relationship

In evaluating the impact of emotionally positive interactions with adults, Subbotskii (1983) worked with seventy three- and four-year-old children and forty-eight five- and six-year-old children to compare their responses to instructions given by a "friend" and by a stranger. The results indicated that the younger children responded positively to the "friend" and negatively to the stranger. The older group responded positively to both the "friend" and the stranger. The three- and four-year-old children appear to be more influenced by the positive emotional interactions with adults than do the five- and six-year-old children.

The opportunity to fulfill an adult role seemed to have a positive impact on both the three- and five-year-old children. The experimenter expressed trust in the youngsters and asked for assistance. The older child was asked to teach the younger one how to perform the task and be sure that all the rules were observed. After this was accomplished the child was asked to monitor the actions of a child his own age in performance of the same task. (The latter child had already broken rules in a previous session.) The results indicated that both the younger and the older children showed significant positive moral actions after this experience (Subbotskii, 1983).

Ward (1979) suggests that much of what we learn about morality we learn from the environment in which we spend our time. People who are treated fairly and honestly, develop faster than those who experience constant injustice. This was supported through a recent study. Alborg (1984) in an effort to train preschool age children to tell the truth and confess wrongdoing, exposed the children to modeling, behavior rehearsal, prompts, praise, rule stating, and material reinforcement. Results indicated that parent attitudes, teacher attitudes, and the consequences experienced from confessing or truth-telling had a more powerful impact on the child than did the training. Those attitudes and consequences are the environment that Ward refers to.

To establish a relationship of respect it is important to provide children with the reasons for the rules. Edwards (1987) provides the following examples of giving the reasons behind rules: "You must wear a smock to paint to keep your clothes clean." "You need to put away materials after using them so that the play area doesn't get all jumbled." "Hitting hurts. I can't allow you to hurt someone else."

Edwards challenges teachers to be supportive and assist children as they work through their conflicting emotions. The following ideas might be incorporated to create a warm, supportive environment:

1. Support children's initiative and self-determination.

2. Encourage children to negotiate. Teach negotiation strategies when appropriate.

3. Help children become aware of other's feelings.

4. Point out the results of the child's actions.

5. Respect the child's own standards of what constitutes a fair or acceptable solution to the problem.

6. Encourage children to take responsibility for their own actions.

7. Encourage children to participate in the process of establishing classroom rules.

8. Allow children the freedom to make mistakes and learn for themselves why it is important to follow specific rules.

The primary responsibility of parents and religious educators is to establish a warm, loving relationship with each child. Without this relationship of mutual affection and respect between the adult and the child most of the efforts to "train up a child" will be unsuccessful. A warm, loving relationship must be the basis for developing an environment in which moral development will flourish.

Such an environment should also include opportunities for exposure to other viewpoints through explanations, discussion, and role-playing. Children must be given an opportunity to develop respect for materials and others' rights as "established" limits are consistently and appropriately enforced. Moral development will be enhanced as children are exposed to appropriate models, are encouraged to practice prosocial behaviors and are given many opportunities to make choices and develop autonomy. Religious educators, including parents, are responsible for carrying out the biblical injunction of "training up a child" using the best information we have available on how children develop morally.

REFERENCES

Alborg, C. G. (1984) *Training truth-telling behavior in preschool age children.* Unpublished dissertation. Rosemead School of Psychology, La Mirada, CA.

Allen, J. E. (1982) *The assessment of moral reasoning in preschool children and the relationship between moral reasoning and peer interaction.*

Benninga, J. S. (1976). *The relation of self-concept, sex, and intelligence to moral judgment in young children.* Unpublished doctoral dissertation, George Peabody College for Teachers, Nashville, Tennessee.

Damon, W. (1977). *The social world of the child.* (San Francisco: Jossey-Bass).

Damon, W. (1983). *Social and personality development: Infancy through adolescence.* New York: Norton.

Eisenberg, N., Pasternack, J., Cameron, E., & Tyron, K. (1984). The relation of quantity and mode of prosocial behavior to moral cognitions and social style. *Child Development, 55,* 1479-1485.

Eisenberg-Berg, N., & Hand, M. (1979). The relationship of preschoolers' reasoning about prosocial moral conflicts to prosocial behavior. *Child Development, 50,* 356-363.

Eisenberg-Berg, N., & Neal, C. (1979). Children's moral reasoning about their own spontaneous prosocial behavior. *Developmental Psychology, 15,* 228-229.

Eisenberg-Berg, N., & Neal, C. (1981). Children's moral reasoning about self and others: Effects of identity of the story character and cost of helping. *Personality and Social Psychology Bulletin, 7,* 17-23.

Eisenberg-Berg, N., & Roth K. (1980) Development of young children's prosocial moral judgment: A longitudinal follow-up. *Developmental Psychology, 16,* 375-376.

Flynn, T. (1984). Age, sex, intelligence, and parents' occupation and the moral development of the preschool child. *Early Child Development and Care, 17,* 177-184.

Gruen, G. E., Doherty, J. & Cohen, A. S. (1979). The moral judgments of preschool children. *The Journal of Psychology, 101,* 287-291.

Hartshorne, H., & May, M.A. (1928). *Studies in the nature of character* (Vol. I). New York: Macmillan.

Hoffman, M.L. (1975). Developmental synthesis of affect and cognition and its implications for altruistic motivation. *Developmental Psychology, 11,* 607-622.

Jensen, L., & Hughston, K. (1971). The effect of training children to make moral judgments that are independent of sanctions. *Developmental Psychology, 5,* 367.

Joy, D. (1979) Proceedings for the Moral Development Conference, Asbury Seminary, Asbury, Kentucky.

Kamii, C. (1982). *Number in preschool & kindergarten: Educational implications of Piaget's theory.* Washington, DC: NAEYC.

Kohlberg, L. (1964). Development of moral character and moral ideology. In M. L. Hoffman and L. W. Hoffman (Eds.), *Review of Child Development Research.* New York: Russell Sage Foundation.

Kohlberg, L. (1970). The developmental approach to moral education. In C. Beck, B. Crittenden, & E. Sullivan (Eds.), *Moral education: Interdisciplinary approaches.* (Toronto: Toronto Press.

Krebs, R. (1980). *How to bring up a good child.* Minneapolis, MN: Augsburg Publishing House.

Lickona, T. (1983). *Raising good children from birth through the teenage years.* New York: Bantam Books.

Matsumoto, D., Haan, N., Yabrove, G., Theodorou, P., & Carney, C. (1986). Preschoolers' moral actions and emotions in prisoner's dilemma. *Developmental Psychology, 22,* 663-670.

Moran III, J., & O'Brien, G. (1983a). Influence of structured group experience on moral judgments of preschoolers. *Psychological Reports, 52,* 587-593.

Moran III, J., & O'Brien, G. (1983b). The development of intention-based moral judgments in three- and four-year-old children. *The Journal of Genetic Psychology, 143,* 175-179.

Moran III, J., & O'Brien, G. (1984). Relationship between parental child-rearing attitudes and preschoolers' moral judgments. *Psychological Reports, 55,* 893-894.

Mussen, P. & Eisenberg-Berg, N. (1977). *Roots of caring, sharing and helping.* San Francisco: W. H. Freeman and Company.

Nelson, S. A. (1980). Factors influencing young children's use of motives and outcomes as moral criteria. *Child Development, 51,* 823-829.

Nelson-LaGall, S. (1985). Motive-outcome matching and outcome foreseeability: Effects on attribution of intentionality and moral judgments. *Developmental Psychology, 21,* 332-337.

Nucci, L. (1982). Conceptual development in the moral and conventional domains: Implications for values education. *Review of Educational Research, 52,* 93-122.

Piaget, J. (1932). *The moral judgment of the child.* New York: The Free Press.

Radke-Yarrow & Zahn-Waxler (1984). Roots, motives and patterning in children's prosocial behavior. In E. Staub, D. Bar-Tal, J. Kurylowski, & J. Rujkowski (Eds.), *The development and maintenance of prosocial behavior: International perspectives on positive morality.* New York: Plenum Press.

Ratcliff, D. (1987). Predicting the moral development of the mentally retarded. *Journal of Psychology and Theology, 6,* 65-67.

Rest. J. R. (1983). Morality. In P. H. Mussen (Ed.), *Handbook of child psychology* (4th ed., Vol 3). New York: Norton.

Rotenberg, K. (1980). Cognitive processes and young children's use of intention and consequence information in moral judgment. *Merrill-Palmer Quarterly, 26,* 359-370.

Ruffy, M. (1981). Influence of social factors in the development of the young child's moral judgment. *European Journal of Social Psychology, 11,* 61-75.

Sears, R. R., Rau L., & Alpert, R. (1965). *Identification and childrearing.* Stanford, CA: Stanford University Press.

Siegal, M., & Francis, R. (1982). Parent-child relations and cognitive approaches to the development of moral judgment and behavior. *British Journal of Psychology, 73,* 285-294.

Siegal, M., Storey, R., & McDonald, (1985). Day care and children's conceptions of moral and social rules. *Child Development, 56,* 1001-1008.

Smetana, J. (1981). Preschool children's conceptions of moral and social rules. *Child Development, 52,* 1333-1336.

Subbotskii, E. V. (1983, Fall). Shaping moral actions in children. *Soviet Psychology, 56-71.*

Suls, J., Gutkin, D., & Kalk, R. (1979). The role of intentions, damage, and social consequences in the moral judgments of children. *Child Development, 50,* 874-877.

Turiel, E. (1983). Interaction and development in social cognition. In. T. Higgins, D. N. Ruble, & W. W. Hartup (Eds.), *Social cognition and social development.* Cambridge: Cambridge University Press.

Ward, T. (1979). *Values begin at home.* Wheaton, IL: Victor Books.

Wellman, H., Larkey, C., & Somerville, S. (1979). The early development of moral criteria. *Child Development, 50,* 869-873.

Yakobson, S. G., & Pocherevina, L. P. (1982). The role of subjective attitude toward ethical models in the regulation of preschoolers' moral conduct. *Soviet Psychology, 22,* 20-39.

Chapter Five:

Faith Development
in the Preschool Years

ROMNEY M. MOSELEY AND
KEN BROCKENBROUGH

For the past decade the concept of faith development proposed by James Fowler (1981) has assumed prominence in religious education. Faith, as defined by Fowler, is an active process of meaning-making by which persons construe their relatedness to a transcendent center of value and power. Following Wilfred Cantwell Smith (1962), Fowler distinguishes faith from religion. The latter Smith defines as the "cumulative tradition," the cultural reservoir of rituals, symbols, and beliefs. Faith is interpreted as a generic feature of the human condition. Both Smith and Fowler attempt to retrieve an etymological understanding of faith as belief or *credo*, a compound of the Latin words *cor* (the heart) and *do* (I give). Faith as the "giving of the heart" captures the surrendering of the total self to an ultimate center of value and power. In theistic terms, faith as *credo* is the giving of the heart to God.

In addition to Smith, Fowler draws on the theology of H. Richard Niebuhr (1960). Niebuhr's radical monotheism preserves a covenantal relationship between God and the community of faith. Faith as fidelity to the sovereignty of God presumes the development of trust and an ethic of interpersonal responsibility. This confidence in the human capacity to be trustworthy bearers of the kingdom of God is the crux of the meaning-making propensity attributed to faith.

The phrase, "kingdom of God," captures the ultimate image of the Christian vocation. As such it is a formal regulative principle whose efficacy is perhaps similar to regulative principles in other traditions, e.g., Nirvana in Buddhism. Faith development theory describes in some normative fashion the affective and cognitive dimensions of the human

capacity to shape life in relation to some transcendent regulative principle or center of value, whether or not the latter is interpreted in theistic
language. This is a formal or generic definition of faith. As far as Fowler
is concerned, it is a point of departure for hermeneutical inquiry into
the normative claims of other perspectives on faith.

The theory that faith is a peculiar process of meaning-making by
which persons apprehend their relatedness to the transcendent involves
both theological and social-scientific language. The former is primarily
concerned with the teleological and ontological dimensions of faith.
Here the *why* questions are pertinent. Why do persons have faith? We
could say with Niebuhr that faith is inherent to the human condition,
that the human is *homo poeta* (maker of meaning) and, furthermore,
that it is the nature of faith to change throughout the human life span.

Then we may ask *how* does faith change? Here we turn to the Piagetian structural-developmental framework. We must remember that the
domain for the construction of knowledge established by Piaget is physical reality, e.g., the construction of the concepts of mass, volume,
number, and so on, and that faith is not simply the acquisition of
competences or skills to be empirically tested. Faith and intellectual
development are not identical. Rather, Fowler defines faith as a process
of knowing, the content of which is not physical reality but a peculiar
relation to a transcendent center of value. In short, faith is a way of
being in the world. The cognitive structure of this activity may be
interpreted in terms of Piagetian cognitive developmental psychology.
We are faced then with the task of making intelligible in theological and
social-scientific language a phenomenon that is elusive and mysterious.
This is especially difficult in the preschool years when the focus of
attention is on the verbal and nonverbal expressions of what constitutes
relatedness to a transcendent center of meaning and value.

The Structures of Faith

A primary assumption is that faith has its own internal logic or
structure. Fowler notes that this is also a "logic of conviction" (1981,
p. 102), referring to the historical symbols, beliefs, and practices that
form the *content* of faith. However, this distinction between structure
and content is somewhat ambiguous. Fowler himself adds to this ambiguity by referring to the "structuring power of the contents of faith"
(1981, p. 276). His intention is to underscore the impact of deeply held
beliefs, symbols, and values that are transmitted from generation to
generation. On this point Fowler does not depart from Piagetian episte-
mology. In fact, he makes explicit what is implicit in Piaget's argument
that knowledge is constructed in the interaction between the individual
and the external environment. Fowler illuminates the texture of the

environment as a reservoir of truth and meaning which not only supplies the content of our meaning-making activities but also evokes our loyalty and commitment.

This is especially critical in the preschool years when much of what the child knows is mediated through stories, images, and symbols. Erikson draws attention to the ritualization of the "numinous" early in the communicative interaction between mother and infant. Erikson depicts the numinous as a transcendent source of power to which persons are related ontogenetically. This is the foundation of basic trust—what Fowler refers to as primal faith. Theologically speaking, it is the encounter of human love and divine grace. Erikson suggests that the social resource for the nurturance of this primary connection to the transcendent is religion. However, he is aware that not all persons acknowledge themselves to be religious. Some even deny the validity of religion.

> Whosoever says that he has religion must derive a faith from it which is transmitted to infants in the form of basic trust; whosoever claims that he does not need religion must derive such basic faith from elsewhere (1959, p. 65).

The burden of faith formation clearly rests on the quality of parenting and the availability of a healthy religious environment for the nurturance of basic trust. At the same time, each child is endowed with unique cognitive and affective propensities for shaping her or his relation to the world. The child's mind is not simply a *tabula rasa,* or blank slate, that absorbs available stimuli from the environment. Rather, the complementary processes of assimilation and accommodation bring about adaptation to a world that is always changing. Assimilation is the activity by which data from the environment are incorporated into existing mental schemata. Accommodation refers to the transformation of existing models or schemata to fit the data of experience. In addition to adaptation to the external environment, existing cognitive models must also assimilate and accommodate to each other, thereby forming a stage of development.

Each stage is organized as a "structured whole." Each successive stage incorporates and advances aspects of preceding stages to bring about a more comprehensive level of functioning. Thus, cognitive development is an ordered process of constructing mental models or schemata of the world, testing these models against experience, and effecting changes in them. Through the dynamic interplay of assimilation and accommodation, equilibration occurs. This is the basic mechanism of cognitive development.

It is the nature of the biological organism to seek equilibrium, but the availability of new and sometimes discrepant data will create disequilibrium. Hence the process of equilibration is unending, even with the attainment of formal operations, Piaget's final stage of cognitive development. Here we observe Piaget's dialectic of the changing organism interacting with a changing world. Both cognitively and affectively, this relationship may be characterized by conflict and contradiction. Moreover, adaptation involves the restructuring of discrepant data, and trusting a world that is sometimes strange and confusing. Herein lies the heart of "primal faith." The meaning-constructive activities of the child involve not only cognitive processes of internal equilibrium and disequilibrium but also affective-relational and symbolic aspects of life history—experiences which may require significant restructuring of the individual's cognitive system. In other words, stage transition is not simply a cognitive developmental phenomenon.

In summary, the relevance of Piagetian constructivism for faith development is not limited to the correspondence between Piaget's stages of sensorimotor, preconcrete, concrete, and formal operations and Fowler's stages of faith. The key factor is Fowler's use of the metaphor of structural disequilibrium as the normative mechanism of change.

Equilibration and Stage Transition

A fundamental assumption of structural-developmental psychology is that children are equipped with the capacity to maintain constancy in the midst of change, the crux of Piaget's equilibrium dialectic. Simply put, the internal cognitive process of equilibration is a developmental process, the products of which may be equilibrated states or stages. Ultimately, the impetus for equilibration is adaptation to the environment. A key issue is the generation and resolution of internal cognitive conflict, without which developmental progression is not possible. At the same time, conflict must be resolved in order for development to occur. But what is the source of cognitive conflict? Here Piaget assumes that the external world will always yield sufficiently conflicting data that will provoke the restructuring of the individual's cognitive system. This is a fundamental metapsychological assertion of Piagetian structuralism. Development then is the result of both historical forces and equilibrated transformations. Our first task therefore is to show how these elements help produce faith development and, second, to demonstrate the implications of faith development for preschool religious education.

Structural Development and Stages of Faith

According to Piaget, the concept of structure is intended to explain the ordered historical progress of the biological organism toward the attainment of intelligence and the cognitive operations involved in the achievement of this goal. Fowler expands the principle of structure beyond Piaget's logical-mathematical operations to include additional affective-relational aspects of psychological development. These are included in the "aspects" or criteria by which a stage is defined. They are: A) form of logic; B) bounds of social awareness; C) form of moral judgment; D) social perspective-taking; E) locus of authority; F) world coherence; and G) symbolic functioning.

It should be noted that Fowler's stages are not limited to Piaget's final stage of formal operations (abstract logical thinking) but extend over the entire life span. Consequently, the governing principle of a stage of faith is its relation to the transformation of the self, thus faith development should be understood within the larger context of human becoming. If faith development is concerned with the human capacity to discern ultimate meaning, then it is particularly important to state the norms of human relations and the necessary components for evoking and sustaining the meaning-making potentialities of children. We learn from Erikson that basic trust is required for ego identity formation. The mutuality generated in this relationship between parent and child sets the stage for the rest of the life cycle. Fowler acknowledges these prescriptions, but their importance in the preschool years is shrouded by the emphasis attached to cognitive development. One of the objectives of this essay is to show how Margaret Mahler sharpens our understanding of the relational and affective dimensions of meaning-making in the preschool years.

Recent research by the Center for Faith Development suggests that the construction of meaning is not adequately interpreted by Piagetian structuralism. While Piaget's criteria for the attainment of a stage of intellectual development are the completion of specific logico-mathematical tasks, the structuring of the affective domain remains unclear. Fowler, on the other hand, argues that Piaget's "logic of rational certainty" needs to be complemented by a "logic of conviction." By conviction is meant those beliefs and values that constitute the parameters of meaning for each individual. The German word *Weltanschauung* (worldview) captures what is intended here. In the preschool years primary attention should be paid to those persons who are bearers of these paradigms of meaning and to the stories and images of the transcendent they transmit from generation to generation. Their trustworthiness and the coherence of their narratives form the foundation of "primal faith" (stage 0). Faith so defined is indeed *credo*. The seriousness of the "giving of the heart" by children to persons whom they trust and whose words they believe to be true should not be minimized. Faith is not merely assent to the truth of propositions but is the surrendering of the heart to a transcendent center of value and power. We may well ask what is the object of such affection for preschoolers? It would be foolish to exclude parents. Nevertheless, Fowler's formal definition of faith leaves ambiguous the object of faith. At the same time his Niebuhrian theology calls for a radically monotheistic faith that is acted out in the relationship between self, community, and God. There is therefore in faith development theory the tension between a formal definition of faith that does not specify any particular content and a theology of radical monotheism. Fowler attempts to resolve this tension by emphasizing the formation of covenantal relationships as the ethical correlate of faith. A pivotal issue of faith development in the preschool years is the shaping of an ecology of parental care that is covenantally grounded. It is in the transmission of virtues such as justice, freedom, love, and truth that the common good is sustained and the transcendent apprehended.

Let us turn to the earliest stages of faith, noting especially the affective-relational dimensions of each stage.

Primal Faith

The experience of consistent primary care mediated through prenatal sensations and intuitions is the point of departure for stages of faith development. Following Erikson, it is assumed that infant cognitive and affective-relational differentiations and separations develop within a psychosocial dialectic of trust and mistrust. The emergence of self-other differentiation during the first two years presupposes the experience of consistent and trustworthy parenting. According to Erikson, the reiteration of this trustworthiness through religious rituals is an important contribution to human development. Foremost is the reenactment of our relatedness to the transcendent (the "numinous") and its recapitulation in the relationship between mother and child.

Primal faith therefore refers to the preverbal experience of a coherent world. In Piagetian terms, this experience is mediated through sensorimotor schemata, e.g., sucking, grasping, and other modes of constructing physical reality. In Eriksonian terms, primal faith is basic trust. Here are to be found the roots of the human capacity for faithfulness.

Stage One: Intuitive-Projective Faith

In this stage, imagination is the principle medium for ordering the many feelings and intuitions of the world. The meaning-constructive activities appear to be structured primarily in a narrative mode. This is particularly evident in the use of narrative to establish causal relations, e.g., to connect events and experience, and in the use of fairy tales to understand good and evil. Questions about what is real and true are raised frequently as fact and fantasy are not easily distinguished. A salient feature of meaning-making is understanding good and evil, particularly their representation through fairy tales, cartoons, television, and so on. The polarities of good and evil are often linked to a mixture of anthropomorphic and nonanthropomorphic images of God (see chapter three), thus reflecting the mixture of preconcrete and concrete cognitive operations. These images of God may assume lifelong significance especially when reinforced by parental or institutional religious behavior. It should be noted that the acquisition of language is marked by thought that is episodic, egocentric, and one-dimensional. Since the child is unable to take the perspective of the other, reliance on his or her own intuitions and projections is paramount, hence the need for a trustworthy parental environment.

Stage Two: Mythic-Literal Faith

This stage is marked by the emergence of full concrete operational thinking. The child constructs the world imaginatively through play, fantasy, and story. In short, the child formulates a literal narrative of the world, projecting herself or himself into the fabric of the narrative. A salient feature of this narrative structuring of experience is the anthropomorphic apprehension of God as one who punishes those who do bad things and rewards the good. Meaning-making also involves experiences of attachment and loss, issues of identity formation such as initiative and guilt, industry and inferiority, and relation to authority figures, especially given the widening network of relationships that extend beyond the immediate familial environment, e.g., day care and kindergarten. The narrative structuring of experience heightens the importance of a trustworthy and coherent environment and educational strategies that stimulate the child's imagination. The typical child in this stage is between ages seven and eleven. Perspective-taking is limited by the inability to reflect on one's own interiority. Kegan (1982) refers to the self at this stage as "imperial," embedded in its perceptions of the physical world. Thus the challenge of transformation is centered on subject-object differentiation—the transition from being subject to one's perceptions to having these perceptions as the object of attention. Piaget refers to this capacity to move back and forth among one's perceptions as reversibility. This allows the child to organize the world into groups and classes and to recognize causal relationships. The meaning-constructive activity which we have defined as "mythic-literal faith" is concerned with the primary efforts at constructing and deconstructing subject-object or self-other relationships. This includes the perception of God as "other" and the causality, reciprocity, and conservation associated with God as one who punishes evil and rewards good. The emerging ability to take the role of the other, i.e., mutual perspective taking, represents an evolution in cognitive-affective development and is considered a characteristic of stage three.

Stage Three: Synthetic-Conventional Faith

The deep structure of this stage is evidenced by interpersonal relationships that involve mutual perspective taking. Mutually shared feelings and conventional virtues upon which the community of belonging rests are tacitly held as the self's center of meaning and value. This dependence on "significant others" and "generalized others" for self-definition corresponds with Erikson's account of the adolescent identity crisis which eventuates from the breakdown in continuity and sameness between self and significant others. Since interpersonal relationships are emphasized as the principal medium through which God is known, much attention is paid to the personal attributes and roles played by authority figures. These assume priority over conflicting beliefs and cognitive dissonance. In effect, the dialectic of thesis and antithesis is resolved by appealing to synthesis, i.e., conventional ideas which do not threaten harmonious relationships within the community of faith. It is not surprising then that this stage may extend from adolescence throughout adulthood.

Three other stages complete Fowler's outline of faith development: Individuative-Reflective Faith, Conjunctive Faith, and Universalizing Faith. This chapter will focus on the concerns of preschoolers, most of whom fall within stage one, and include both theological and psychological considerations. In the first stage the presence of the divine (the "numinous") is presumed to be incarnate in the relationship between child and parent and remains as a vital part of the deep structure of each stage. The aspects of each stage illuminate how the transcendent is apprehended cognitively and affectively. But here the organismic/biological metaphor of Piagetian constructivism is of limited usefulness. The dialectical tensions of attachment and separation, presence and absence are not evident in the preconcrete operational structure of intuitive-projective faith. Yet it is precisely at this stage that Erikson suggests that the numinous presence of the transcendent is mediated in the sensations and intuitions experienced in the interaction between child and mother. This suggests that in addition to the organismic/biological metaphor we have a *covenantal* metaphor of interaction that extends beyond the child-mother dyad to include the relation to the transcendent. This is what Fowler means by the triadic structure of faith.

Mahler and Faith Development Theory

Mahler's work on early child development (Mahler, Pine, & Bergman, 1975) supplements Erikson's and Fowler's hypotheses regarding the importance of the primary familial community in mediating the child's first experience of the numinous. Drawing on Mahler, we propose that the earliest parent-child interactions compose a presymbolic dialogue. The images which emerge from this dialogue are often vague representations of parent and child. This proposition requires a more detailed examination of symbolic functioning in the preschool years.

Mahler's essential contribution to psychology has been the intricate discussion of psychological birth, principally in the first three years. A seminal idea emerging from her work is the dialectic of union and separation.

Mahler's dialectic refers to a parent-child mutuality in which the child has separated and individuated well enough that the threats of premature self-sufficiency or re-engulfment by the powerful mother are avoided. Mahler uses the term "constancy" to describe the balance of self-love and other-love in the mother-child dyad. Thus the child is not threatened by short separations or momentary loss of the mother's love. The mother-child dyad powerfully predetermines decisions regarding autonomy and identity in the life-course, though Mahler qualifies the predictive capacity for later outcomes. Kaplan (1978) refers to the dialectic of union and separation with words most parents can understand: "Constant love is the reconciliation between self-love and love for others. Those who love themselves just enough will turn themselves to the arms of others—without clinging to them in desperation" (1981, p. 44). This reconciliation includes the loved self and the loved object images coexisting in relative peace.

Mahler probably overemphasizes the mother as the sole source of nurture. The father is treated more as a reality principle, a "powerful, uncontaminated, helpful ally" (McDevitt & Mahler, 1981, p. 413) associated with a wider scope of external reality and autonomous functioning. However, neither parent is idealized or negatively distorted if the reconciliation between self-love and love for parent is optimum. Negative or harsh images and experiences need not be "split off"; the extreme outcomes of fusion or isolation are avoided intrapsychically. The critical period in which the omnipotent toddler is most liable to split off negative or positive images of the parent is *"rapprochement,"* around the middle of the second year.

Most parents have witnessed a sort of second attack of stranger anxiety with their toddlers around the age of eighteen months. The earlier stranger anxiety (at about eight months) occurred when the threat of actual parent loss was imminent. The latter anxiety owes its power to the threat of the loss of parental love. The unspoken question becomes, "If I venture out into this frightening world, in which I seem to be quite small, will my mother's love still be there when I return?" The reason that the latter takes more time to surface than the former is that we are discussing far more than perception. What is at stake is the object of our first love as well as the newly developed concept of the self.

Here we will not discuss in detail the phases and subphases engaged in by parent and child but instead attend to that early schematization of the world during the early years following rapprochement. The ambivalence arising in the second year of life may be observed in the later preschool years, specifically in indications of potentially hazardous post-separation issues or, conversely, the relatively successful navigation of these waters. Specifically, we look for symbolic evidence of mutuality with mother, father, caretaker, and God. God is understood symbolically in this, not as a projection, but rather as the experience of the numinous which is at least partially constructed of ideal parental images. Is there evidence of trust, constancy, and autonomy while symbolizing these ideal images? On the other hand, is there pretentious self-sufficiency, mistrust, an urge for fusion with an adult caretaker or a precarious splitting of images into the all-good and all-bad? Is the God imagery consonant with ideal parental images or is the imagery compensatory, covering up mistrust of the parent or the self?

Mahler argues that at critical life transitions it is normal to experience the "temporary limbo of suddenly not knowing who we were or who we might become. . . . What few of us have understood is the choreography and rhythms of our personal cycles of breaking loose and returning were set in motion by the events of our (psychological) birth" (1975, p. 59). Should this pattern persist, however, there is the likelihood that the person in question will require some holding environment in order to develop toward a more reflective faith.

In order to understand an environment that fails to hold, it is necessary to define a proper holding environment. First, it holds as much as is needed by the child or adult; that is, it reads signals from the individual and reacts with adjustments of holding and letting go. It embraces without intrusion. Therefore it lends a sense of warmth, nurture, and filling as the individual is able to internalize its qualities. It provides a sense of continuity with manageable increments of dissonance or the strange. The greatest irony of a holding environment is that its ultimate purpose is to enable separation and individuation, with a hope for mature intimacy in the future. Its holding is firm but tentative because it remains in dialogue with the person held.

Mahler explains that the child has a confident expectation of his or her environment when that environment meets the needs for love and the reduction of aggressive tensions in play. Demonstrations of confidence and trust should have some means of becoming public in behavior: bodily presence, symbolic play, and so on. Mahler suggests her own categories of attachment, not unlike Ainsworth's (1979). Every outward description requires a leap of imagination in theoretical interpretation. No scheme or image theory is without such leaps; some just require more imagination than others. Our task is to describe spontaneous symbols as they are revealed in the physical presence of the child, in the manipulation of materials, and in the spoken context. These interpretations are meant to expand upon previous research. We are interested in the visions of ultimacy implicit or explicit in the preschool years and their implications for religious educators, parents, professionals, and other caretakers. The following case studies exemplify the importance of constancy, the dynamics of individuation and symbolism in the preschool years.

Peter, Age Six

Peter is principally mythic-literal. His play is intricately woven with narrative, but evocative and episodic outbursts penetrate the fabric of his story like molten lava through a fragile crust. Most of Peter's responses are characteristic of transition to or equilibration at stage two. His use of symbol allows his stories to be evocative, fantastic, and fluid. Power, aggression, and father/son tensions are consistent themes. While it is clear that Peter is able to distinguish fantasy from reality, the distinction becomes blurred when his figures get aggressive beyond his ability to control them. When his own creations become too overwhelming he regains control with statements like, "He's a good guy, but I pretend like he's a bad guy." Otherwise, he abandons the story altogether, making him appear episodic and fragmented as a stage one child would be.

For Peter the narrative itself is an important part of the holding environment. Because it is spontaneously constructed, it has the power to hold only so long as the images are not too transparent. He plays with parent and child symbols gleefully until they threaten to reveal too much about their groundedness in his own experience. For example, he offers to tell the interviewer a story before the stage for an interview is even set. He asks to sit in the male interviewer's lap, and he strokes the adult's knee as he launches into his story. The story has Jesus and God alternately saving one another from "Slimemacher," a demonic figure living under a manhole. The protagonists and the narrative milieu have been chosen from the world of the boy's father, a university professor. The son in the story tries to save the father from the demon, only to be brutally blinded and killed. As the son's body is dragged through the manhole to hell with a cold chain, the father (God) breaks the chain with his love and the two live happily in heaven thereafter. (Keep in mind, the adult interviewer has said nothing about the purpose of the visit yet. This is spontaneous material.) When asked whether his own father might not like to hear this wonderful story, Peter urgently requests that the story remain a secret. It is our opinion that his ambivalent aggression toward his own father, at a time when the father is idealized as role model, is understood by the child to be too transparent. He projects upon his father his own anger by telling us that his father would be very upset about his story.

The family paradigm is critical to most of Peter's responses. We discover after the interview that a recent divorce is thought to have had repercussions in his classroom behavior, predominantly in heightened aggressive behavior and attention demanding outbursts. Family relations are also reflected in some of Peter's story content. Viewing a picture of the nativity, he says that Mary is turning her head away because "Joseph is saying a very, very foolish thing." Subsequently she is forced to send Jesus away, wishing that he will not be hurt. Joseph must leave also "because Mary's happy then, and she doesn't need him right now, but he trusts." "And Jesus said 'I love you' when she said goodbye to him." Peter's ambivalence about his mother's imminent remarriage is again disclosed in his response to Mary: "She's still not smiling very much. She is nice."

Later, working with the creche figures, Peter clusters the figurines tightly around the baby as if to protect it. In perfect dualistic fashion, typical of stage two, but more thorough than most children, he divides all of the figurines between God and the devil. God has "power, but his power's not like the devil's powers." A "stranger" is introduced to the scene by the interviewer (a spaceman figure). Peter announces, "May I have your attention! May I have your attention!" He proceeds to transform the stranger from a baby killer to a "good guy" and then later into himself. Now the stranger, (representing Peter), brings a "box of love" to the Christ child, but actually hands it to Mary. The baby kisses the stranger for the present, and Peter yells "Yahoo!" This is an incredible example of the subject/object dilemma: Mary and the baby must be able to accept this strange little boy who so desperately needs to get someone's attention. In this story the father is distant and powerful. The subject (Peter) as stranger has the potential of killing the baby at first.

As a "good guy" he can become Peter. By being good he is able to win the mother's love as well as that of the baby. While the story ends on a happy note, one must ask what became of the baby killer. Why did the baby need such close attention? Where was the father's power made evident? A balance between self-love and object-love was developed, but at what cost?

The issue of persistent dualism may indicate more than a new stage in cognitive development. It may reveal a splitting of images, a lack of reconciliation. For instance, when Peter drew a picture to tell about God, he sketched two pictures much like the interviewer's puppet, calling them "Googies" from planet "Starflower," which is "tiny, like a little speck of a crumb, that small." Peter assumes control as a teacher, instructing the two Googies about God, because they "skipped that at school." He demonstrates confident command of the story until these defenseless creatures must reckon with "two gods." One "small . . . good" god is male, and one "giant" female god is "bad." Peter closes abruptly; he cannot continue. He is asked, "Do you think that's *really* the way it is?" He pauses and then replies cautiously, "I don't know at all." The narrative has ceased to hold; the images have become too powerful. He identifies with the powerless male god as well as the "speck of a crumb" from which his drawings emerge as living creatures. The female god is overwhelming, yet commands respect, awe, love, and fear. Once again he splits his images into two clear camps. Yet he remains ambivalent about the side with which he is identified. Once more male and female figures represent separately both the loved and the hated; Peter is unable to integrate them. (We hasten to point out that Peter's images do not necessarily correspond to the images held by adults in the boy's interpersonal world. What is essential is that Peter's internalized images have not been reconciled and may impact future faith development in a less than optimum way.)

Whether what we observe is indicative of splitting as Mahler describes it is still open to question. Mahler tells us that splitting occurs most easily under two conditions:

1) Under conditions of high arousal, where the child is too suddenly helpless.

2) When the power of one's own aggression outweighs the constancy of partnership with the love object.

The dualisms of love and rage, God and devil, male and female, along with the projection onto small creatures of the boy's heroic wishes give us reason to suspect an element of splitting. The interview has helped Peter temporarily vent rage and maintain the good self. This transitional space has held the child and given him opportunity to recreate meanings in less threatening symbolic forms.

Ann, Age Four

Ann's responses have all been scored as intuitive-projective (stage one), as we would expect from her age. However, her use of authorities confronts our scoring with difficult questions. For instance, she uses TV, books, parents, and family traditions to justify her responses. If this indicates the use of orthodoxy or appearance of choosing one's authorities, then we should score these responses stage two, despite the lack of rational mediation or reciprocity. Perhaps the constellations of authority have changed in our culture since the original faith development research. Yet, another possibility presents itself, as possibly indicated in the following exchange:

Q: "Who do you pray to?"
A: "Jesus."
Q: "Can he hear you?"
A: "Nope."
Q: "Why do you talk to him?"
A: "Because, we say the blessing?"
Q: "Uhuh. And why do we say a blessing?"
A: "Because we eat supper, and that's what you do."

Every parent has probably heard such a tautology. Several things are worth noting about this child's use of authority and ritual to create narrative. First, she uses what McLean has referred to as multiple "reference groups" (1986, p. 168). She draws upon a loosely connected list of authorities to weave a simple story.

More importantly, the story is permeated with ritual. Ritual provides an internal continuity and logic of its own. Ann's blessing ritual is one which carries a surplus of meaning that she may later identify with new insights. Presently its meaning lies in its parental sanction as a regular event. The parents are still the principal authorities, as we would expect, but they mediate or possibly point to a larger referent. An event or series of events may have relational continuity which give them both immediate meanings and make themselves available for future meaning-making. Ritual provides a peculiar vehicle for the repetition and potential power of these relational symbols.

Nan, Age Five

Nan is solidly on her way to mythic-literal faith (stage two). While in some respects she is still at stage one, as the interview proceeds she gives increasingly mature responses (as we have found with many adult interviews). Nan is a budding empiricist, yet not able to submit her observations to any manipulations. Appearance and convention are extremely important to her in decision making and in choosing authorities, yet Nan's symbolic functioning is easily her most mature aspect by our criteria. In only one instance does she fail to discriminate a symbol from its referent object; reality and fantasy are clearly differentiated.

Nan's use of familial imagery to portray religious themes leads us to suspect that identification with mother and peacemaking with father, sibling, and self are well under way. There appears to be a degree of constancy in these primary images which may account for her precocious symbolic development. On the other hand, her ability to manipulate symbols may assist her consolidation of primary images. God's family is structured exactly like Nan's. God is father. Mary is mother. Joseph, because he cannot also be father, is Jesus' older brother. Jesus is the youngest and has a sister, which is obviously Nan. Females dominate the heavenly family in Nan's drawing—Mary is most prominent along with her girl-child. Nan projects herself into both the roles of sister and mother: She says "if I were Mary," and "Mary says the stranger can hold" the baby. Mother's importance is central, but Nan's own importance is also prominent. When asked more about this family, Nan responds that Jesus is "still way up there in the sky." In fact, "the whole family's up there."

A preliminary deduction we might derive from the foregoing symbolism is that Nan's mother is very important to her conception of authority, her relationship to her younger brother, and her premonitions about the unseen world. The young empiricist recognizes the possibility of the unseen and seems to be comfortable with it due to her identification with the mother who governs the heavenly family. Her own symbolic and pictorial proximity to Mary demonstrates that her power within the family is derived from her identification with the mother. A healthy relational world would appear to exist, giving symbolic function a leading edge in Nan's faith development.

Mary, Mother, Age Early Thirties; Drew, Son, Age Three

As a family interview, this particular dyad presented us with the opportunity to compare a mother's responses with some of her son's. Mary is clearly a stage three (synthetic-conventional) adult. Nearly all of her responses were consistent with this stage, with the exception of a few transitional answers to questions probing for her social perspective-taking. While she appears equilibrated here, this interview is clearly distinct from stage three adolescent interviews in its content as well as in the nature of its social embeddedness, which appears to be holding back this woman from maturing toward individuative-reflective faith. Unlike the teenager, this woman appears to have become embedded in a story from her familial past which seems compelled to be repeated in the present.

Somewhat like Peter in the first case-study, Mary relates a story of dual images tied to father and mother figures. As Kaplan has so capably described human love, "Demons are transformed into ordinary human passions by the down-to-earth devotion of one human being for another" (1981, p.247-8). "Demons" in this sense need not be absolutely bad; they may be absolutely good. The fact is that they are not whole or real. When images of the other are split, there is a likelihood that the images of the self will be split as well. A certain partnership between good and bad images (within the self) ceases to exist. One may not even call it a state of war, as neither side recognizes the other. While the internalized objects differ from their real personal counterparts, we believe that the mutual regard possible within the family covenant is essential to becoming real, being human in the face of contradictory images of self and other. Splitting keeps the world in absolute dichotomies of the angelic and demonic, thus distorting its potential for offering real recognition and direction.

Mary demonstrates, by her radical dualisms, a failure to construct an environment which is whole. It is likely that her environment did not hold in the past, nor is it expected to in the future. Her mother is "maternal, loving, and nurturing . . . I never thought of her as having a mind, I don't think," she concludes. The irony of her remark ("I don't think") is unintentional and repeated in several places. Her father, on the other hand, is "bad, bad, all his life . . . naughty. . . naughtier than anybody else." Remembering her childhood, she says "I would die if my mother did. . . . I wanted to die if my mother died." When Mary's adult life was threatened by appendicitis she remembers, "That will be fine, as long as my mother is not too upset." The interviewer learns that she was almost spontaneously aborted in the first trimester. The theme of abortion appears over and over, and it is the one ethical principle she cannot relativize. We learn indirectly that she was pregnant prior to marriage, but felt she had no real reason to marry.

There is every evidence that the pattern of a "strict authoritarian . . . bad . . . naughty" father and a "nurturing" mother continue to dominate her world as a married woman. Just as her father moved her mother from a hyper-clean Dutch community to a mosquito-infested trailer park, she now feels compelled to remain in a threatening community in a house her husband had chosen for her. She rationalizes that she sometimes wants to remain in order to be a "good example . . . something stable." When a mother across the street brutally murders her infant, it is ironic and frightening that her son Drew must pin the blame on "GI Joe."

Her dualities extend to her spiritual life. She wants to be a "good person" at church. She adds, "I need to believe in sin so I can feel forgiven." Her conflict in church is most evident in the following statement: "I feel guilty, guilty, guilty. . . . I was blameless." She describes God with nurturant images similar to those of her mother. But she feels the weight of God's burdens on her own shoulders. She wants to be "loving and secure" for her son so that God will seem loving and secure. On the other hand, Drew, who reportedly was thinking of hurting his baby sister, said, "I wish God made me Lynn (the sister) instead." Mary tells him to stop thinking bad thoughts and he replies, "I want him to be a good person, my way."

Mary appears to be reliving the disorder of her childhood. Her appeal for help in the interview is most poignant as she recounts a prayer beside her sleeping husband, "I need help! I need help!" Her partially stable resource is a nurturing God-image that draws its energy from the perfect mother internalized. Unfortunately, just as the mother is not real, this God must be upheld by her own efforts and appearances. Critical to this interpretation, Mary reports that she does not like to be "held," which is precisely what she appears to need from her community. The split of her all-good mother and all-disordering father appears to extend to her own self-image. This may partially account for her delayed ability to take the perspective of others; she fails to be able to construct another's viewpoint due to her own lack of integration. She lives with the fear of almost being aborted and realizes this possibility existed for her son.

On the basis of the mother's interview, one might expect to find that the three-year-old son with an infant sister is precariously balanced between union and separation and possibly fearful of strangers. On the contrary, we were confronted with an outgoing and precocious little boy ready to launch into conversation with adults.

Two important phenomena dominate much of Drew's interview. First, he uses father images throughout. He appears to be bridging the past into the present situation by reminding himself of a father's presence. Second, he creates the illusion of control over the unknown or unfamiliar by mastery in the manipulation of small objects. A final point is that he seems to titillate himself with the novel, particularly "bad things."

The interview with Drew is particularly striking because the names of his parents happen to correspond to those of the holy family in the paradigm (Mary and Joseph). The three protagonists in all of his stories are a mother, father, and a stranger. (It should be noted that a stranger is introduced into the format by the interviewer.) The presence or absence of the father appears to mediate the possibilities for the other two. Consider, for instance, a projective remark with a picture of Mary and Jesus:

Q: "She's going over to the baby. What is she going to do?"

A: "Pick her up. I mean, pick him up."

Q: "So all Mommies love babies?"

A: "Yes. No, Mommies love boys."

Q: "Who is that holding the little girl?"

A: "Ah, nobody."

Q: "Where is his Daddy? Where is Joseph?"

A: "Joseph must have run away."

Q: "Where did he go?"

A: "I guess he went to help other people, that have problems, and then tell God . . . he might have gone to see God."

Q: "What does God look like?"

A: "He has that black hair like my Daddy."

When the father is symbolically absent, the presence of the mother has ambivalent significance for Drew. The father is described not only as looking like God, but as performing personal missions for him as well. When the father figure has been present and then fails to reappear, Drew quickly seizes control over the entire play-drama. For instance, he is asked if the boy carrying a lamb is a shepherd. He replies, "No. He's just a plain boy. . . (pause) . . . that, but his Daddy died." He then hides the more aggressive figurines (snake, dragon, dinosaur) so they cannot get the baby and says, "This is real scary!" Then he uses a lion to "chase all the mean things away." Finally he turns all of the figurines surrounding the baby around to face him. Some would argue that this is only an example of egocentric perspective-taking. A further interpretation is possible however: The father is absent, in fact dead. Drew assumes control in this symbolic absence by exercising his own aggressive abilities, removing all threatening animals from the proximity of the baby (who may be Drew or his sister, necessitating two alternate explanations for the final movement). The child who is "just a plain boy" achieves the mirroring attention he needs by turning the figurine to face him. This is arguably an interpretative leap on our part. However, Drew seems to periodically realize that he has not brought the father into a scene, and his reaction is to bring up and ultimately control "scary" subjects.

In the mother interview, Mary brings up her concern that Drew is choosing "bad" playmates in order to tease her. He also identifies with Oscar the Grouch on TV. It appeared in the interview with the son that these identifications were evidences of personal attempts at self-control or mastery. He appears much less helpless than several other three-year-olds we interviewed. For one thing, he consciously chooses media for play that his mother will not like: "I like boring colors. I like black and brown." When other colors are offered, he refuses with authority. He goes on to draw God and Jesus in their personal rocketship (the shuttle disaster has just occurred, and his grandfather is a NASA engineer). "God moves real fast!" Why? "So that no strangers, no bad strangers will come out and get Jesus, so they can put Jesus in a bed." Then he makes another rocket full of strangers. He is asked, "Is it safe?" He replies emphatically, "No!" He proceeds to make a police rocketship to "scratch them out." Asked, "They just scratched them out?" he responds, "But, it's really that I did it." Besides demonstrating a mature differentiation of the real and the imaginary, the symbol and the object, Drew also takes a great deal of control and responsibility. He puts the father and son in a precarious situation and then saves them with his police rocket. Incidentally, the strangers are exploded without really being hurt.

It would be presumptuous of us to argue that Drew faces any kind of crisis in development, particularly faith development. Neither can we argue that there is any hard evidence for a "negative identity," to use Erikson's term (1968, p. 172). However, the child is undoubtedly facing the challenges of a new sister along with his strong need for an ordering presence, hoped for in the form of his father. Unlike Peter, Drew does not seek the physical proximity of the male interviewer. Like Peter, he demonstrates a strong need to continue the interaction, while maintaining a certain autonomy through the use of aggressive symbolization.

At this stage in her life the mother feels herself to be losing control. Drew appears to have taken more than his share of control over matters. He hopes for a father and a God who will provide protection, but falls back upon lions and police to frighten away the unknown and the threatening. Both Ainsworth (1979) and Mahler (1975) describe a type of child who appears to separate prematurely and to be ambivalent toward the mother. Interestingly, Mahler nearly always uses boys as examples. These children are open to the strange adult. They seem to bounce off of life, seeking to define their own boundaries, and they appear independent. On the basis of the faith development scoring system, Drew is very mature (Moseley, Jarvis, & Fowler, 1986). We suggest, however, that he has constructed a precarious holding environment that may fail to hold as his faith will require. More particularly, he seems to need to consolidate his paternal identification. A confluence of environments (home, preschool, church) could also help him to spend less energy ordering his world. This is precisely the crux of the structure/content dilemma, the holding power of the particular contents of the faith environment and their impact on the structural transformation of faith.

IMPLICATIONS FOR RELIGIOUS EDUCATION

Several implications for religious education are possible, using the seven aspects of faith development as Fowler defines them as an ordering principle for these applications. The major themes, in keeping with the previous material, will be the holding environment and the dialectic of separation and reunion. All of these highlight the importance of the trustworthiness of the environment. The main point is that the faithfulness of the environment is critical to the faith of the child, consistent with Erikson's emphasis upon basic trust in the first stage of life.

Aspect A: Form of Logic

The most important point to be made here is that conceptualization is related to sensation at this age. The environment should offer opportunities to touch, smell, hear, see, and taste. If ultimate concerns are mediated through the everyday milieu, then it is incumbent upon us to offer a milieu that matches the interests of the preschooler.

Next, we believe that with the expanding marketplace the child must face (home, preschool, Sunday school, etc.), a congruence of themes and models leading to a coherent worldview is important. If the child grows optimally under conditions of incremental dissonance, then the child's various worlds should be in communication with each other. Issues of authority, role modeling, and handling (even feeding schedules, naptime) should have some degree of agreement. As we will see in the section on symbolism, the child will bridge his/her worlds naturally through play. We can assist by offering a holding presence in which bridges may be built.

Aspect B: Social Perspective Taking

Throughout our work, we have addressed the question of perspective on the self. The self is in fact an object of conscious and unconscious construction and manipulation. The theory we have been reviewing suggests that the self and other are always dialectically related as development progresses (or regresses). At this stage the child is not fully aware of having a perspective at all. We might say that the youngster is embedded in his or her narrative or prenarrative stories. Therefore it is important that we offer the child opportunities to construct stories for others to hear and appreciate. It should be clear at this point that matters of ultimate concern, which are generally the focus of religious educators, are reflected in the early play-dramas and storytelling by the child.

Aspect C: Moral Judgment

There is clear evidence in our preschool interviews that children are not always preoccupied with punishment, reward, and reciprocity as the principal matters of their moral judgments. Perhaps their more gracious accounts of parental or divine rulership are simply learned responses. We suggest, however, that mutual regard provides an undercurrent for grace, especially for the preschooler. Of course, parents are the first people that come to mind when we think of mutuality. Other adults, however, have opportunities to mirror back to the child the valued self. Mutual love provides the rapport within which the loved self and loved object may be held in balance.

Role-play provides occasions for moral dilemmas from real life to be played in a safe space. Finally the church has the distinct responsibility of providing the child with opportunities to participate in its mission: visiting shut-ins, serving in soup kitchens, or simply helping to prepare for a special celebration. The child is thereby safely introduced to environments not otherwise encountered.

Aspect D: Bounds of Social Awareness

We need to take seriously the evidence that intergenerational events provide unique chances for children to be exposed to multiple perspectives and other stages of faith. Along with the enlarging of experience, the child has opportunity to empathize, imagine, and imitate a wider variety of respected elders. Isolation and age-grading, while they have provided some degree of protection for children in the economic sphere, have radically reduced the child's opportunities for exposure to potential futures. By providing times when old and young can participate in ritual together we offer the child a connectedness within his or her experience which is obliterated when we exclude the young from the powerful experiences of community among their elders.

Second, if children are allowed to be co-planners with their teachers and parents for the curriculum, they become acquainted with connectedness. A holding environment is meant to hold and let go as the child indicates need for each, and the child will give signals of those needs explicitly if given the chance. Preschoolers, for example, understand when they no longer need stars, smiley faces, or physical positive reinforcers. They will tell the adult when a touch or kind word will do.

Aspect E: Locus of Authority

The main point to be made here reiterates the suggestion made about "Ann." We find that while she had multiple authorities, her parents were the cohesive principle behind their sanctions or restrictions. This extends to the power of family rituals. The involvement of parents in the religious life of the youngster provides a message to the child that someone can be depended on to sanction and help make sense of experience with the unknown. There is good reason to expect that the authority pattern chosen by the parent is closely correlated with the religious worldview chosen by the child for adult life. While this work requires further study, it seems clear that when parents have basic trust in the child and supply reasonable but firm limits, the child is likely to trust the world and God.

Aspect F: Form of World Coherence

Our pilot project suggests that the child needs opportunities to create worlds, both fantastic and real. More specifically, it appears that children are quite provoked in their thinking by ultimate matters, particularly the pictures of what heaven, God, or family might be or become (see chapter three). These images need to be accepted by the adult in their idiosyncratic forms. Children need to be given chances to distinguish real and make-believe, symbol and object. Again, a concrete approach is recommended. Religious ritual provides a coherent environment in which continuity of experience exists alongside the incremental dissonance of fresh and challenging symbols. The potential exists for the expanding of horizons within a safe space.

Aspect G: Symbolic Function

Prior interpretation and scoring of symbolic function indicated that it might develop independently, yet by understanding symbol within the Mahlerian framework, some association is discernable between this function and the other aspects. First, it is necessary to reiterate that symbol does not refer to some peculiar theme or word such as "God," "church," "heaven," or "prayer," in which transcendent phenomena are apparent. Symbols act as bridges in two distinct ways: 1) They bridge the experience of the prelingual (or sensorimotor) child with the later experience of the child for whom speaking is a principal form of communication. When children have achieved what Piaget called "representational competence," they are able to sustain mental representations independent of object cues. The boy or girl can manipulate the inner pictures, but realizes that the object has an existence of its own. 2) Symbols are tools for union and reunion of places and persons, even the self. In this regard they serve to bridge rather than split mental images by representing them in the outer world so they can be manipulated. They may appear in a linear format, such as in speech, or in more pictorial and nondiscursive forms.

Analogy is fundamental to our experience. Generally it deals with relationships of the self and some object. Play and ritual provide powerful arenas for the expansion of analogical symbolism. Play provides a safe space for the free manipulation of these pictures of life. It is a transitional space, a place between the worlds of more mundane demands, where the child can experiment with relational hopes and dilemmas. Langer (1957) argues that play distinguishes human from other life. Intentional and nonintentional representation give a place for conscious and unconscious images to find expression. Moreover, ritual provides a communal context for imaginal life. It is here that the relational and imaginal can come together in ways that transcend our conscious awareness. In intergenerational religious rituals, the child (or adult) has the unparalleled opportunity to participate in matters of ultimate concern to the entire community. We are convinced that these experiences help precipitate and nurture faith development in the preschool years.

REFERENCES

Ainsworth, M. (1979). *Patterns of attachment: A Psychological study of the strange situation.* Hillsdale, NJ: Lawrence Erlbaum Associates.

Erikson, E. (1959). *Identity and the life cycle.* New York: International Universities Press.

Erikson, E. (1968). *Identity, youth, and crisis.* New York: Norton.

Fowler, J. (1981). *Stages of faith: The psychology of human development and the quest for meaning.* New York: Harper & Row.

Kaplan, L. (1981). *Oneness and separateness: From infant to individual.* New York: Simon and Schuster.

Kegan, R. (1982). *The evolving self: Problem and process in human development.* Cambridge, MA: Harvard University Press.

Langer, S. (1957). *Philosophy in a new key: A study in the symbolism of reason, rite, and art.* Cambridge, MA: Harvard University.

Mahler, M., Pine, F., & Bergman, A. (1975). *The psychological birth of the human infant: Symbiosis and individuation.* New York: Basic Books.

McDevitt, J. & Mahler, M. (1981). Object constancy, individuality, and internalization. In Greenspan and Pollack (Eds.), *The course of life: Psychoanalytic contributions toward understanding personality development.* Washington, D.C.: United States Government Printing Office.

McLean, S. (1986). Basic sources and new possibilities: H. Richard Niebuhr's influence on faith development theory. In C. Dykstra & S. Parks (Eds.), *Faith development and Fowler.* Birmingham, AL: Religious Education Press.

Mosely, R. M., Jarvis, D. & Fowler, J. (1986). *Manual for faith development research*. Atlanta, GA: Center for Faith Development.

Niebuhr, H.R. (1960). *Radical monotheism and western culture*. New York: Harper & Row.

Smith, W. C. (1962) *The meaning and end of religion*. New York: Macmillan.

Chapter Six:

Religion and Socialization

MARY ANNE FOWLKES

It may be helpful to begin by framing religious socialization in the current matrix of religion education, specifically the work of Scott (1984) and Barker (1981). Scott's (1984) "Ecclesial Enculturation" model encompasses what is described as "catechesis," "Christian nurture," or "religious socialization" by Nelson (1967), Westerhoff (1985), Marthaler (1978), and Foster (1982). Ecclesial Enculturation serves as a means of induction into the community, the tribal phase of religious education, concerned with its own tradition and borders. The processes involved are initiation, adaptation, transmission, translation, and maintenance, all of which are utilized to develop commitment to a particular ecclesial community.

Guiding and passing on a tradition is particularly important for the religious education of the *young* child. A rootedness in one's own religious tradition—developed through the rituals, sacraments, language, and symbols of the community—forms a sound basis for religious nurture for Protestants, Catholics, and Jews.

The "cultural" approach to religious education utilizes the community as bearer of a particular heritage, way of life, and worldview to be transmitted to the next generation. Drawing heavily on the work of Nelson and Westerhoff, Barker (1981) focuses on the anthropological themes of belonging and identification, as the community engages in cultural transmission. While acknowledging his debt to cultural anthropology, Barker nevertheless credits both Nelson and Westerhoff with adding the theological or transcendent dimension to the model to allow for change. The ability to change allows for the dimension of freedom which is the focus of Barker's work.

The particular type of freedom engendered by the cultural transmission model is freedom *from* chaos, confusion, and fragmentation and freedom *for* creative living together in a community bound together by a coherent symbol system. Lifestyle and learning become synonymous terms in this framework. While attending to story, ritual, and values, members are initiated and develop their sense of identity and belonging. As members are shaped, they in turn have the freedom to reshape their community.

Processes of Socialization

Nelson in *Where Faith Begins* (1967) posits that children are basically shaped by the culture in which they dwell. If that culture is the community of faith, the children will become believers through three processes utilized in cultural transmission. The first is formation of an identity which answers the question, "Who are we?" As the young learn a language, they likewise appropriate a meaning system which provides a particular way of seeing the world.

The second process has to do with the formation of conscience or values which are initially shaped by parents and later internalized. While moral development theory may explain character development, Nelson claims that the church must shape the minds and hearts of parents if the Christian family's goals are to differ from those of society in general.

The final process of self-identification ("Who am I?") takes place only in the context of belonging to a group with significant persons (parents, adults, groups) as role models to imitate. Nelson sees the congregation, or community of believers, as the school of faith in which learning takes place by participation in events with those who belong. According to Nelson, worship incubates faith and fellowship makes faith operational.

If Nelson's view is taken seriously, the preschool child will be socialized in the community of faith by adults who will interpret the meaning of events such as the birth of a new sibling, a natural disaster, the death of a grandparent, the discovery of a butterfly emerging from a cocoon, a quarrel and reconciliation, all in terms of God's action and often recognized by spontaneous prayer. One's identity as a member of God's family will be communicated to the child in innumerable events of everyday living. Symbolic behavior and gestures of the faith—such as grace at table, bowing heads, giving gifts—all become avenues of communicating the way we do things in our family and congregation. As the preschool child moves from the toddler stage of "What's that?" to the preschool stage of "Why?" and "How does that work?" the community's perception system and its ways of doing things become appropriated by the child. While Nelson claims that the young learn faith, hope, and love by enacting them, Barber (1981) details more precisely how this happens and how parents and adults may intentionally go about attitude development as the foundation for religious education.

Westerhoff (1985) supports Nelson's view of Christian nurture as a function of the faith community. In his terminology "nurture" and "catechesis" are synonymous and imply a communal understanding of persons who share a common vision, memory, hope, authority, rituals, and symbolic actions. However, he distinguishes formation and education. Formation is described as enculturation or socialization and is based on experiences in the faith community which shape perceptions, consciousness, and character.

For a clear understanding of how enculturation takes place, Westerhoff looks at the community in terms of its ritual life, experiential life and life in the world and asks, "What does it mean to be Christian together?" Enculturation involves interaction among persons of all ages as they discover, share, and celebrate life.

Rejecting developmental stages of knowing, Westerhoff posits four *styles* of faith which may operate throughout life—experienced, dependent, searching, owned—with no one better than another. Experienced faith based on actions rather than words is foundational to faith and is the primary mode of preschool children as they observe, imitate, act, and react. In his enculturation theory, Westerhoff would eliminate age groups and provide diverse communities small enough to provide purposeful, meaningful interaction among all ages. This approach is an antidote to Suransky's (1982) picture of young children being warehoused into meticulously age-graded preschools, to be considered later.

A third model of religious socialization comes from Marthaler (1978) who draws heavily on Berger and Luckman's secular conception of socialization and thus reduces the definition of socialization to the interaction of an individual with a group. Like Westerhoff, Marthaler does not see the child as "tabula rasa" or lump of clay, but as an actor in forming his or her own identity, which emerges from reciprocal relations within a group. Children are both actors and acted upon.

Marthaler explains identity formation in terms of a process based on strong and emotional attachment, in which a person develops a social identity and symbol system. He sees catechesis as a specialized form of religious socialization continuing throughout the lifespan as one comes to know structured meanings and behaviors which have been defined by previous generations. Gradually these become internalized into one's own identity through transformation as well as transmissions.

Although Darcy-Berube (1978) praises Marthaler's foundational work in religious socialization, she raises several criticisms which deserve careful attention. First, although Marthaler states the aims of socialization to be both transmission and transformation, Darcy-Berube sees the model as tending to imprison religious education in a maintenance mold self-perpetuating its own image. Westerhoff attempts to remedy this problem by his separation of catechesis into the two dimensions of formation and education.

Darcy-Berube also criticizes the neglect of personal and spiritual dimensions of faith in stressing assimilation and identification. She contends that the socialization model can produce religious church members who lack a real faith experience. On the preschool level it may produce "good children"—those adapted and assimilated into the community. Inherent in the model is the risk of fostering "ideological internalization" rather than faith; children can be socialized into a system of beliefs, become good solid church members in the mold of their elders, and never be converted. She challenges us to look at the long-term effects of religious socialization in adolescence and adulthood.

Religious Socialization and the Family

How is the religious socialization model implemented with the preschool child? Obviously the family plays a major role, although Nelson and others urge us to neither place too much of a burden on the family nor to discount them by turning religious education over to church school and trained teachers.

A study by Hunsberger and Brown (1984) entitled "Religious Socialization, Apostasy and the Impact of Family Background" surveyed college psychology students and found that intellectual orientation and emphasis placed on religion in the childhood home were predictors of apostate/nonapostate status. Those who had a strong religious home environment in childhood were likely to remain in the religious field while weaker home environments were likely to produce apostates. Forty percent of all respondents claimed parents to be the strongest religious influence, most frequently the mother.

Insight into religious socialization through the family can be traced back to Horace Bushnell's *Christian Nurture* which proclaims, "The child is to grow up a Christian and never know himself to be otherwise." Miller (1979) highlights Bushnell's view of family and children by claiming that the nurturing process begins at birth in the organic unit of the family. Stressing the power of parents as unconscious, intimate, and contagious, Miller illuminates Bushnell's views of how strongly parents influence character development. By three years of age more than half of character formation has taken place, leaving the preschool child to concentrate more on refinement and reflection of behaviors.

The spirit of family life is pervasive, communicating the love of God through caretaking activities. What the parents *are* is more important than what they *say.* In this sense religion is caught not taught, and the family functions as the child's church. Bushnell believed in mothers staying home with children and modeling prayer in godly conversation. They were to let children play and ask questions, not indoctrinate them by memorization of catechism or Bible verses. For this role the church should offer support and training so that the foundation of trust would later result in the autonomy and emancipation of the child.

Authority should be based on love plus rules in a dependable environment. The whole notion of Christian parenting in Bushnell's scheme relied heavily on the infant's baptism into the full life of the church. Preschool children, then, belong as full participants in the life of the faith community as they move from faith in parents as gods, to faith in the parents' God, to a faith of their own (Miller, 1979).

Bushnell's emphasis on the family's child-rearing function as the key to religious socialization is seen in current Greek Orthodox and Catholic treatises. Boojamra (1985) attempts to restore the family's nurturer/educator role as a priority in the Greek Orthodox communion. He sees the family, in the context of the church, as the formative agency of community and the matrix of trust, personhood, and intimacy. As the child's primary world, both psychologically and spiritually, the parents are to guide children into spiritual realities.

With Westerhoff and Nelson, Boojamra sees faith as a gift to be given, not something to be taught in didactic fashion. He defines religious socialization as a process focusing on the origins of religious thought, attitudes, and behaviors and how and to what extent these are translated by the family from one generation to another. He does not believe in faith development theory, but rather that agents of socialization should set the stage for grace in the life of the child through a live encounter with Christ.

Interestingly, Boojamra moves away from a child-centered focus into a family systems approach for parish planning. Claiming that the family exists for all members, especially the spouses, the model concentrates upon family interaction patterns as models for living in the world. This larger perspective places children in a complicated series of relationships which influence their development and nurture. An effective model of religious socialization in the local church community would not separate family ministry from childhood education nor contribute to family disorientation by strict age-grading in community activities.

Socialization in the Church

Integrating theological, sociological, and psychological views of children in the faith community is a major task. Bedouelle (1985) makes a case for children in Catholic ecclesiology, through infant baptism with communion and also for children to be children in the church. Children, claims Bedouelle, can contribute to the building up of the Body of Christ. He develops a concept of the "catholicity of childhood" couched in the mystery of the Christ image unfolding in each of its parts, including his infancy. He then elaborates the gifts of childhood to the church: spontaneity, openness to revelation, playfulness, and hunger for learning.

Attacking a proliferation of children's Masses which isolate children from the church community, Bedouelle advocates liturgy "in which the beauty and joy of celebration unite Christians of all ages." The catholicity alludes to the diversity and beauty of all God's people, including children in their natural state, as recipients of grace. Although somewhat romantic in his view of childhood, this priest calls our attention to both the rights of children and the importance of their inclusion in the sacraments. Both issues will be discussed in detail beginning with the latter.

Children and the Sacraments

The inclusion of children as full participants in the community of faith is closely allied with an understanding of the sacraments. This theme, developed by Browning and Reed (1985), attempts to broaden a narrow concept of catechesis with a vision of God's action in the world beyond the church. They claim that churches tend to codify the truth within religious education programs thereby reducing the mystery of the Kingdom of God. While drawing heavily from Westerhoff's concepts of faith enculturation and catechesis, Browning and Reed opt for a model of sacraments which interrelates religious education and liturgy, as well as word and sacrament, in a holistic manner.

The aim of this model is to appropriate a *vision* while maintaining the integrity of the self and integrating faith with all of life's experiences *beyond* the faith community. Socialization into a community is not enough. Rather, persons must be socialized into a vision of the Kingdom of God as present beyond the faith community in the very structures of life. This view of religious socialization implies an exploration of a wide range of options to answer life's basic questions and provides a rebuttal to those critics of the socialization model who claim that the church only deals with the questions for which they have answers (Campolo, 1983).

What does the participation model offer to our understanding of the religious socialization of the preschool child? Infant baptism is regarded as the initiation rite and the open communion table allows for ongoing participation. Browning and Reed concur with Boojamra (Greek Ortho-dox) and Bedouelle (Roman Catholic) in advocating a threefold initi-ation rite by water, laying on of hands or "chrismation," and participa-tion in communion for children *within* the faith community. For those *beyond* the faith community they recommend postponing baptism until a later confirmation. Infant baptism (or dedication in some traditions) involves a commitment of the entire congregation and confirms the child's identity as a member of the household of faith. It provides a whole complex set of relationships for the child, parents, sponsors, and congregation to support ongoing nurture in times of stress. The socializ-ing role of parents, godparents or sponsors, and congregation members may take on religious significance and require congregational orienta-tion and support in the forms of counseling and education. The church might recognize anniversaries of the child's baptism instead of birthdays to highlight the importance of the event in the religious life of the child.

The Eucharist or Lord's supper in Browning and Reed's treatment is a life-giving joyous experience in the community to be shared with young children. The child learns through the ritual actions of sharing, feeding, touching, and lifting up what is important in the community. Relating the meaning of the sacrament to Fowler's stage 1, Intuitive-Projective Faith (see chapter five), Browning and Reed see communion as a love feast to be shared with God and one another. Communion then is central to Christian nurture and socialization in its participatory and intergenerational dimensions. It can be further enhanced by the family's ongoing celebration of the liturgical year and the lectionary or Bible reading integrated into home and family life.

Preschool children might more fully participate in communion by assisting the family in the baking of communion bread, taking shut-in communion with pastors and elders, or collecting empty communion cups from the sanctuary in churches where the common cup is not used. In this way preschool children can become participants in the service as well as the sacramental aspects of community life. After all, preschool children thrive on being given some responsibilities and are proud to be called "helpers."

A final word is needed about the participatory function of sacraments and preschool children. When younger siblings are baptized, pre-schoolers can participate as part of the family. Likewise, all preschool children might be included in worship when a baptism takes place even though they may not always attend a complete worship service. Some advocate communion as well. But, like baptism, adequate preparation of child, parents, and the congregation enriches the child's participation in the worship life of the community.

Congregational Support for Parenting

While religious socialization takes place in the family and through the sacraments, it can be done in a more intentional manner when specific training is provided for parents of preschool children. Barber, Hiltz, and Skoch (1979) describe a research-based program called *Realistic Parenting*, utilizing a two-tiered training program. The first level focuses on communication in marriage, while the second involves communication between the parents and young child. Based upon the family systems theory that a strong parent dyad is the key to family functioning, the developers evaluated what happened to young children as a result of training. The results showed that while the Realistic Parenting Skills Program was generally successful, it had a more measurable effect on parents of two- and three-year-olds than on those of older preschoolers.

Another program designed for parents and sponsors draws upon the work of Foster (1982), another advocate of religious socialization in the Christian community. Browning and Reed (1985) include the following components in their suggested program:

1) Priesthood of Parents
2) The Child, the Unique Gift of God to the World
3) Family Ministries Through Rituals Which Affirm the Child's Sacred Destiny and Unique Gifts
4) Education Concerning the Unity of the Initiation of the Child Through Infant Baptism, Confirmation, and Communion
5) Orientation to the Unified Service of Initiation coupled with training for parents and sponsors.

Browning and Reed provide further suggestions for educating the congregation in the meaning of the sacraments. However, they make clear that the sacraments involve more than simply a nurturing function and plead for religious education and liturgy to be kept in creative tension.

Religious socialization of the preschool child can be enhanced through courses of study in the church school which stress learning by doing in the family of faith, either in age-specific or intergenerational contexts. The particular emphasis of the *Living the Word* resource material (Fowlkes, 1983) lends itself to equipping children to be full participants in the life of the congregation. The corresponding *Doing the Word* model of awareness-analysis-action-reflection equips children to share in the full ministry of the church in the world and meets the general criteria for religious socialization, described by Nelson and Marthaler.

Child Care and the Preschool

The family, worship life, and religious education programs are seen as the most obvious arenas for religious socialization of the preschool child. Fellowship functions and service activities are not to be overlooked as opportunities for participation by young children. Yet probably the impact of the church-related weekday preschool, child care center and "mother's morning out" program as a channel for religious socialization has not adequately been measured. *When Churches Mind the Children* (Lindner, Rogers, & Mattis, 1983) is a study funded by the Carnegie Foundation documenting the vast scope of daily child care and child rearing in the nation's churches. From this study has come a National Council of Churches policy statement which supports this avenue of socialization of preschool children. While many of these programs do not have particular religious content in their curricula, they make a statement by their existence in church buildings. Young children and their families are important to the faith community and the act of providing this service speaks loudly.

The buildings, how the facilities are cared for, and how well they are suited to the developmental needs of preschoolers make a religious statement to young children. The quality of the programs, the personalities of the caregivers, the relationships with church staff and members in the hallways, all communicate messages about belonging and acceptance. Those churches which are meeting the needs of the "latch key" child before and after public school kindergarten are saying, "Here is a safe place—a place where you can be loved and protected while your parents work." Thus buildings and programs to meet the needs of preschool children provide a context for socialization which may have strong religious dimensions.

If the program is a church-related preschool it may function as a parochial school with a strong religious education function. However, Lindner, Rogers, and Mattis (1983) found that most church-housed child care programs do not have heavy religious content in their curriculum. But most do celebrate religious holidays, say grace at meals, and engage in a number of activities which constitute various degrees of religious socialization.

Can we really tell the difference between secular and religious socialization? This is a difficult question because so many of the categories and tools for analysis from sociology, psychology, and anthropology are utilized in understanding religious socialization. Thus far, we have discussed religious socialization primarily in the context of the ecclesial body or the community of faith, although Westerhoff, Browning and Reed talk about the church in the world and the Kingdom of God in a much broader perspective than simply the congregation or parish.

Religious Socialization in Non-Church Communities

In a provocative article on "Transmission of the Faith in the U.S.A." Elizondo (1984) admits that while the traditional agents of family, parochial schools, religious education programs, radio, television, and revivals are still operative, much religious socialization is taking place in the following five settings which he calls nonchurch institutions or movements.

1) Social justice movements (civil rights and peace) where total commitment and unity attract a diverse group of enthusiastic followers.
2) Personal experiential groups like the Jesus movement, where persons join in fellowships of loving, caring, and forgiving while seeking a transcendent God.
3) Voluntaristic efforts based on discipleship where persons band together to serve the poor and create new forms of family.
4) Self-help groups related to alcohol and drug addiction and finding God's strength, such as Alcoholics Anonymous.
5) Fundamentalist and Bible-centered groups which have clear-cut answers, high moral demands, and emotional fervor.

Children of parents deeply committed to and involved in these movements transmit to their offspring the values and visions of the particular community. A particularly good example of this kind of socialization was offered by Ellis Nelson at the Caldwell Lectures at Louisville Presbyterian Seminary. He was riding on the bus that runs from the Presbyterian Seminary at St. Anselmo across the San Francisco Bay Bridge to Berkeley with a young mother and her preschool child who could barely talk. Halfway across the bridge the child spotted a submarine and began to shout adamantly "No Nukes! No Nukes!" That child had been well-socialized by a particular community! Elizondo regards each one of the movements mentioned above as a community of discipleship engaged in transmitting its faith to the next generation.

The Community as Context for Transmission of Faith

Just what is it about the community that makes the process of socialization work? To better understand the process Mette (1984) utilizes sociological analysis along with theological insight to articulate religious socialization in our present society. Mette claims that the criteria for community education are as follows:

1) Close-knit durable social networks where people can relate in holistic fashion rather than in roles.
2) Interaction with people who live as Christians in everyday life and can articulate what they are doing.
3) Exposure to a variety of intellectual and social movements in order to permit different styles of faith.

The family, Mette asserts, is too privatized, and wider networks have too low a durability and density of communication. Therefore the parish or congregation offers the optimum social form between family and the larger institutional church, providing a point of intersection between the private and public spheres. Such a value-forming and norm-building community can lead to transformation and innovation in church and society by reshaping lifestyles. All this can only happen when the process is open to the Holy Spirit. Mette points out that base communities or small grassroots groups have more potential than much of the present church.

In order to be effective communities for learning faith, the whole person must be involved without compulsion or manipulation. This issue is a frequent criticism of the socialization model which is often regarded in terms of indoctrination and conformity. In addition, learning must be done in solidarity, with commitment and innovation, and in an intergenerational context. Thus the formation of community is an integral part of the learning process.

The generative issue is a major one to raise under the umbrella of socialization. The question of Westerhoff's—"Will our children have faith?"—is now being reversed: "Will the faith have children?" In other words, what is the future of the church? This question has been addressed in two ways. First, Vander (1984) looks at socialization models from a worldview similar to that of Barker (in terms of freedom) and Mette (the ability to change). A second more radical stance asks, "Will there be children through whom transmission can take place?" The issue is what is happening to childhood in our contemporary society and how that affects traditional views of socialization. Obviously the process of transmission works best in a stable social situation in which generational boundaries are clearly defined.

Parent-Child Interaction

How do children become socialized so that they can form relationships, get along well with others, belong to a group, adapt their behavior according to social norms and rules, and so forth? There are a variety of explanations of the process.

A large body of literature compiled by Maccoby and Martin (1983) places family socialization of the young child within the context of the parent-child dyad. Although Maccoby and Martin give credit to the role of the psychoanalytic and cognitive-developmental theories in the socialization process, their matrix of parent-child interaction includes the following four major theories under the rubric of social learning theory: 1) reinforcement, 2) observational learning, 3) attribution, and 4) interaction. Reinforcement in the social learning framework focuses on the use of contingencies in the production of a learned response. In dealing with the preschool child, this theory is concerned with the consequences of behavior controlling whether or not a certain act will occur. The application of this method of behavioral control seems most feasible for molecular behavior and suited to the child in the preconventional level of moral development.

Observational learning based on Bandura's work involves children imitating or copying the behavior which they have observed in others. Observational learning is potent for acquiring novel behaviors, combining elements from different models, and vicarious learning (observing the consequences of various acts without ever engaging in the acts themselves). For preschool children this theoretical approach is used to explain the acquisition of certain linguistic expressions, gestures, mannerisms, sex role behaviors, and frequently the accompanying attitudes of salient persons in the environment. Observations of young children in sociodramatic play provide a rich source of information about what they have learned from persons in the environment.

While the first two theories focus more on behavior, the third, attribution theory, explains how children internalize adult values. Three processes—compliance, identification, and internalization—describe the child's acquisition of prosocial behavior by adult influence. The amount of pressure required to secure compliance is still an unresolved issue in attribution theory. The study of influence in attitude change is a ripe area for further research.

Of particular interest for socialization is interaction theory which finds it roots in Mead's concepts of the "looking glass self" and the "generalized other." In Mead's theory one develops a core of understandings about relationships which can be applied to new persons or whole groups and forms the basis of script or role theory. The nature of interactions is dialogical (Stern, 1980, Gottman, 1979), with emphasis on reciprocity providing a framework for understanding basic social exchanges of young children. The beginnings of altruistic behavior in young children is of particular interest to students of religious socialization. Youniss (1980) employs the interactionist model to study this behavior in relationships rather than as discrete behaviors. Thus new research methodology has emerged to study the reciprocal interactions of partners through sequential analysis (Gottman & Bakeman, 1978; Brazelton, Koslowski, & Main, 1974). Originally used with mothers and infants, the methodology has been applied to such behaviors as hitting among nursery school children (Bakeman & Brownlee, 1980) and play episodes in preschool groups.

Maccoby and Martin's review of socialization literature highlights a fourfold scheme of parenting styles: 1) Authoritarian-Autocratic is associated with low social competence and has an external moral orientation in children. 2) Indulgent-Permissive is linked to impulsive, aggressive children who lack independence. 3) Authoritative-Reciprocal parenting produces independent, self-confident, socially responsive children. 4) Indifferent-Uninvolved parenting has mixed results revealing the need to research an optimum level of parent involvement. Although children with noninvolved parents seem to suffer more than those with involved parents, there is a problem with overinvolved parents who become intrusive and controlling. Studies of internalized discipline and other-oriented induction techniques which lead to voluntary compliance by children in parent's absence show that effective parents may use multiple methods of childrearing depending on the situation and the developmental level of the child. While research shows that withdrawal of love yields weak correlation with moral development, Maccoby and Martin include it as a powerful technique which generates anxiety in young children and is similar to physical punishment in achieving desirable behavior for the short term only.

Family Systems Theory

While extensive research has been done on the parent-child dyad, family systems theory requires that second order effects be studied, such as the influence of the father on mother-child interaction, the effects of birth of a baby on mother-father or mother-preschool sibling interaction, the effects of grandparents on childrearing practices or the effects of marital discord on parent-child, child-child relationships. Bidirectional processes are being studied to reveal the effects of children on parents, particularly in terms of temperament, handicapping condition, or the child's readiness to be socialized (compliance). The complexity of relationships among family and social network members who play a large role in socializing the young child requires new tools for analysis.

The usual contexts of socialization for the preschool child are parent-child relationships, the family system, the family's social network, the neighborhood or playgroup, child care or preschool settings, and if the family is a member of a religious body, the congregation or parish. While all of these have been looked at separately, and some more widely studied than others, it seems helpful to apply Bronfenbrenner's (1979) ecological systems theory to see how these various settings relate to one another regarding the religious socialization of the preschool child.

Bronfenbrenner offers a comprehensive framework for studying the developing child with a complex social system. The first level is the immediate setting in which the child engages in personal face-to-face relationships with persons, who engage in activities, play roles, and operate according to certain rules, all in a physical and emotional setting. For the preschool child these may be the home, preschool, day care, playground, church school classroom, other settings at church (worship, family night supper), or in another home such as the grandparents' or a close family friend's. The next level, involves the linkages among the microsystems, such as the church school and home, home and preschool/day care, preschool and church school. The third level considers how economic, political, and social policy affect the child even though he or she has no direct encounter with the system. Examples of this level include whether the father travels a lot, the sick-leave policy of the mother's job, the policy of the church about preschool rooms (can the children cook, have animals, use church school material during the week? Are the children put in the basement?), the school board's policy on age of school entrance, the church's curriculum material selection process, and whether or not children are included in worship. The fourth and final system incorporates the level of subculture along with the belief system or ideology which holds it all together. For the pre-school child this may be membership into a white Anglo-Saxon Protestant middle-class community or a black, low SES Holiness group, or a particular ethnic working-class Catholic parish, or an Orthodox Jewish family and synagogue.

For optimum socialization to take place there must be as much continuity between settings as possible. For example, it helps for parents to be closely allied to the preschool or day care setting through visits, newsletters, and telephone calls, but of even greater importance is continuity in childrearing and discipline, expectations for celebrations, and common rituals observed at home and school. If the childcare setting is located in the family's church, a sense of continuity between the Sabbath and weekday worlds of the child confirms and reinforces the child's ecclesial affiliation. Choosing a childcare setting in accord with the family's religious values can aid the socialization process in the formative years. However, public policy on funding and parent's employment benefit packages are factors affecting such decisions.

This does not mean that child care facilities must always be homogeneous; the preschool may reflect values of racial/ethnic and socio-economic diversity by providing sliding scale fees, scholarships, even a particular quota system. Clear policies on the mission of the preschool—such as serving the community or a particular population (handicapped, refugee, migrant) or nurturing one's own children—need to be stated and clarified by the governing board. The relationship between the weekday use of facilities and the ongoing Sabbath or church-related preschool programs speaks loudly about the nature of the community and the quality of its models on a day-to-day basis.

For the preschool child to feel an identity with the entire church family, he or she needs to participate in worship, fellowship, and service activities with the rest of the parish. The continuity of persons, rituals, and things bridges the shift in settings from preschool religious education classroom to fellowship hall to sanctuary. The pastor's visit to the children in preparation for baptism, seeing the friendly face of the church school teacher in the worship service, practicing the responses, hymns, and rituals in church school, hanging the children's pictures in the church halls, having children set tables or make table decorations for a fellowship meal, all help to link the various settings children are likely to inhabit within the parish setting.

Participation with persons of all ages in the community service and mission projects is a far more effective learning/socialization experience than holding an age-graded class. Bronfenbrenner bemoans the fact that children can be educated in schools without ever having learned to care for another person, particularly the very young or the very old, and urges the development of a "curriculum for caring." This might well be implemented in a religious socialization model by preschool children making scrapbooks for the nursery and visiting in nursing homes either with their families or as a church school group. For young children the formation and education aspects of catechesis seem to go hand in hand as they are enculturated into the faith community. The *Living the Word* (Fowlkes, 1983) approach to curriculum seems particularly compatible with religious socialization.

Bronfenbrenner (1979) provides a framework for analyzing the complex process by which socialization of the young child takes place. He has applied this framework to day care and children's institutions. Suransky (1982) has done a comprehensive descriptive analysis of five child care settings which vividly reveals the categories which Bronfenbrenner considers: the nature, variety, and complexity of activities, as well as changes in children's behavior and their relationships with adults and peers. All of these provide images of socialization influenced by the settings (space, time, arrangement) in which they take place.

The Institutionalizing of Children

Suransky's interpretive ethnographic study of childhood in preschool settings reveals differences in institutions, but overall the children she studied were not allowed freedom to play or to be different or to have the power to impact their environment. Those incompletely socialized (those who break rules) were regarded as deviants, trouble makers, and

pathological. Suransky concludes that the nature of children is antitheti-
cal to life in these child care institutions. The result is an early childhood education which she labels "domestication." Champions of children's rights frequently frame the dilemma as, "Do we fit the child to
the school, or do we mold the school to fit the child?"

Suransky's data demonstrate that in many early childhood institutions the lives of children are made to fit the needs of the school
program. This situation becomes serious as the child care institutions
appropriate more of the role of the parents. She refers to Berger and
Luckmann's discussion of the formation of the "reflected self" through
identification with intimate significant others and internalization of
roles and attitudes in the development of identity. The child care environment falls short as a primary socializing agent when the child has no
consistent "significant others" in a world of rapid turnover of caregivers
and impersonal interactions. Suransky's picture of socialization in institutional preschools portrays children as aliens, homeless, and deprived
of their capacity as meaning makers.

Attempts to deinstitutionalize childhood, suggests Suransky, include
public support for parenting, fathers taking on greater household and
childrearing responsibilities, and cooperative child-friendly centers run
by parents. Suransky's model of child care includes intimate face to face
encounters, the elderly and young together, consensual organization,
and in essence a community very much like those models of the faith
community described as the optimum setting for religious socialization.
A family-like community which respects childhood as a natural state is
where all generations can live and grow together.

The religious community has done much to revalue children through
the work of Bedouelle (1985) and Foster (1982). In *Teaching in the
Christian Community,* Foster restores the concepts of children of God
and child-likeness as critical to the notion of a community of faith with
a common history and shared vision of the future. Children are necessary bearers of the culture, linking past and future, as well as being
agents of God's ongoing activity in the world. Understanding childhood
from a biblical and theological perspective is the core of religious socialization, particularly in a cultural milieu where childhood is under attack.

The Decline of Childhood

The conception of childhood is receiving attention as commentators
bemoan its demise. A spate of publications describe the state of childhood on the contemporary scene: Postman (1982), *The Disappearance
of Childhood*; Suransky (1982) *The Erosion of Childhood*; Winn (1983),

Children Without Childhood; Elkind (1981), *The Hurried Child.* Each author has a slightly different thesis about the condition of childhood which in turn influences one's understanding of the socialization process in today's world.

Postman (1982) considers childhood as a social construct, induced by the printing press, which once required children to be socialized into the world of literacy. Childhood had to do with schooling (originally *schoolboys*). The major task required for becoming adult was learning to read so that one could gradually be initiated into the secrets of adult life. In today's world of electronic media, print literacy is no longer necessary for cultural and social survival. Children, through the avenue of the television screen, are exposed to the most intimate and sophisticated issues of adult life, within a thirty or fifty minute episode. All ages are party to the same information. As a result, we see images of adultified children and childified adults documented in TV commercials. Postman claims that the media culture in which we are enmeshed has no past, no future, only NOW. Therefore there is no cultural heritage to be passed on and there are no initiation rites. There is no need of intergenerational learning, for the very notion of generations has disappeared. The major socializing agent is the television rather than the family, school, church, or peer group. Postman documents the number of hours a day children spend in front of the TV set, becoming socialized into a cult of "Couch Potatoes."

Suransky (1982) raises the critical question: "Is childhood a social invention or is it a natural state of being?" Postman follows the interpretation of Aries (1965) that childhood is indeed a social idea emerging after the Middle Ages, while other commentators rely on the work of psychohistorian De Mause (1974) and his psychoanalytic interpretation of childhood. De Mause paints a picture of the cruelty and brutality to children throughout the ages. Suransky points to the fact that the movement away from images of children as miniature adults was class- and sex-based, with the children of the lower classes regarded as property. Women and servants were treated as children, while the notions of childhood innocence and children at play was an upper-class phenomenon. Schooling for young children of all classes came with the Reformers, and Robert Owen's infant schools in New Harmony, Indiana, in 1826.

Froebel, the father of the kindergarten movement, is credited with instituting childhood as a special state of being. The scientific study of childhood in America began by G. Stanley Hall has shaped the era of the child for the last hundred years. A movement which began as a celebration of a natural state of being has become a means of segregation and containment, says Suransky (1982). Her view is that childhood is indeed a special way of being which needs respect and belongs to the fabric of a healthy society. However, in our society childhood has become so institutionalized that we are warehousing the very young and the very old out of the mainstream of society, allowing them little control over their own lives.

Obviously all of the commentators on contemporary childhood claim that what is happening to our children is negative. Elkind's (1981) "hurried child" is pushed to grow up fast and is schooled in factory-modeled institutions. Postman's (1982) children are adultified children socialized by the media with no sense of past or future. Winn's (1983) children are participants in a sex and drug culture, and Suransky's (1982) are contained in bureaucratic institutions which are downward expansions of the corporate paradigm. In all of these views, children are being socialized into the mold of the existing society where the status quo can be maintained. How much can churches, which operate from a transcendent and transforming perspective, buy into traditional means of socialization? Many of the models of religious socialization discussed have incorporated ways of promoting freedom, change, and criticism in their design. In terms of the preschool child, it seems crucial to focus on Suransky's seminal question, "Is childhood a natural state or a social construction?"

Suransky's approach to methodology is the key to understanding. The era of the scientific study of childhood has observed, counted, compared, and made hypotheses about children through the quantitative research lens. We have studied the parent-infant dyad, manipulating and controlling all possible variables. Frequently studies are conducted in laboratory and hospital settings in order to define the characteristics of each discrete behavior and age group. Thus we have arrived at a body of theory regarding children which is indeed a social construction of reality culled from fragmented and atomized components. We have abstracted the child from family, friends, social class, and meaning systems and constructed theories of child management. Suransky rejects the positivist approach on the grounds that it yields a model of socialization designed to produce conformity to social norms and rules, adjusting the child to fit society's mold. Her criticism is not limited simply to the behaviorist and observational learning models described by Maccoby and Martin, but her critique extends to Kohlberg's cognitive-developmental stage theory of moral development. Suransky objects to the methodology of using hypothetical moral dilemmas abstracted from real experiences. Further, she claims that adult-defined stages of moral reasoning are removed from the real crises and dilemmas of children's everyday lives. She is equally critical of Hoffman's research on measuring empathy in children. She bemoans the fact that taxonomies, typologies, measurements, and evaluations have helped us dissect childhood as a field of scientific study and in the process have lost its meaning. For an antidote she touts the work of Robert Coles in *Children in Crisis* and moves toward her own anthropological methodology of studying the child as meaning maker. She acknowledges her indebtedness to the Dutch phenomenologist F.J. Boytendijk who claims that "the child is not something with characteristics, but an initiative of relationships to a world where he chooses and by which he is chosen." Although Suransky opts for qualitative rather than quantitative research methodology for studying children, it seems that the interactive theory described previously is compatible with her intent and certainly does not treat the child in isolation. However, mere understanding is not enough for Suransky, whose methodology includes transformation through a dialectic of critical reflection, affirming the claims of religious educators that praxis and socialization models need to be complementary.

Suransky is in sympathy with Barker's (1981) notion that freedom is essential for an adequate model of education. Contrary to traditional socialization, she advocates that children in child care have *freedom to disobey* if they are to experience intentionality in the world. It is in the dialectic of freedom to disobey, as well as to obey, that children experience the world of the "other" and engage in learning about relationships essential to communal life. Thus a conflict or crisis model of human development is contrasted to one of smooth continuity and gradual change. Traditional models of socialization have flowed more readily with the continuity stream.

Campolo (1983) in *A Reasonable Faith* accompanies Suransky in attacking psychoanalytic and behaviorist views of socialization, while appreciating G. Herbert Mead for his suggestion that our view of the future determines social behavior. From a Christian perspective, Campolo utilizes the theories of Mead and Peter Berger to illustrate how the past is reconstructed and given new meaning. Methodologically, Campolo uses secular scientific analyses to articulate questions which he then answers theologically. For Campolo socialization is the process by which we become human as forgiving people. Becoming human takes on theological dimensions as persons become conformed to the image of God. Although Campolo's focus is on youth, his notion of achieving humanity from being with loving, sensitive, aware, and emphatic people is consistent with the notion of religious socialization of the young child. Likewise he finds the concepts of freedom, transformation, and transcendence essential to an adequate formulation of religious socialization. In essence, Campolo sees humanity as the gift of society with children becoming like those who socialize them. For Christians, Jesus is fully human and becomes the "significant other" in our struggle for self-realization. Campolo's "Christian humanism" calls for a community in which socialization involves becoming loving, forgiving persons.

Friendship in Childhood

Socialization for participation in community life requires that the preschool child become competent in social behaviors and interactive skills which will allow him or her to participate fully and assure a sense of belonging. Descriptions of the child's overall development frequently include physical, cognitive, and affective capabilities (see chapters one and two), and may cover moral development from the stance of social cognitive theory (see chapter four). This treatment of religious socialization will address specific dimensions of the development of friendships, beginning with peer relationships. In religious socialization the issue is how can preschool children be encouraged to "love one another."

An extensive body of literature on the development of children's friendships has emerged in the last fifteen years (Asher & Gottman, 1981; Gottman & Parkhurst, 1980; Lewis, Young, Brooks-Gunn, & Michaelson, 1975; Corsaro, 1981; Damon, 1977, 1983; Youniss, 1980; Selman, 1981; Hartup, 1983; Berndt, 1981). Two trends have brought attention to a broader range of social relationships: 1) family and social network theory and 2) extensive research on the origins of peer relationships. Earlier, the parent-child relationship was regarded as the prototype of all social experiences for the young child, thus the main focus of research on socialization (noted previously). With the advent of family systems and social network theory new research questions are raised. Do children learn about relationships simply from adult-child interactions or do other members of the family and social network make unique contributions to social development? At what age do children begin to interact with each other? What is a peer?

The studies in origins of peer social interaction (Bronson, 1975; Lee, 1975; Mueller & Lucas, 1975; Eckerman, Whatley, & Kurtz, 1975; Ross & Goldman, 1975) have shown toddlers to be quite skillful in social encounters. The notion that children were not social beings until three years of age and therefore would not benefit from earlier group experience can be traced to Parten's (1932) study of social play which showed cooperative play to increase with age (see chapter two). Bakeman and Brownlee (1980) challenged this assumption in a study of free play among three-year-olds. By using sequential analysis, they found that parallel play would probably be followed by associative or cooperative play during the course of a play episode. Parallel play served as a warm-up period for higher levels of play with the transition taking a brief time rather than months in a developmental sequence. Rubin (1980) has also challenged Parten's serial play hierarchy on the grounds that solitary play is not necessarily a less mature form of play. Now research has shown that children's social interactive capabilities are present at a much younger age than previously conceived.

Closely related to the origins of social interaction are the questions, "what is a peer?" and "what is the role of peers in stimulating social development?" Peers, according to Lewis and Rosenblum (1975), are those who share parallel levels of maturation and function in a particular activity or interactive episode. Therefore they may not always be strict age-mates. For example, siblings are regarded as a subset of peers who are slightly older or younger. As Dunn's research shows, preschool siblings in many families contribute greatly to the socialization of the infant (Dunn, 1985; Dunn & Kendrick, 1982). If we accept Lewis and Rosenblum's assumption, then adults may sometimes operate as peers, for example, when playing a game or in the religious milieu as *children of God*. Thus peers are similar on some dimension and share equally in a particular relationship or event.

However, peers are more frequently conceived of as near age-mates who contribute to the developing social skills of the young child. The term most often used to describe peer relations in the preschool years is "friendship" meaning "affiliation"—engaging in a joint activity, an alliance of bonding for a particular purpose. Selman (1981) and Ruben (1980) have studied children's conceptions of friendships and arranged them into a developmental hierarchy. Stage 0 is that of a *momentary playmate,* a person who is in near proximity and with whom one happens to be playing at the moment. Older preschoolers may be in Stage 1 friendships; one-way assistance, i.e., she does what I want, and has some knowledge of what I like and dislike.

While the development trend in children's friendship is confirmed by Berndt's study of children from kindergarten through grade six (Berndt, 1981), Damon (1983) points out that Berndt's scheme is not a hierarchical stage model like Selman's. Rather the earlier notions of play and association exist side by side with later notions of intimacy and loyalty. Therefore a qualitatively different stage model does not fit his data.

Like moral development, studies of friendship have been based on children's reports of how they *think* about friendships (the social-cognitive paradigm) rather than how they act in particular situations. As an alternative Gottman and Parkhurst (1980) studied children at home, comparing differences in play between friends and strangers. Friends engaged in more pretend play and communicated more with younger children, avoiding disagreements. Gottman and Parkhurst suggest that preschool children create a joint "climate of agreement" which promotes bonding. The younger children increased in this solidarity through social comparisons, while older subjects tolerated more disagreements and differences.

Extensive observations in preschools have revealed data about children's social knowledge and social skills as related to the formation and meaning of friendships, the amount of same-sex and cross-sexed play, the modes of entering into episodes and the exclusion of others ("You're not my friend," "You can't play"), the emergence of altruism, helping and caring behaviors, and the training of unpopular or handicapped children in the social skills necessary to maintain friendships. Personal characteristics related to popularity are attractiveness, compliance, cooperation, possession of social knowledge, and nonagressiveness. Popularity and status are often equated with friendship due to the sociometric techniques used. The measure of popularity is, "Who do you like best?" or "Who is your (best) friend?" (Hartup, 1983). Familiarity is another criteria for extended social interaction which is often related to friendship. However, in preschool groups the stability of playmates and best friends is much lower than with older children. Exclusiveness of friendships is likewise more prevalent with older children. Often when a preschool child is asked to name, point out, or identify the picture of "friends" in the group, the child will say, "everybody." Whether or not this is what the child has been taught (socialized) to say, the phenomenon indicates that the preschool stage and setting provide an opportunity for developing an attitude of inclusiveness for friends in God's family and social network.

The power of socialization in building group cohesiveness can be seen in Levy-Shiff and Hoffman's (1985) study comparing urban and Kibbutz preschool children in Israel. In free play settings the Kibbutz children exhibited more highly developed group functioning skills such as more coordinated play and less competition than did urban preschoolers who spent more time exchanging toys and struggling over them. However, the affective behavior of Kibbutz children was less warm and intimate and was more verbally aggressive than their urban counterparts. This pattern of group cohesion coupled with affective distancing has also been found with older children and adults in the Kibbutz. Thus inclusiveness may not always incorporate intimacy. At the preschool level, peer relationships may well be described in terms of affiliation, proximity, and joint activity.

However, Youniss (1980) emphasizes the voluntary aspects of friendship in which either party is free to either pull away or accept obligations to sustain the friendship. Among preschool peers there are more opportunities for autonomy and freedom than with adults who have power over children. This difference is social interaction patterns between adult and child play partners was found by Fowlkes (1979) in a group of twelve-, eighteen-, and twenty-four-month-olds. The equal status of the peer dyad allowed same-age children to negotiate, refuse to play, reciprocate, switch leadership, and engage in role reversal (from runner to chaser, catcher to thrower, etc.) more frequently than with an adult play partner. Among preschool peers the possibility of forming friendships in a more egalitarian, cooperative social organization is more likely than in groups with adults. Therefore all activities in the community of faith need not be intergenerational. Opportunities to develop friendships among same age-mates is important in the socialization process.

The notion of sibling as slightly older or younger peers provides a useful tool for broad-age grouping in smaller congregations where close-age grading is not feasible. Since families are having fewer children, a preschool child who has no siblings may engage in sibling-like interactions with others in the church family and become bonded to them in the household of God. Insights from social learning theory have shown the efficacy of modeling by slightly older children who have competence, status, and some power, yet still are enough like the child who imitates them that the younger child can identify with the model. As some congregations promote adopted grandparent figures for preschoolers, they might arrange for Big Brothers and Big Sisters as well.

While most of the research on friendships has been done on close-age groups due to the similarity dimension (those alike attract), there are untapped possibilities in the parish community for both cross-age relationships and diversity in friendship options if structured carefully. Linking the preschool child with a single adult who lives alone as they share a fellowship meal meets the criteria of a Stage 0—momentary playmate (meal-mate) friendship. If the congregation has ethnic and socio-economic diversity, careful structuring of joint activities can enhance formation of social ties. Pairing a preschool child who sees a friend as helper with a handicapped member who requires special assistance at least provides the possibility for a friendship to develop. Kindness, empathy, caring, and giving can be fostered consciously rather than taught directly in the congregation. This is what intentional socialization means. A community where persons come to "love one another as I have loved you" is built on an understanding of how friendships develop and fits nicely into Barber's (1981, p. 157) Venn diagram of her model of "*The Religious Education of the Preschool Child.*"

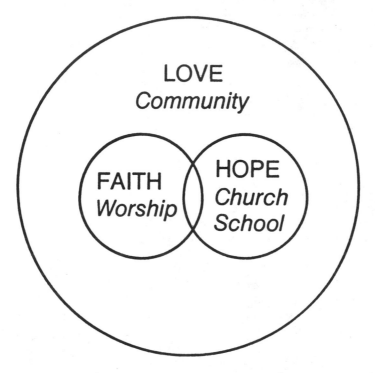

REFERENCES

Aries, P. (1965). *Centuries of childhood.* New York: Vintage Books.

Asher, S., & Gottman, J. (1981). *The development of children's friendships.* New York: Cambridge University Press.

Bakeman, R. & Brownlee, J. (1980). The strategic use of parallel play: A sequential analysis. *Child Development, 51,* 873-78.

Barber, L. (1981). *The religious education of the preschool child.* Birmingham, AL: Religious Education Press.

Barber, L., Hiltz, J., & Skoch (1979). Ministry to parents of little children. *Religious Education, 74,* 263-270.

Barker, K. (1981). *Religion, catechesis, and freedom.* Birmingham, AL: Religious Education Press.

Bedouelle, G. (1985). Reflection on the place of the child in the church: Suffer the little children (E. Tillman, Trans.), *Communio, 12,* 349-367.

Berndt, T. J. (1981). Relations between social cognition, non social cognition and social behavior: The case of friendship. In J. H. Flavell & R. D. Ross

(Eds.), *Social Cognitive Development.* New York: Cambridge University Press.

Boojamra, J. L. (1985). Theological and pedagogical perspectives on the family as educator, *Greek Orthodox Theological Review, 29,* 1-34.

Brazelton, B., Koslowski, & Main, M. (1974). The origins of reciprocity. In M. Lewis & L. A. Rosenblum (Eds.), *The effect of the infant on its caregiver.* New York: Wiley.

Bronfenbrenner, V. (1979). *The ecology of child development .* Cambridge, MA: Harvard University Press.

Bronson, W. (1975). Peer-peer interactions in the second year of life. In M. Lewis & L. N. Rosenblum (Eds.), *Friendships and peer relations.* New York: Wiley.

Browning, R., & Reed, R. (1985). *The sacraments in religious education and liturgy.* Birmingham, AL: Religious Education Press.

Campolo, A. (1983). *A reasonable faith.* Waco, TX: Word.

Corsaro, W. A. (1981). Friendship in the nursery school: Social organization in a peer environment. In S. R. Asher & J. M. Gottman (Eds.), *The development of children's friendships.* Cambridge: Cambridge University Press.

Damon, W. (1977). *The social world of the child.* San Francisco: Jossey-Bass.

Damon, W. (1983). *Social and personality development.* New York: W. W. Norton.

Darcy-Berube, F. (1978). The challenge ahead of us. In P. O'Hare (Ed.), *Foundations of Religious Education.* New York: Paulist Press.

de Mause, L. (1974). *The history of childhood.* New York: The Psychohistory Press.

Dunn, J. (1985). *Sisters and brothers.* Cambridge, MA: Harvard University Press.

Dunn, J., & Kendrick, C. (1982). *Siblings: Love, envy, and understanding.* Cambridge, MA: Harvard University Press.

Eckerman, C. O., Whatley, J., & Kutz, S. (1975). Growth of social play with peers during the second year of life. *Developmental Psychology, 11,* 42-49.

Elizondo, V. (1984). Transmission of the faith in the USA. In N. Greinacher and V. Elizondo (Eds.), *The transmission of faith.* Edinburgh: T&T Clark Concilum 174.

Elkind, D. (1981). *The hurried child.* Reading, MA: Addison-Wesley.

Foster, C. (1982). *Teaching in the community of faith.* Nashville: Abingdon Press.

Fowlkes, M. A. (1979). *Social roots of play in early maternal, sibling and peer games.* Ph.D. Thesis. Georgia State University.

Fowlkes, M. A. (1983). God's family of friends. CE: SA, Living the Word, Level Three, fall, 1983.

Gottman, J. M. (1979). Detecting cyclicity in social interaction. *Psychological Bulletin, 86,* 338-348.

Gottman, J. M., & Bakeman, R. (1978). The sequential analysis of observational data. In M. Lamb, S. Suomi, G. Stephenson (Eds.), *Methodological Problems in the study of social interaction.* Madison, WS: University of Wisconsin Press.

Gottman, J. M., & Parkhurst, J. T. (1980). A developmental theory of friendship and acquaintanceship process. In W. A. Collins (Ed.), *Minnesota symposia on child psychology* (Vol. 13). Hillsdale, NJ: Lawrence Erlbaum.

Hartup, W. W. (1983). Peer relations. In E. M. Hetherington (Ed.), Socialization, Personality and Social Development, Vol. IV. In Paul Mussen (Ed.), *Handbook of Child Psychology.* New York: John Wiley.

Hunsberger, B., & Brown, L. B. (1984). Religious socialization, apostasy and the impact of family background. *Journal for the Scientific Study of Religion, 23,* 239-251.

Lee, C. L. (1975). Toward a cognitive theory of interpersonal development: Importance of peers. In M. Lewis & L. Rosenblum (Eds.), *Friendship and peer relations.* New York: John Wiley.

Levy-Shiff, R., & Hoffman, M. (1985). Social behavior of urban and Kibbutz preschool children in Israel. *Developmental Psychology, 21,* 1204-5.

Lewis, M., Young, B., Brooks-Gunn, J., & Michaelson. (1975). The beginning of friendship. In M. Lewis and L. Rosenblum (Ed.), *Friendship and peer relations.* New York: Wiley.

Lindner, E. W., Rogers, J. R., & Mattis, M. C. (1983). *When churches mind the children.* Ypsilanti, MI: High-Scope Press.

Maccoby, E., & Martin, J. (1983). Socialization in the context of the family: Parent-child interaction. In E. M. Hetherington (Ed.), Socialization, Personality and Social Development, Vol. IV. In P. Mussen (Ed.), *Handbook of child psychology.* New York: John Wiley.

Marthaler, B. L. (1978). Socialization as a model for catechetics. In P. O'Hare (Ed.), *Foundations of religious education.* New York: Paulist Press.

Mette, N. (1984). The Christian community's task in the process of religious education [trans. R. Nowell]. In N. Greinacher & V. Elizando (Eds.), *The transmission of faith.* Edinburgh: T&T Clark.

Miller, R. C. (1979). Bushnell, the family and children. *Religious Education, 74,* 254-262.

Mueller, E., & Lucas, T. (1975). A developmental analysis of peer interaction among toddlers. In M. Lewis and L. Rosenblum (Eds.), *Friendship and peer relations.* New York: John Wiley.

Nelson, C. E. (1967). *Where faith begins.* Atlanta: John Knox Press.

Parton, M. (1932). Social participation among preschool children. *Journal of Abnormal and Social Psychology, 27,* 243-269.

Postman, N. (1982). *The disappearance of childhood.* New York: Dell Publishing Company.

Ross, H., & Goldman, B. (1975). Establishing new social relations in infancy. In T. Alloway, L, Krames, & P. Plinar (Eds.), *Advances in communication and affect, Vol 4 .* New York: Plenum Press.

Rubin, K. (1980). *Children's friendships.* Cambridge, MA: Harvard University Press.

Scott, K. (1984). Three traditions of religious education. *Religious Education, 79,* 323-339.

Selman, R. (1981). The child as a friendship philosopher. In S. R. Asher & J. M. Gottman (Eds.), *The development of children's friendships.* Cambridge: Cambridge University Press.

Stern, D. (1980). *The first relationship.* Cambridge, MA: Harvard University Press.

Suransky, V. (1982). *The erosion of childhood.* Chicago: University of Chicago Press.

Tennant, D. (1985). Anabaptist theologies of childhood and education (3). Anabaptist schooling: Education or socialization? *Baptist Quarterly, 31,* 118-136.

Westerhoff, J. (1985). Living the faith community. Minneapolis: Winston Press.
    1976 *Will Our Children Have Faith*? New York: Seabury.
Winn, M. (1983). *Children without childhood*. New York: Penquin.
Vander V. J. (1984) The future of the Church as an intergenerative problem. In
    N. Greinacher & V. Elizondo (Eds.), *The transmission of faith*. Edinburgh:
    T&T Clark. Concilium 174.
Youniss, J. (1980). *Parents and peers in social development* . Chicago: University of Chicago Press.

Chapter Seven:

How to Teach:
Foundations, Processes, Procedures

JAMES MICHAEL LEE

"Children are God's apostles, day by day
Sent forth to preach of love, and hope, and peace."[1]

—James Russell Lowell

INTRODUCTION

Teaching young children is far more complicated than standing in front of a group of preschoolers and simply talking. In actuality, teaching is a complicated process of structuring or orchestrating a whole host of variables in such a way that a desired outcome is achieved.

Religion is far more complicated than a collection of theological truths. In actuality, religion is not even theology. Rather, religion is a holistic lived experience which a person has with the Holy. This lived experience is composed of many intersecting areas of human existence.

Teaching religion to young children is not simple. Furthermore, it is hard work. This chapter will explore the nature and structure of the teaching process so that early childhood religious educators can become more effective teachers.

A Word About Content

In the ultimate analysis, preschool religious educators do two major things. First, they teach. Second, they teach religion. Both the teaching process itself as well as the religion they teach are contents in their own right.

---

1. James Russell Lowell, "On the Death of a Friend's Child."

The teaching process is a genuine content in and of itself.[2] It is for this reason that it can be called structural content. A content is that which is learned. Young children not only learn the religion that is taught; they also learn religion from the way it is taught. If a young child is taught religion in an unloving way or in a way that emphasizes the legalistic character of God's justice, then the content the young child acquires will be an unloving and legalistic religion. As a matter of fact, the way in which something is taught usually has more lasting cognitive and attitudinal impact on learners than what is taught substantively. Indeed, the way in which religion is taught is also the religion that is taught. Teaching procedures constitute a powerful content of religion teaching. Hence, the preschool religious educator should strive to improve the quality and effectiveness of her instructional procedures.

Religion is the second major content of religion teaching. The term given to this molar form of content is substantive content. In the here-and-now religion teaching act, structural content and substantive content merge to produce a unified activity.[3] The teaching process and the religious content both undergo transformation during this merging. This is why, as George Albert Coe (1929, p. 23) observed many years ago, religion changes in the act of teaching it.

There are two important attributes of the substantive content we call religion which are of great importance to the early childhood religious educator.

The first of these attributes is that religion is not theology. Virtually all theologians agree that theology is a cognitive science which intellectually investigates God.[4] The purpose of theology is to find out more about God's nature and activities. In contrast, religion is the lived relationship which a person has with God. The purpose of religion is to constitute an enriched metier for a person to live as full a religious lifestyle as possible. Theology and religion, then, belong to two very different zones of reality. From both the philosophical and the psychological dimensions, then, theology does not produce religion; it only produces more theology. Hence, if the early childhood religious educator wishes to teach religion, she must teach religion and not primarily theology. Theology has a certain place in religion teaching depending on which dimension of religion is being taught at the time. Moreover, the

---

2. The whole book *The Flow of Religious Instruction* is devoted to this crucial point (Lee, 1973).
3. For a fuller discussion of this point, see Lee, 1982a, pp. 173-174.
4. For a summary of what leading theologians think about the nature of theology, see Lee, 1985a, pp. 4-7. In and of itself, theology is an areligious activity.

place of theology is contributory; it does not comprise the whole of religion or even the major part of it. Theology will not directly help the young child get to heaven; religion will, however.

Theology is a science and, therefore, can be completely and genuinely contained in books and other scientific treatises. Religion, on the other hand, is a human activity and hence can only be completely and genuinely contained in the human person.[5] Because there are four primary domains in human existence, there are four primary domains in authentic religion. These four domains are the psychomotor, the cognitive, the affective, and lifestyle. Just as fully functioning human beings smoothly integrate these four domains in their own lives, so too fully functioning religion meshes all four domains into one smooth harmonious flow. This meshing or integrating of the four domains is called holism and is absolutely central to the effective teaching of religion.

There is a hierarchy of domains in the human act called religion. The most important of these domains is lifestyle, the next most important is affect, the third most important is cognition, and the least important is psychomotor. Of especial importance to early childhood religious educators is the fact that affect is more important for religion than is cognition. Since young children learn affect more readily and more deeply than they learn cognition, the preschool religious educator is in a more favored position to profoundly influence the religious development of the persons she teaches than are educators of any other age group. Indeed, the pertinent research, especially from depth psychology,[6] suggests that the deeper attitudes and values and love-orientations (all affects) are learned before the age of six—all that teachers of older children can do is to direct or deflect these deeper learnings.[7] There always has been an abiding and near fatal temptation in the churches to embrace rationalism.[8] Early childhood religious educators would do

---

5. Theology is a product of the left hemisphere of the brain. As a holistic reality, religion involves both hemispheres (bicameral). Notwithstanding, the finer forms of religion seem to involve a great deal of right hemisphere activity. On this point, see Lee, 1985a, p. 503.
6. For an especially helpful and clear overview of the major schools of depth psychology with explicit reference to the unconscious, see Caputi, 1984.
7. In contrast, the research seems to suggest that though cognitive stimulation or cognitive deprivation in early childhood does indeed affect a young child's intellectual growth, nonetheless these good or bad effects can by and large be reversed by later experiences such as high cognitive stimulation given to an elementary school child who was intellectually deprived in early childhood. (Clark-Stewart with Apfel, 1978, p. 94).
8. Elsewhere I define rationalism as "the attempt to assign to reason the first place and fundamental role in personal and social development." Rationalism seeks to validate human existence and human activity by cognition. (Lee, 1985, p. 33).

well to resist this temptation. Such resistance is relatively easy since young children operate more at the experiential and affective level than at the cognitive level.

The second important attribute of the substantive content we call religion is that, like all substantive contents which are taught, it is an amalgam of nine discrete subcontents. These distinct subcontents are product content, process content, cognitive content, affective content, verbal content, nonverbal content, conscious content, unconscious content, and lifestyle content.[9] Each of these contents interact with one another. Each modifies the other and in turn is modified by the other. Religion consists in a special valence or thrust of all these interactive contents—a valence or thrust toward the Holy. If any one substantive subcontent is missing or is not brought to sufficient salience in the religion lesson, to that extent is the lesson less religious. Authentic religion is holistic, not fractionated.

THE NATURE, STRUCTURE, AND DYNAMICS OF TEACHING

Definition and Characteristics of Teaching

Simply stated, teaching is the intentional facilitation of desired learning outcomes. Thus, teaching and learning are reciprocal activities. Teaching is defined by the learning outcomes which are intentionally produced through instructional activity. Where there is no learning, there has been no teaching, even if the teacher tried hard to bring about learning.

Of the many characteristics of teaching, four are particularly germane to the early childhood religious educator.

One important characteristic of teaching is that it is basically a process of prediction. When planning her lesson, the early childhood religious educator predicts that one pedagogical procedure will be more effective in bringing about a particular learning outcome than another. If, during the course of the lesson, she discovers that the teaching procedure she has chosen is not bringing about the desired learning outcome, then the religious teacher shifts to another specific procedure which, on the basis of what has happened thus far in the lesson, she predicts will now produce the desired learning outcome. Teaching as prediction means that the early childhood religious educator has mas-

---

9. The whole of the book *The Content of Religious Instruction* (Lee, 1985a) is devoted to an extended treatment of each of these nine major subcontents, with the exception of conscious content.

tered a wide repertoire of instructional procedures so that she can easily move from one procedure to the other as the dynamics of the lesson unfold.[10]

Another important characteristic of teaching is that it is an art-science. The early childhood religious educator is an artist because she fashions substantive content and structural content into a concrete form which facilitates learning. This fashioning takes place tentatively during the planning phase of teaching and reaches its zenith in the concrete pedagogical act. (It is very helpful to recall that the word art comes from the Latin word *ars* which means making. Hence, the teacher as artist is a person who makes, forms, and fashions.) But the teaching art, like any true art, is not free-floating. Rather, the teaching art is based on scientific principles.[11] Just as painters such as Michelangelo and Caravaggio were constantly in touch with the scientific principles of perspective, contrast, and pigmentation during all phases of their painting, so are artistic teachers in close touch with the scientific principles of teaching and learning which underly all phases of the pedagogical task.

Successful teaching, like all successful artistic endeavors, is the skillful and aesthetic fashioning of scientific principles and data into a form which yields the desired results.[12] Such skillful and aesthetic fashioning requires that the early childhood religious educator maintain constant and intimate contact with the research in her field. The first of these contacts consists in keeping abreast of the important research taking place in early childhood religious education. This is best done by regular and frequent reading of the serious (not just the popular) journals and the serious (not just the popular) books in early childhood teaching, learning, and religious education. The second intimate contact with research consists in a research mentality which the early childhood religious educator brings to bear on all the here-and-now concrete teaching in which she is engaged[13] (see chapter ten).

The effective teacher is a researcher-on-the-hoof. She is always encountering learners not only through the prism of what they are actually

---

10. For a further discussion of this point, see Joyce, Wald, and Weil, 1981, pp. 141-156).
11. For a helpful treatment of this point, see Gage, 1978.
12. This fashioning is not a mechanistic application of scientific principles and data. Rather, it is the admixing of these scientific realities with the artist's own vision, personality, and artistic skills which forms the aesthetic shape into which scientific principles and data are placed.
13. This point is one of the central themes in Barber, 1981. This book is the finest single-authored volume on early childhood religious education, and has become "the bible" of persons working in this field.

learning at any given moment but also what the empirical research says about this learning. In this way, the teacher may be able to instantly alter her pedagogical procedures to better facilitate desired learning outcomes. Furthermore, the teacher as researcher-on-the-hoof is also gathering impressionistic and objective data about these particular learners as they are here-and-now concretely engaged in the learning task so that she can sharpen (or revise) the overall research matrix out of which she plans and implements her pedagogical procedures for these learners. To the extent to which an early childhood religious educator is in constant touch both with the ongoing research in her field and with her own on-the-hoof research in the present pedagogical situation, to that extent is her skill and vision as a pedagogical artist actualized.

A third important characteristic of teaching is that it is a cooperative art-science. An operative art-science can be done alone, such as sculpting. But a cooperative art-science requires that two or more persons dynamically participate in the fashioning of the final result. This fact suggests that the more the early childhood religious educator actively involves the young children in the lesson, the more cooperative and artistic (effective) that lesson will be. Teacher-centered pedagogical procedures such as that of telling minimize the cooperativeness in the instructional act and hence tend to minimize the artistic (effectiveness) benefits which can result from the teacher's activity.

The final characteristic of teaching is that each person in the lesson changes in and through the teaching activity (Lee, 1973, pp. 221-225). The teacher, then, is not a catalyst because a catalyst by definition is an element in an interaction which does not undergo any change during the interaction. On the contrary, the teacher is a person who not only changes learners but who in turn is changed by learners by what she teaches and by how she teaches. This fact is very good news for the early childhood religious educator because it enables her to grow as a person and as a religious person during each lesson and during each phase of her career.[14] It is precisely because the teacher undergoes changes during the lesson that one often hears the very finest teachers say that they have learned more from their learners than the learners have learned from them.

Can Everything Be Taught?

As a general rule, anything which can be learned can be taught. Put differently, things are learned because they have been taught in one way or another. Hence the range of learnings which the early childhood

---

14. For a further discussion of this point, see Lee, 1985b, pp. 7-42.

religious educator can facilitate are virtually limitless.

Unfortunately some early childhood religious educators seriously limit their effectiveness as teachers by believing discredited pedagogical fallacies which suggest that some outcomes cannot be taught. The underlying theme of most of these erroneous pedagogical fallacies is that only cognitive outcomes can be facilitated, and that affective outcomes and lifestyle outcomes cannot be facilitated. For example, many early childhood religious educators incorrectly believe that outcomes such as attitudes, values, and good conduct are outside the range of pedagogical possibility. Let us look briefly at each of these three outcomes.

A famous—but erroneous—pedagogical fallacy is that attitudes are caught, not taught. In actuality, attitudes are caught because they are taught. There is abundant empirical research to suggest that attitudes can indeed be taught; conversely there is no body of empirical research to suggest that attitudes cannot be taught.[15]

Another erroneous pedagogical fallacy is that values are not able to be taught. Once again, there is abundant empirical research to suggest that values can be taught and indeed have been taught throughout history. In her impor ant book *Teaching Christian Values,* Lucie Barber (1984) offers a whole gamut of Christian values and shows clearly what teachers can do to insure that they can teach solid Christian values to their learners.

A good Christian lifestyle can also be directly taught to learners. Again, there is no empirical evidence to suggest that early childhood religious educators are unable to teach learners to conduct themselves as good Christians in life.

In order to appreciate the fundamental reason why everything which is learned can be taught, we have to gain a proper appreciation of the nature of teaching and of the importance of differential pedagogical procedures to attain differential learning outcomes.

As mentioned at the beginning of this chapter, teaching is not just standing up in front of learners and telling them things. Teaching consists of an extremely wide repertoire of strategies, methods, and techniques which are employed to facilitate desired learning outcomes. Indeed, standing in front of a group of learners and telling them things has been proven to be one of the least effective and most restrictive of all pedagogical procedures. Expressing care to a learner in distress, putting a learner in a situation in which that learner will have to make an

---

15. For a still-valid summary of some of the pertinent empirical research on this point, see Lee, 1973, pp. 106-119. See also Barber, 1981, pp. 8, 10-11, 50-51, 118-119, 153-156, 160-161, 169-171.

affective choice, punishing or praising a learner, role playing, praying with a learner—all these are examples of *direct* teaching because these pedagogical procedures are just as direct as telling learners things—and in almost every case, are even more direct because they are not as heavily mediated through abstracted verbal symbols as is telling learners things. If early childhood religious educators are to effectively teach learners the whole gamut of possible learning outcomes, then these religious educators will have to expand their concept of the nature of teaching.

There is a lineal relationship between the pedagogical procedure which an early childhood religious educator uses and the type of outcome which is facilitated. If the teacher wishes to facilitate a cognitive outcome, then the teacher will have to select a pedagogical procedure which highly correlates with cognitive learning. If the teacher wishes to facilitate an affective outcome like attitudes or love, then the early childhood religious educator will necessarily have to use that kind of pedagogical procedure which is affectively oriented.[16] If the teacher wishes to facilitate a lifestyle outcome, then she must select a pedagogical procedure which lies in the same domain as the lifestyle outcome. The matching of teaching procedure and desired learning outcome is a central and indispensable task of every religious educator.[17]

While it is possible to teach *all* kinds of substantive religious content to learners, it is not possible to teach these substantive contents in exactly the same way to each and every person. The learner's age and, even more importantly, the young child's level of maturation and development shape the way in which that person is able to learn a particular substantive content.[18] It is unjust, immoral, and pedagogically impossible to attempt to teach one or another substantive content in basically the same way to learners of all ages. Young children learn differently

---

16. On this point, see Lee, 1985a, pp. 196-275. See also Ringness, 1975, pp. 3-37, 134-174.
17. The choice of teaching procedure, of course, takes place within the broader existential matrix of the living out the variety of complementary roles and tasks which the teacher is required to play in the pedagogical setting. On this last point, see Schickedanz et al., 1983, pp. 14-16. See also Doyle, 1979, pp. 42-74.
18. Evangelical Protestant religious educationists and educators, who normally posit the Bible and theology as the starting points for religious teaching, seem to agree on this point with respect to preschool children, at least. Thus, Gail Linam (1978, p. 235) writes: "The needs, skills, and developmental levels of preschoolers suggest the approaches to be taken in teaching young boys and girls. Therefore, the program begins with the preschooler." Also see Beechick, 1979.

than older children; and children in general learn differently than
adults. The pedagogical standard for teaching young children and evaluating the quality of their learning should not be determined by adult
standards. Contrary to a certain baseless ideology which has swept
much of Christian religious education and Christian leadership since
1970, Christianity is not an adult religion. Rather, Christianity is a
religion for persons of all ages and stations.[19] Christianity is just as much
a religion for preschoolers as it is for adults. (Jesus made this point very
clear in Matthew 19:14.) We should not attempt to teach adult religion
to young children because children are not miniature adults,[20] nor
should they be judged by adult standards or by any standards other than
young children's standards.[21] Christian standards for children are not
perforce immature because they are children's standards. To be sure,
maturity properly considered means that a child is where that child
should be maturationally and developmentally. If a four-year-old child
acts like an adult or learns like an adult, then this child is just as
immature as if it acts like or learns like a two-year-old.

The important point I made in the previous paragraph can be graphi-
cally demonstrated by the reaction of some religious educators to the
celebrated empirical research investigation conducted by Ronald Goldman (1964). Goldman's investigation found that children under the age
of twelve tended to grossly misunderstand biblical stories such as Moses
and the burning bush, the crossing of the Red Sea, and the temptation
of Jesus. The reaction of some religious educators to Goldman's research findings was one of shock. What Goldman had discovered, they
erroneously concluded, is that it is impossible to teach the Bible to
children, and especially to young children. This conclusion is clearly
fallacious, and results from the mistaken belief on the part of these
religious educators that the heart of religion teaching is the communication of cognitive content. The truth of the matter is that Goldman's
research found what every parent and every perceptive teacher has
known for centuries, namely that children, especially young children,
are not developmentally ready to learn higher-order cognitive material
(1964, pp. 51-67). As Goldman himself states, the full understanding of

---

19. In this view John Westerhoff (1980, p. 18), the tractarian, states that "bibli-
    cal tradition affirms that the [religious] status of children is equal to that of
    adults."
20. There was a time in the Sunday School Movement when children were
    urged to model themselves after adult religious standards. See Lynn and
    Wright, 1980, pp. 70-76.
21. For an interesting history of childhood as a state of existence in its own right
    and not just a passage to adulthood, see Aries, 1962.

Moses and the burning bush, the crossing of the Red Sea, and the temptation of Jesus involves rather high-level cognitive thinking.

What do Goldman's research findings suggest for the religious education of children, in our case, young children? These findings suggest that religion should be taught holistically. In other words, religion should not be taught from the cognitive perspective only, but should also include a great deal of affective content and even more of lifestyle content. Thus, exclusively cognitive pedagogical methods such as the reflection-reflection teaching procedure known as "shared praxis" should be assiduously avoided in the religious education of young children.[22] Because of the developmental level of young children, the cognitive content of religious instruction in the Bible (and in every area of religion, for that matter) should revolve around the way in which a young child thinks, namely, very concretely and very personally (1965, pp. 77-101) Thus, the proper way to teach the burning bush, the crossing of the Red Sea, and the like, is to help the preschoolers cognitively relate these biblical stories to their own lives, such as wading in shallow water and then going in so deep that the water is over one's head.[23]

Even more importantly, teaching the Bible, and indeed any other religious content, to young children should incorporate much more affective content than cognitive content. The singular importance of

---

22. "Shared praxis" is a highly cognitive teaching procedure devised by Thomas Groome (1980, pp. 184-232), a religious educationist. To date there has been no real empirical validation for the pedagogical efficacy of this method. Furthermore, the evidence suggests that Groome was not conversant with the nature, structure, and range of teaching procedurology when he concocted his "shared praxis" procedure.

23. Goldman himself advocates excluding the teaching of more cognitively complex biblical passages such as the three which he investigated. His rationale is that the children will grossly misunderstand the real message of the biblical passages. I contend, on the contrary, that Goldman is erroneously making adult understanding the norm for "correct understanding." Strictly from the cognitive standpoint, I believe that it is more important that young children gain intellectual familiarity with the biblical passage and place that passage within their overall interactive cognitive repertoire than it is to have an adult understanding of this or that biblical passage. On another level, if Goldman were right in claiming that more cognitively laden biblical stories should not be taught to persons until they are able to intellectually grasp these stories, then many adults would be deprived of encountering large portions of the Bible. Adults, after all, vary considerably in their levels of intellectual development, intellectual attainment, and intellectual ability. It should never be forgotten that one of the many wonderful features of the Bible is that it can be understood to an appropriate degree by all persons regardless of age or level of intellectual development.

this point is highlighted in three well-conducted studies in which David Elkind (1964, pp. 635-646) investigated the religious identity conceptions of Jewish, Catholic, and Protestant children aged five to twelve. These studies found that the child is most like the adult in the affective domain and least like the adult in the cognitive domain. Thus, in teaching the burning bush or the temptation of Jesus and the like, the early childhood religious educator should have the learners spend considerable time in trying to feel what it was like to encounter a burning bush or be tempted by the devil. Putting biblical stories in the form of a song is one successful way to develop these feelings (Brusselmans & Wakin, 1977, pp. 65-83). The teacher should try to help learners develop attitudes toward the power of God (crossing the Red Sea), and the craftiness of the devil (temptation of Jesus). And the early childhood religious educator should help learners come to a greater love of the Bible and a greater love of God through encountering the scriptural verses in a warm, loving manner—and ending the little Bible lesson with a short affective prayer, such as, "I love you, God, for helping Moses cross the Red Sea."[24] Finally, and most holistically, teaching the Bible to young children should accord the most attention to lifestyle content, namely, helping young children live a Christian life appropriate for their own level of development. The teacher can stage a little play having someone tempt another learner. Or the teacher can light up a bush and have the learners experience a burning bush (especially good after Christmas when families throw away dry Christmas trees).[25] Or the early childhood religious educator can structure a special children's liturgical service in church during which one or another biblical story becomes the focus of the liturgy.[26] Worship is an especially potent lifestyle-soaked content of religious instruction.[27] Or again, the early childhood religious educator can have the preschoolers engage in holistic life projects of a distinctly religious nature.[28]

---

24. The great masters of the spiritual life have over the centuries consistently ranked affective prayer more highly than cognitive prayer. On this point, see Lee, 1985a, pp. 672-676.
25. For some helpful pedagogical procedures for teaching the Bible to preschool (and also to older children) in a manner which emphasizes affective content and lifestyle content, see Furnish et al., 1979, pp. 37-116.
26. For a discussion of the intrinsic relationship between religion teaching and worship, see Neville and Westerhoff, 1978, pp. 91-106.
27. For a nice little article on children's liturgies, see Haas, 1976, pp. 148-150.
28. In this vein F. Franklyn Wise (1978, p. 235) writes: "Preschoolers are not skillful enough to provide fine-quality, useful objects for the church or home. Yet they should be encouraged to do simple creative things that express love for their parents, for the church, and for God." Wise calls these activities "projects for service."

From the Christian perspective, the center of religious instruction must be the core virtues of faith, hope, and love.[29] Can these three virtues be taught, or is there nothing the early childhood religious educator can do to help young children grow in faith, hope, and love? We have no evidence that faith, hope, and love result only from the direct infusion of God's grace into the learner. But we do have abundant empirical evidence all around us that faith, hope, and love have indeed been successfully taught to learners of all ages. It should be remembered that faith, hope, and love are simply theological and psychological constructs which describe in a logical fashion both a set of global behavioral orientations and a set of interrelated specific behaviors. To effectively teach faith, hope, and love, the early childhood religious educator must find out which overall behavioral orientations go to make up faith, hope, and love in young children. After this has been done, the early childhood religious educator breaks down these global behavioral orientations into specific teachable behaviors.

Lucie Barber, one of the twentieth century's premier psychologists of early childhood religious development, has dissected faith, hope, and charity into what her decades of empirical research have shown to be among the basic developmental orientations of young children (Barber, 1981).[30] The early childhood religious educator can profitably take these orientations and then break them down into more specific human behaviors which are by their very nature amenable to being framed into performance objectives[31] (see chapter ten).

GLOBAL BEHAVIORAL ORIENTATION	VIRTUE
• Trust nature	
• Trust the predictability of events	
• Trust the dependability of parents	FAITH
• Have a joyfully expectant attitude toward life	HOPE
• Have a joyfully expectant attitude toward learning	
• Have a positive self-image	
• Have a positive valence toward others	LOVE

---

29. Paul the apostle stresses this point in one of the most famous verses of scripture, namely 1 Corinthians 13:13.
30. See also Barber's fine book *Celebrating the Second Year of Life* (1978).
31. One of the best basic books on performance objectives remains Mager, *Preparing Instructional Objectives* (1962).

One of the most important learning outcomes for all Christians is religious experience. Persons of all ages, including preschool children, can and indeed should learn religious experience.[32] Religious experience is the foundation and the justification both for Christian faith and for Christian theology. To Christians, faith is far more than a set of cognitive beliefs. Faith is holistic in that it comprises the meshed involvement of a person's cognitive, affective, and lifestyle functions. As I observe elsewhere (Lee, 1971, pp. 109-110), faith is 1) an amalgam of total, unqualified, and free assent on the part of the whole person to God (cognitive domain); 2) a total trust and commitment of the person to God and his revelation (affective domain); 3) an encounter between God and the human person (lifestyle domain); and 4) an existential compact between God and the person (lifestyle domain). For its part, theology is nothing more than a cognitive reflection or verbal afterword about the personal religious experience of each individual and about the corporate religious experience of the ecclesia. To teach religious experience to young children should not be construed simply as setting some sort of base for the later learning of theology, since religious experience is of a different order of reality than theology, and religious experience is far more important than theology in Christian living. Rather, to teach religious experience to young children is to educate them in the most important form of their entire lives, a form into which all other dimensions of Christian existence have their being, their action, and their completion.

Religious experience can be taught to children because unlike theology which is exclusively an objective cognitive content, religious experience is a personally lived subjective affair which occurs authentically in the life of each person regardless of age or station.[33] Like all other kinds of human experience, religious experience takes on the contours of the developmental level of the person having the experience—in our case, young children. Religious experience may be passive or active; furthermore, religious experience runs the gamut from simple encounters with the sacred all the way up to the all-encompassing mystical state (Lee, 1985a, pp. 649-652, 676-678). For developmental reasons, young children in all probability can never attain the mystical state, precisely because they are so young. But young children can and should engage in that level of religious experience appropriate to their developmental level.

---

32. The last part of this statement is especially true from the psychological (subjective) aspect of the act of experiencing (as contrasted to the objective dimension of the experiential act). See Godin, 1985, pp. 17-22, especially p. 22.
33. On some fundamental contrasts between religious experience and theology, see Lee, 1985a, pp. 42-49.

All the research evidence indicates that religious experience can be intentionally 1) discussed, 2) intensified, and 3) facilitated by a religious educator. And there is no research evidence to indicate that the kind of religious experience which is intentionally discussed or intensified or facilitated is of a lower level than the kind of religious experience which occurs spontaneously.[34] Thus, the early childhood religious educator can and indeed ought to discuss, intensify, and facilitate religious experience in the young children she is teaching.[35]

Some pedagogical procedures have proven to be successful in discussing, intensifying, and facilitating religious experience in young children. Because the cardinal pedagogical principle underlying all teaching is to take the learner where that person is developmentally, the teaching of religious experience to young children must revolve around the psychological fact that preschoolers construe reality in a concrete and affective fashion (Paloutzian, 1983, pp. 71-72). Far from being a detriment to the successful discussion and intensification and facilitation of religious experience, the fact that young children encounter the world in a concrete and affective fashion is a distinct advantage. Religion in general is far more concrete than abstract, far more affective than it is cognitive. Indeed, the relevant empirical research suggests that ratiocinative cognition and abstraction are formidable barriers to having religious experience.[36] When one reads the writings of the mystics, even when they are not discussing their own mystical experiences but just simply giving a religious view of the world, one is struck by the all-pervasive concreteness and affectivity of the language which they use.

Four pedagogical procedures can be quite helpful for the preschool religious educator who wishes to effectively teach religious experience to their young learners.

First, have the learners actively engage in religious practices such as worship services specifically designed for young children, performing visible charitable deeds for other persons, and so forth. For young children, religion—and religious experience—consists primarily in religious practices performed with adult approval (Paloutzian, 1983, p. 74).

---

34. For a review of the pertinent research on this point, see Lee, 1985a, pp. 667-670.
35. One of the very few books on religious education for children to stress the importance of providing children with increasingly high (intense) levels of religious experience is Chaplin, 1948, pp. 209-223. Her point is that if children do not have experiences of the transcendent early in life, then how are they going to be ready to receive experiences of God when they grow up.
36. This fact is especially true for intense religious experience. See Lee, 1985a, pp. 670-671.

Second, when dealing with expressly religious matters, emphasize affectivity. Young children live at the all-important affective level of life, a level far more central to religion and to religious experience than the cognitive level. When teaching prayer, when teaching an event in the life of Jesus, or when teaching Christian love, the early childhood religious educator should not stress the abstract nature of prayer, or the meaning of an event in the life of Jesus, or the nature of love. On the contrary, the religious educator should stress what different kinds of prayer feel like, what Jesus might have personally felt during this or that event in his life, and what love feels like (Armstrong, 1971, pp. 288-289).

Third, have young children share their dreams with one another. If possible, have children act out their dreams during the lesson. Religion is very much enmeshed in the unconscious aspect of a person's life (Frankl, 1975), and as Sigmund Freud (1953, p. 647) remarked, dreams are the royal road to encountering the activities of the unconscious. Indeed, the Bible is filled with accounts of God speaking to persons through dreams.[37] Young children have dreams, and some of these dreams have expressly religious significance. The perceptive early childhood religious educator helps young learners get in touch with their dreams in a childlike manner so that these learners now and in the future will befriend their dreams and the God who encounters the children in dreams.

Fourth, use religious language rather than theological language whenever possible. All verbal language, by its very nature, is abstract and symbolic and thus is not really congruent with the developmental level of the young child. But because religious language consists of those linguistic symbols which are used in a person's direct encounter with the Holy it is far more pedagogically potent than theological language whose axis is exclusively cognitive reflection about God.[38] By using metaphor and imagery, by using words which perform things rather than which just predicate things, and by using emotive language the early childhood religious educator can make the lesson more religiously charged than if she used abstract theological language.

SOME BASIC PSYCHOLOGICAL PRINCIPLES

If the early childhood religious educator is to teach religion successfully, then she must weave basic psychological principles into the fabric

---

37. For an excellent account of dreams in the Bible, see Kelsey, 1968.
38. For a discussion of the essential difference between religious language and theological language, see Lee, 1985a, pp. 280-282.

of her pedagogical activity. Psychology tells the teacher how learners actually learn. If the early childhood religious educator is ignorant of, or deliberately neglects psychological principles and psychological research data, then in all likelihood this teacher is thereby dooming herself to instructional failure.

Before dealing with some of the more important psychological principles of effective preschool religious instruction, let me mention two cardinal points which undergird these principles. *First,* every person learns psychologically, not logically. While an effective scientific treatise is necessarily written logically, an effective religion lesson is necessarily taught psychologically. This means that the religion teacher does not fit the learner into the logical parameters of religion but rather teaches religion in such a way that it is first and foremost adapted to the psychological contours of learners—in other words, completely tailored to the way in which learners do in fact learn. This axial point is especially true for a personal holistic pattern of living. *Second,* a person learns religion in exactly the same way in which that individual learns any other holistic reality having the same general characteristics. There is no empirical research data to suggest that a person learns religion any differently from the way that individual learns anything else. A famous principle of philosophy which is also a touchstone principle of psychology is that *all* learning, including religious learning, takes place according to the nature and operations of the learner.[39] Religion is part and parcel of life; it is not something which can be separated from life, something spooky or ethereal or "out there." So also, the learning of religion is part and parcel of an individual's personal life; it is not something which can be separated from the person's overall process of learning, something spooky or ethereal or "out there."

Principle #1: Young children learn primarily through personal relationships. There is abundant empirical research to indicate that personal relationships are especially significant in influencing the degree, thrust, contours, and tint of each person's learning (Hyman, 1968, pp. 147-152). The establishment of a personal relationship with a learner is nowhere more important than with young children. This factor is true because, among other things, young children operate at a much higher level of affectivity and at a much deeper level of holistic human encounter than do adults.[40] In contrast, adults tend to use cognitive abilities

---

39. For a further discussion of this point, see Lee, 1973, pp. 58-59.
40. As a corollary to this, it is well to note that adults frequently substitute cognition and all sorts of defense mechanisms to prevent or at least retard the growth of close personal relationships with other individuals.

and defense mechanisms to prevent or retard the growth of close, personal relationships. Another reason why the establishment of personal relationships is so very important when teaching preschool children is that a very basic thrust of the young child's overall development as a human being is the achievement of personal relationships with peers and adults (Griffin, 1982)—and in the case of religious instruction, the attainment of a personal relationship with God, Jesus, and the communion of saints dead and living. Psychologically, young children learn things primarily through personal relationships. Thus, the young child learns God's love and care and providential relationship to human beings by what the religious educator does to and for the preschooler. A teacher's sympathetic voice, a soothing hand, an encouraging pat on the back—all these teacher behaviors directly and forcefully say to the young child: "God loves you. He cares about you personally."[41] While the teacher of the Bible to adults can often get away with totally basing the lesson on cognitive concepts about the Bible in the name of biblical instruction, the early childhood religious educator must be far more biblical—she must act in a biblical way with learners since young children learn the Bible in and through their personal relationships with the Bible and with the teacher.

Principle #2: Affect constitutes an extraordinary powerful factor in the young child's overall learning process. This principle is a more specific extension of the previous one, since personal relationships are always heavily affective. The feeling-function of the personality, namely, the affective domain, is the predominant one in early childhood. Indeed, affect is learned and comes to flower prior to cognition and prior to voluntary action in the developing person. This fact leads to two important psychological conclusions. First, affect strongly textures and colors a person's basic psychological *structure* through which and in which cognition and voluntary action are later shaped. In Freudian theory, the unconscious (which is basically affect) is primary process and is thus ultimately dominant in persons of all ages. Cognition and voluntary action are secondary processes which occur later as the person attempts to control or channel primary process (Freud, 1953, pp. 626-648). In Jungian theory, the unconscious (which also is basically affect) has prior temporal existence not only in each person but also in the historical development of the human race as a whole: thus, affect is a doubly powerful force, namely, a personal force and a collective force (Jung, 1954, pp. 626-648). Second, affect strongly textures and colors both the general and the specific *responses* a person makes to a reality. There is a

---

41. On this point, see Yoder, 1966, p. 30.

growing body of empirical research to suggest that a person's responses to various realities are first affective and only later arc cognitive.[42] It should be noted that psychophysiological research is increasingly suggesting that the same area of the brain (right hemisphere) which is the seat of affect tends also to be the seat of religion—in contrast to the left hemisphere which is the seat of cognition.[43] It is comforting for the early childhood religious educator to know that the relevant empirical research suggests that cognitive behavior can be enhanced by prior or simultaneous attention to the affective dimension of life (Kelsey, 1971, p. 71). It is also encouraging to the early childhood religious educator to recall that the empirical research strongly suggests that the affective development of a young child can be influenced, developed, and taught by a teacher.[44] The enhancement of the young child's affective life (and thus of a major portion of the young child's religious response to the world) must be deliberatively taught by the preschool religious educator—it cannot be left to chance. Specific pedagogical skills which the preschool religious educator can learn and then effectively deploy in lessons include attending to the learner's affective behaviors, communicating empathically with the learner, responding to the learner's feelings, expanding the use of feeling-toned words, increasing the use of nonverbal behaviors, and personalizing the meaning and reference of things (Carkhuff, 1981, pp. 153-157).

Principle #3: The socioemotional climate of the learning environment impacts significantly upon learning outcomes. Virtually every review

---

42. See for example, Zajonc, 1980, pp. 151-175. It should be noted that research on the affective domain by nontheraputically oriented psychologists is very sparse contrasted to the research on cognition undertaken by these same psychologists. Research on cognitive processes is much easier and more "methodologically clean" than hard-nosed empirical reasearch on affective processes.

43. For a review of some of the pertinent research, see Lee, 1985a, pp. 500-504. While religion is primarily a right-hemisphere activity, theology (cognition) is a left-hemishpere activity. Thus the essential differences between religion and theology has a profound psychophysiological foundation.

It should be noted that the division of left and right hemisphere capabilities is more variable than some simplistic writers believe. The described lateralization is not the case in some left-handed persons, who may reverse the pattern or process information bilaterally. In addition, brain damage may result in tranfer of function to the undamaged hemisphere (Myers, 1986). Thus left and right hemispheres are not completely discrete. Also, *strict* linkage of brain with religious activity is elusive in the research (Dodrill, 1976; Wong, 1984).

44. For a review of some of the classic research on this subject, see Brophy, Good, and Needler, 1975, pp. 47-74.

of the pertinent empirical research supports the contention that the socioemotional climate in the pedagogical situation predicts not only affective learning outcomes but cognitive outcomes as well.[45] This principle represents an expansion of the first two principles mentioned already in this section. Paramount in the socioemotional climate of all preschool learning settings, and especially in preschool religious education settings, is love and all that love implies—care, unconditional acceptance, warmth, giving, forgiving, and so forth. The love dimension of the socioemotional atmosphere is a two-way street, since the child needs to love (Barber, 1984, p. 241) as well as to be loved.[46] For a preschool religious education setting, a warm socioemotional climate is especially important since teaching young children to love God in a personally committed manner is a major desired learning outcome (Kelsey, 1977, pp. 39-75). Without the dynamic presence of love in the teaching-learning situation, the young child might well be taught to be religiously apathetic instead of religiously committed.[47] A preschool religious education setting which is weak in love-soaked socioemotional climate can also teach young children a distinctly areligious, and possibly even an anti-religious view of right and wrong. In Christianity, right-wrong is not based ultimately on abstract intellect, nor is Christianity fundamentally a matter of "objective" right-wrong. On the contrary, right-wrong is based ultimately on a person's holistic existential orientation to God and on the degree of one's actual love of God as manifested in personal generosity toward God and his creation. Unless there is a warm socioemotional atmosphere in the lesson, an atmosphere in which love is both underlying and salient, there can easily result a juridic (intellectually judgmental) religion in which the young child is taught to be virtuous for the wrong reasons or at least for reasons which do not represent a fine form of Christianity. Early childhood religious instruction should not teach young children to perceive that they have lost God's love if they fail to conform to one or another abstract principle of right and wrong.[48] Love is something which can be taught by the early

---

45. See, for example, Khan and Weiss, 1973, p. 778.
46. For a psychoanalytic examination of the reciprocal dynamism between the need to love on the one hand and the need to be loved on the other hand, see Reik, 1963.
47. "Apathy is particularly important because of its close relation to love and will. Hate is not the opposite of love; apathy is. The opposite of will is not indecision . . . but being un-involved, detached, unrelated to significant events . . . apathy or a-pathos, is a withdrawing of feeling." (May, 1969, pp. 29-30).
48. For a development of these last two sentences, see McDaniel with Richards, 1973, pp. 26-27.

childhood religious educator both by the overall socioemotional climate which she establishes in the pedagogical situation and by the specific love-correlated instructional behaviors which she deploys throughout the lesson.

Principle #4: The learner's self-concept exerts enormous influence on the genesis, form, and outcome of learning.[49] The self-concept is a person's image of self. It is the unified set of perceptions which an individual has of self. Thus the self-concept can be described as a sort of perceptual prism through which the person perceives every experienced reality, including one's own self (Lee & Pallone, 1966, pp. 36-37). The self-concept is multidimensional, holistic, active, forceful, and capable of change (Markus & Wurf, 1987, pp. 299-307).[50] Included in a self-concept is a valuation and an evaluation of self—self identity, self worth, self goals, and so forth. (There is a reciprocal relationship between self-concept and self-assessment, each dynamically affecting the other.) Also central to self-concept is differentiation, namely the recognition that the I (that is to say, the self) is different in many large and small ways from other persons and objects. From this last mentioned perspective, self-concept is the awareness that though the self shares many commonalities with other realities, nonetheless there exists a dynamic collection of multifaceted differences which are unique to one's own self. The growth of self-concept is strongly influenced by direct interaction with others (Markus & Wurf, 1987, p. 305) as well as by the configuration of the immediate social environment (McGuire, 1984, pp. 73-120).[51] Persons also form and later revise their self-concept through social comparisons with others, such as saying, "I am not as smart as Pete" and "I am stronger than Jane." Children learn how to use social comparison to evaluate their own self-concepts and become progressively more skillful at doing this throughout their school career (Frey & Ruble, 1985, pp. 550-562). During early childhood, the person's self-concept is developing—body image, social self, cognitive self, emotional self, and a self capable of bringing about change in the environment

---

49. Technically the child does not have a *generalized* self-concept until middle childhood. Yet the concept of "me" is in gradual development during the preschool years at a more concrete level (Hall, Lamb, & Perlmutter, 1986).
50. It should be added that "researchers have defined the self-concept from various perspectives, including hierarchies, prototypes, networks, spaces, phenomenal fields, and schemas" (Markus & Wurf, 1987, pp. 301-302).
51. Anent this point, it should be underscored that I am virtually the only major religious education theorist to emphasize the great importance of the environment in the religious instruction act. See, for example, Lee, 1973, pp. 65-73, 234-235, 240-248.

(Cartwright & Peters, 1982, p. 484). In early childhood, too, the emerging person is gradually learning to differentiate self from others and to evaluate who self is, what self is like, and what self ought to be (Hess & Croft, 1975, pp. 183-186).

There are many reasons underlying the enormous power and practical importance of the self-concept in the behavior of persons of all ages, including young children. First, there is a very close correlation between one's self-concept and how one behaves in a cognitive fashion, in an affective fashion, and in a lifestyle fashion. The unifying conclusion of virtually all the pertinent empirical research is that the self-concept does not simply mirror a person's ongoing behaviors but more importantly mediates and regulates these behaviors (Markus & Wurf, 1987, p. 299). When placed in its proper context, this research finding means that "behavior is a reaction to the field as perceived" (Rogers, 1951, p. 494).[52] Second, the self-concept may itself become an important source of the young child's motivation (Wicklund & Gollwitzer, 1982, pp. 205-207, 224-226, and Markus & Nurius, 1986, pp. 954-969). Third, together with needs and values, the self-concept is a central factor in the process of setting goals, in the selection of the goals to be attained, and in the actual attainment of these goals (Harter, 1983, pp. 292-297). Like persons of all ages, young children tend to set goals whose process and outcomes are consistent with their self-definition and their self-concept (Markus & Wurf, 1987, pp. 309-310).[53] Fourth, the self-concept plays a very strong role in helping to determine a person's present and future success, regardless of the criteria of success (Coopersmith, 1967, pp. 38-42). Derivatively, the empirical research has also discovered that a young child's self-concept also constitutes a powerful factor in predicting and determining success in school (Cartwright & Peters, 1982, p. 484). In a strong sense, then, one's level of success consists in the implementation of one's self-concept. Fifth, the research suggests that "a positive self-concept leads to a perception of oneself as important, as capable of performing at a normal or superior level, and capable of utilizing learning experiences" (Saracho, 1980, p. 99).

The available empirical research suggests that conditions do in fact exist which help in the development, not only of a self-concept, but more importantly in our case of a positive self-concept in young chil-

---

52. The proper context of the research finding just mentioned in the body of the text is supplied by Hazel Markus and Elissa Wurf who note that the vast body of empirical research suggests that there is a reciprocal interactive influence between self-concept and a person's repertoire of active behaviors. (Markus and Wurf, 1987, p. 329).
53. It should be recalled that goals are related to expectancy.

dren (Samuels, 1977, p. 111). The task of the early childhood religious educator is to know these conditions and to bring them into active salience in the lesson. One of the most important general pedagogical tasks of the preschool religious educator is to organize her instructional activities and objectives in relation to the young child's developing self-concept (Saracho, 1980, pp. 104-106). Some more or less specific pedagogical procedures which the early childhood religious educator can use to facilitate and enhance a positive, healthy, and realistic self-concept in the young child are as follows: First, strive to be as empathic as possible toward each learner. Through the use of empathic teaching behaviors, the early childhood religious educator inserts herself cognitively and affectively into the young child's existential frame of reference so that she can know and feel the young child's world as the young child knows and feels this world. The best vantage point for properly understanding and effectively dealing with the young child's behavior is the internal frame of reference of the child himself.[54] Second, deploy those kinds of teaching devices and structural contents which expand the child's horizons and which help him to become progressively open to new forms of experiences. A closed and narrow world tends to foster a closed and narrow self-concept in the young child. Third, expect a good deal from each young child in accordance with his ability and present self-concept. The teacher's level of expectation for the young child often serves as a self-fulfilling prophecy with respect to the degree to which a child will develop his self-concept and acquire substantive learning outcomes. The young child will tend not only to behave in accordance with what others expect him to do; the young child will also tend to develop his self-concept within the context of expectancies which significant others have for him.[55] Fourth, set realistic standards of achievement for the young child. Excessively high standards can cause the child to develop a low sense of self-esteem. On the other hand, excessively low standards can cause the young child to develop an unrealistic self-concept which will later lead to a distorted sense of self-worth and an unfounded belief that he can accomplish virtually any task easily and with perfection.[56] It

---

54. The kernel of the last sentence is found in Rogers, 1951, p. 494.
55. For a review of the research in this regard, see Samuels, 1977, pp. 96-110.
56. It is my personal observation that many American schoolteachers at all educational levels from preschool through high school hold learners to excessively low standards thus producing unduly bloated self-concepts in young persons. When these young persons graduate and enter the world of work, they often undergo severe shock to self-esteem and indeed to the whole of self when they discover that their self-concepts are founded on self-deception, a self-deception fostered and nourished all along the line by their

should be noted that the empirical research suggests that high-achieving children with high self-concepts tend to evaluate themselves with realistic self-criticism only (Samuels, 1977, p. 108). Fifth, maximize realistic success experiences and eliminate excessive failure experiences in the young child. The young child should be allowed to fail in order to develop a realistic self-concept; however, he should not be placed in situations in which he fails most of the time. Sixth, reward young children when they behave competently. Self-concept is intimately bound up with a sense of competence. The early childhood religious educator should treat competence as a learning task and help the young child realize that he is not incompetent because he is unable to perform a task but is only incompetent when he either refuses to perform the task or will never be able to perform the task. Competence comes with learning, and that is why the young child is in the preschool program (Felker, 1974, pp. 46-57). Seventh, reassure the young child when he makes a mistake (Bills, 1981, pp. 27-29). This reassurance should be given to the young child as a person. It is always important to separate the child as a person from his mistakes and his misconduct (McDonald, 1980, pp. 55-56). Eighth, provide the young child with appropriate role models. Role models exert a significant impact upon the developing self-concept of the young child. Ninth, develop intrinsic motivation in the child.[57] Intrinsic motivation can be produced by giving little children learning tasks which are congruent with their own personal and social needs rather than imposing from the outside learning goals which might not have some root in their developing selves. Tenth, overtly recognize and reward the individual differences of each young child (McDonald, 1980, pp. 54-57). Such public recognition and reward helps the young child capitalize on his own particular strengths and thus contributes to the development of a sense of worth about self as a different (and hence special) self.

Of interest to all early childhood religious educators is the empirical research finding which suggests that there is a positive relationship

---

former teachers. Some of these graduates attempt to cope with this sense of shock to self by defensively declaring that the world is too tough, is oppressive, and possesses inordinately high standards of minimum performance. Some social critics of the American scene claim that the lack of orientation to quality in goods and services exhibited by most Americans from the 1960s onward can be explained by the large number of Americans who seem to possess unrealistic self-concepts which were formed through interaction with excessively low standards set for them by their schoolteachers all along the line.

57. The research suggests that intrinsic motivation and positive self-concept are significantly correlated. On this point, see Samuels, 1977, p. 111.

between the self-concept of the teacher and the cognitive growth of the children under her charge (Aspy, 1969). The empirical research also indicates that the teacher's own self-concept is not independent of the pedagogical procedures she uses. Rather, the teacher's own self-concept tends to influence the instructional procedures she uses and the all-important attitudinal components present in the deployment of these procedures (Spaulding, 1964, pp. 313-318; Gooding, 1969).

Of crucial importance to every preschool religious educator is to insure, as far as possible, that religion becomes not only an integral part of the young learner's self-concept but even more importantly becomes the basic substantive superstructure of that self-concept. Many years ago, Horace Bushnell (1916, p. 5) expressed this point beautifully when he wrote that the central purpose and metier of all religious education is "that the child is to grow up a Christian and never know himself as being otherwise." Thus, for example, in helping enhance the young child's self-concept, the early childhood religious educator can give prominence to biblical personages, saints, and contemporary religious figures as role models for young children. (These religious role models should include a healthy dose of outstanding Christian laypersons in various careers and not just clergy.) Or again, when using expectation-oriented pedagogical strategies to foster positive self-concepts in learners, the preschool religious educator would do well to repeatedly and overtly link the expectation she has for young children with the expectation which God has for all persons young and old as expressed by Jesus when he said that we must be perfect just as his heavenly Father is perfect (Matthew 5:48).

Principle #5: Reinforcement constitutes an especially potent and pervasive specific process through which the young child learns. Reinforcement describes the process by which a consequence serves to strengthen, weaken, or eliminate a preceding behavior. The significance of reinforcement in teaching is that reinforcement increases the probability that a given response or set of responses will recur. In general, the occurrence of a reinforcer strengthens the initial behavior whereas omission of a reinforcer weakens or eliminates that behavior. This lack of reinforcement is called "extinction." Extinction produces a decline in likelihood of a behavior occurring by removing the contingency which reinforces the behavior.[58] Positive reinforcement, such as praise, nonverbal approval, or other kinds of reward for performance, is particularly effective in stimulating learners of all ages to repeat the behavior for

---

58. For a discussion of the basic principles of reinforcement within the special context of religious instruction, see Lee, 1973, p. 79.

which they have been rewarded. Conversely, punishment such as re-proof, nonverbal disapproval, and other kinds of punitive or aversive behavior suppresses undesirable behavior. It should be noted, however, that positive reinforcers seem to be more effective in stimulating repeat behavior than punishment is in decreasing unwanted behavior (though punishment can be highly potent as well). Because reinforcement is so crucial in all learning, and especially with young children, preschool religious educators should make constant and intentional use of those kinds of pedagogical procedures which tend to reinforce the young child's learning.[59] The empirical research has shown unambiguously that reinforcement is one of the most powerful pedagogical tools in the teaching of young children, whether at home, at play, in the classroom, or wherever (McCarthy & Houston, 1980, p. 25). This fact holds true not just for cognitive learning but for all kinds of affective learning (including attitudes, emotions, values, and love), as well as for lifestyle outcomes. The younger the child, the more reliance the early childhood religious educator must place on reinforcement.

Summarizing both the available empirical evidence plus her own decades of careful research with young children, Lucie Barber (1981, p. 19) categorically states that reinforcement constitutes the one most effective instructional process in preschool religious education. It should be underscored that reinforcement does not produce automatic results for the simple reason that learners are not automatons. Young children, like learners of every age, are different and so the results of reinforce-

---

59. Some religious educationists and preschool religious educators might enter-tain severe reservations about reinforcement because of its close association with B. F. Skinner and behaviorism. These religious educators might wish to consider two fundamental points. First, reinforcement, of the operant conditioning variety (Skinnerian) is a proven fact and hence is independent of any psychological theory or theological system. As Skinner remarks at the very beginning of his book *About Behaviorism,* behaviorism is basically a philosophy and not a set of psychological facts. Second, Skinner might not be as threatening to Christianity as some religious educationists and educators seem to believe. There are many, many psychological principles advanced by behaviorism which are not only congenial to Christianity but which have been used by great religious educators from Jesus down to the present time. Furthermore, there are key elements of Skinnerianism which can help Christianity become more true to itself and more fulsome in scope. In my professional career, I have met many religious educationists and educators who have thoroughly opposed Skinner. But not in a single case had any of these persons read Skinner's writings either at all or with requi-site care. In virtually every instance, these persons were not opposing Skin-ner but their erroneous perceptions of Skinner.

ment tend to vary somewhat according to the personality and developmental level of the young child. Thus, the relevant empirical research suggests that praise produces a positive effect in certain persons and not in other individuals. For example, the research has discovered that praise tends to be more effective with girls than with boys. Indeed, boys often perform better and reach higher levels of achievement by being reproved; just the opposite tends to hold true with girls.[60] It should be noted, however, that if the child has intrinsic interest in an activity, external reinforcement may in fact *decrease* that interest (Green & Lepper, 1974).

The empirical research suggests that there are many things which the early childhood religious educator can do to utilize reinforcement to optimum pedagogical advantage. I will list only a few of these. First, reinforcement should be given as shortly after the young child's behavior as possible. The more immediate the reinforcement, the more effective it tends to be. Second, reinforcement procedures should be as varied as possible because sameness often breeds ineffectiveness over the long haul. Reinforcement using the same reinforcers may produce "satiation" or loss of desire (who wants ice cream after eating a half gallon of it?). Third, there should be an axis of consistency in the development of reinforcement processes. Thus, a teacher should not reward a young child's behavior one day and either punish or ignore the same behavior on a different day.[61]

Fourth, reward even the smallest improvements in the young child. Learning is gradual and normally takes place in small incremental steps. Fifth, use primary reinforcers when possible.[62] Unlike parents, schoolteachers are not often in a position where they can use primary reinforcers and so must use secondary reinforcers most of the time. A major advantage of early childhood education is that this age level intrinsically affords the preschool teacher with far more opportunity to deploy primary reinforcers than is possible in elementary school or secondary

---

60. A great deal of the research on reinforcement which is pertinent to to religious educators can be found in Lee, 1973, pp. 79-89.
61. Consistency is one of the three major elements in Kevin Walsh's famous "trinity of discipline." See Walsh and Cowles, 1982, pp. 119-124.
62. A primary reinforcer, it will be recalled, is that which derives its power from an innate or elemental human need such as food, water, and sleep. A secondary reinforcer is one which does not directly derive from such a need, but rather owes its power either to the level of its exchange rate for goods or privileges (for example, money), or to its symbolic value as representing an accomplishment (for example, praise).

school. Sixth, when it is necessary to use extinction or punishment, try to reinforce alternative behavior soon afterwards. It is important to remember that punishment only suppresses the undesirable behavior; it does not tell the child what to do specifically. Telling the young child which behavior is desirable and reinforcing the desired behavior should follow the application of punishment or extinction whenever possible.[63] Seventh, provide the young child with frequent information on how he is performing in the learning task. This kind of information has been shown by the research to result in feedback, namely that the information itself tends to generate desired and improved learning on the part of the young child.[64] The information which the preschool religious educator gives to the young child should be at once tailored to the developmental level of the young child and should be realistic. In the latter connection, over-optimistic reports on the young child's progress can easily cause the child to develop an unrealistic self-concept and a deluded notion of self-progress, both of which will possibly result in religious problems and life difficulties with the passage of time.

WAYS OF TEACHING

The early childhood religious educator should be acutely aware that neither the principles of learning outlined in the previous pages nor the psychological theory undergirding these principles constitute a valid theory of teaching. The principles and theory of teaching are fundamentally different from the principles and theory of learning. Psychological principles and theory are concerned with how and why learning takes place (descriptive). The principles and theory of teaching, on the other hand, describe and explain how to produce learning (prescriptive). A teacher who only knows psychological principles and theory will not, on this account, be an effective teacher. A successful teacher is one who, in addition to knowing the requisite subject-matter content and psychological principles, is also conversant with instructional principles and theory and is skilled in using concrete instructional procedures.

Theory of Teaching

Theory is absolutely essential for effective practice. It is in this sense that theory is extremely practical.

---

63. For a fuller discussion of this point, see Lee, 1982b, pp. 211-222.
64. Timothy Arthur Lines shows how feedback works in a total systems approach to religious education. (Lines, 1987, pp. 195-196).

Theory is indispensable for successful practice because theory explains, predicts, and verifies practice. Thus, a theory of teaching is necessary for the successful practice of teaching.

A theory of teaching explains why a particular teaching procedure works or fails. Without the explanatory power of a teaching theory, the early childhood religious educator would be powerless to capitalize on successful teaching procedures and to correct unsuccessful procedures. A teaching theory predicts the conditions in which a particular teaching practice will work and the conditions under which it will not work. Without the predictive power of a teaching theory, the early childhood religious educator would be incapable of ascertaining whether a particular teaching procedure will work with her group of learners tomorrow, next week, or whenever. Finally, a teaching theory verifies whether a particular teaching procedure has yielded the desired learning outcomes or not. Without the verificational power of a teaching theory, the early childhood religious educator would be unable to determine whether the learner has indeed learned what she wished them to learn.

As I wrote elsewhere, "theory helps save the religious educator from the very failures which theory would have been able to predict. Religious educators of the practicalist variety who imagine themselves to be exempt from the influence of theory are often the unwitting slaves of some defunct and inoperable theory" (Lee, 1982a, p. 119).

Theory is far different from speculation. Speculation consists in armchair reflection on reality. It is a particular form of thinking, and as such is contrary to empiric. For its part, theory is a statement or group of statements organically integrating interrelated concepts, facts, and laws in such a fashion as to offer a comprehensive and systematic view of reality by specifying relations among variables. A valid theory of teaching is not constructed solely by engaging in armchair reflection. Rather, a theory of teaching is constructed by careful, systematic observation of concrete, existential teaching situations. A theory of teaching is always bound up with the reality from which it is drawn. Thus, the concrete existential teaching situation is always refining and expanding a theory of teaching. A theory of teaching is never "spacey" or out-of-touch since a theory is always interacting with the here-and-now dynamics of the pedagogical act.

The source of a valid theory of teaching has important practical consequences for early childhood religious educators because every theory takes its direction and indeed its very existence from its source. The source of a valid theory of religious education is a controverted one. The older, more traditional view is that the source of religion teaching theory (and thus of religion practice as well) lies in theology. The newer view is that the source of religion teaching theory (and practice) lies in social science.[65]

Advocates of the theological approach to religious instruction contend that theology explains, predicts, and verifies everything which occurs in the teaching of religion. In this view, religious instruction is a branch of theology. Theology constitutes the starting point, total process, and goal of the religion lesson (Benson, 1988, pp. 214-215; Terry, 1978, pp. 24-34; Sanner & Harper, 1978, p. 84; and Smart, 1954, pp. 41-43). It is theology which determines the religious readiness of a child, youth, or adult (Miller, 1980, p. 156). It is theology which determines the concrete scope, design, arrangement, and timing of the curriculum (Wyckoff, 1961; Hofinger, 1962, pp. 51-61; Westerhoff, 1981, pp. 293-303). Theology determines which teaching procedures are to be used and which are to be rejected (Goldbrunner, 1961, pp. 108-121; Hofinger, 1962, pp. 62-67). Theology also judges the effectiveness of the teaching procedures used (Darcey-Berube, 1978, pp. 118-120).

Advocates of the social-science approach to religion teaching maintain that it is social-scientific theory which explains, predicts, and verifies all teaching procedures. In this view, religion teaching is a branch of education (and education, of course, is a branch of social science). This position is directly expressed in the term religious education itself: The noun education indicates the general nature of the activity, while the qualifying adjective specifies the particular kind of education taking place. Educational activity provides the starting point, total process, context, and goal of the religion lesson (Lee, 1971, pp. 182-224; Lines, 1987, pp. 211-240). It is social science which determines when and whether a person is ready to learn religion (Goldman, 1965, pp. 11-57; Lee, 1983, pp. 27-33). It is the educational dynamic itself which decides the concrete scope, design, arrangement, and timing of the curriculum (Lee, 1977, pp. 125-130; Barber, 1984, pp. 222-223; McKenzie, 1982, pp. 15-16; Piveteau & Dillon, 1977, pp. 173-211; Bickimer, 1983, pp. 40-92). Educational knowledge and awareness govern which teaching procedures are to be used and which are to be rejected (Burgess, 1983, pp. 174-187; Lee, 1985a, pp. 746-766). It is social science which authen-

---

65. Social science is far different from the broad-fields school curriculum known as social studies. Social science is a generic term for the collection of those disciplines which are focused on the detailed, systematic, and empirical study of human beings and their interrelations with individuals, groups, and institutions. Disciplines under the generic name social science include anthropology, economics, education, geography, history, political science, psychology, and sociology.

tically judges the effectiveness of the teaching procedures used (Lee, 1973, pp. 274-294; Bowman, 1986, pp. 89-112; Hemrick, 1983, pp. 200-204, 209-212).

The proper response to the controverted issue of whether religion teaching is part of theology or part of social science has immediate significance and great practical consequences for the early childhood religious educator. For example, does the preschool religion teacher look to theology or to educational science for answers on which teaching methods to use in helping learners acquire religious outcomes? Does she read primarily theological books on grace or educational books on curriculum for suggestions on how to organize learning experiences? Does she consult a theologian or an educational psychologist when she is experiencing difficulties in helping a learner with emotional difficulties? Does she attend theological conferences or educational workshops in order to learn how to construct that kind of instructional environment which will help preschoolers learn better? Should she talk with a theologian or with an educational reading specialist when she is trying to lay the affective foundations for reading readiness?

The answers to the practical, action-oriented questions in the previous paragraph are obvious. It is education (a branch of social science) rather than theology which is the most fruitful source for the theory and practice of early childhood religious education. Theology often has a vital ancillary role to play in religion teaching. However, this role is always supporting and external. Furthermore, theology is not religion. Theology is only one theory or explanation of religion. To teach theology is not to teach religion. Furthermore, it is possible for a person to learn and live religion with only a little knowledge of theology.

Timothy Lines (1987, p. 233) is historically correct when he observes that the search for a religious education since 1965 appears to be oriented toward social-scientific underpinnings rather than toward theological structures. After all, the theological approach to religious instruction has never directly generated a single new teaching procedure or curricular plan whereas the social-science approach has produced many. The theological approach to religious instruction has never directly constructed a single evaluative device to adequately ascertain whether a young child has learned what is supposed to be learned; social science has, of course, directly built all sorts of very helpful evaluative devices. The theological approach to religion teaching almost completely neglects the very important environmental variable present in every pedagogical situation; the social-science approach, on the other hand, gives great research-based attention to structuring the environment for optimal instructional advantage. The theological approach pays scant atten-

tion to the way in which a teacher actually teaches, contenting itself
instead with vague and sometimes spooky answers such as "It is the
Holy Spirit who really teaches and not the teacher," or that "Teaching is
a mystery"; in contrast, there is a vast amount of social-scientific literature on those teacher activities which are correlated with learning. In
short, theology simply lacks the theoretical structure and the methodological tools to do what every adequate theory or macrotheory should
do, namely to explain, predict, and verify teaching/learning practice.
Theological imperialism (Lee, 1971, pp. 242-243) and, what is worse,
theological positivism (Lee, 1982a, pp. 146-148) are no substitutes for
that kind of early childhood religious instruction based on the concrete
realities of teaching and learning. Indeed, as the later Gabriel Moran
remarks, "the hegemony of theology over religious education programs
in Christian circles is one of the obstacles to the emergence of religious
education as a field of study and a field of work." Moran (1982, p. 43)
also notes that while theology at times can provide a part (but only a
part) of the substantive content of religion teaching, it has nothing
directly to offer concerning the method, structure, and institutional
form of religious education.[66]

General Procedure

General procedure refers to those teacher behaviors which are universal throughout all teaching and are present to one degree or another in
every specific instructional activity. Ultimately, the success of any specific instructional procedure depends on the effectiveness of the general
procedure in which that specific procedure inheres. Put somewhat differently, specific procedure is enacted within the shape, flow, and context of general procedure.

Two of the most important general procedures in all teaching, including preschool religious instruction, are structuring the pedagogical situation and engaging in antecedent-consequent behavioral linking.

Teaching as Structuring the Pedagogical Situation. Fundamentally, all
teaching is the deliberate arrangement of the relevant variables in the
situation so that the probability of attaining learning outcomes is enhanced. As I wrote elsewhere (Lee, 1973, p. 207), "it is here that the
teacher as artist works to fashion from a host of variables and subvariables a pedagogical process in which the richness of each variable and

---

66. Moran goes on to argue for an approach to religion directly through revela-
    tion and faith, an approach which disavows the assumptions of Christian
    theology and instead places faith and revelation within the living context of
    religious education.

subvariable is so blended with all the others as to at once bring a new dimension to the process and serve also as a reinforcer to all other constituent variables and subvariables."

Probably the most serious misconception that all educators have about teaching is that instruction is one or another variant of the teacher standing in front of a group of learners and talking. As a result, most teaching is exclusively verbal rather than verbal and nonverbal, most teaching is exclusively cognitive rather than cognitive and affective and lifestyle, most teaching is exclusively product-oriented rather than simultaneously product-soaked and process-thrusted. Indeed, teacher-telling (little lecture) represents only one of countless pedagogical procedures. Furthermore, for a great deal of teaching, especially preschool religion teaching, teacher-telling is one of the least effective pedagogical procedures. By switching her view of teaching-as-talking-in-front-of-the-classroom to teaching-as structuring-the-learning-situation, the early childhood religious educator can free herself from the tight confines of only one specific teaching procedure (teacher-telling). As a result she will become able to devise a whole set of new and appropriate instructional procedures, procedures which combine and permute all four major variables involved in every pedagogical situation into new and highly effective forms of teaching.

The four major variables present in each and every pedagogical act are the teacher, the learner, the subject-matter content, and the environment. These four elements are termed variables because each of them changes or varies as each interacts with the other elements in the here-and-now instructional dynamic. The quality of the instructional act, as well as the specific and general learning outcomes of the instructional act, are contingent upon the configuration of the interaction among the four major variables. The shape and flow which this interaction takes depend in large measure on the way in which the teacher structures this interaction at the outset of the lesson and on the way the teacher continually restructures this interaction during the course of the lesson. To the extent to which the teacher deliberately structures and restructures the dynamic interaction among all four variables to that extent is the teacher really teaching. Like the maestro of a symphony orchestra, the teacher will at one time give prominence to one variable, at another time to a different variable, at a third time to yet a different variable, and so forth—but all within the participatory interaction of all the other major variables.[67]

---

67. For an elaboration of teaching as structuring the pedagogical situation, see Lee, 1973, pp. 230-268.

In its authentic actuality, then, teaching is the deliberative structuring of the pedagogical situation to attain the desired learning outcome. This realization can free the preschool religious educator to devise a whole host of different teaching procedures and to enact them consciously and with success.

Teaching as Antecedent-Consequent Behavioral Linking. The ongoing interaction among the four major variables always present throughout the lesson suggest a second fundamental characteristic of all teaching, namely antecedent-consequent behavioral linking. By antecedent-consequent behavioral linking is meant that a teacher's initial behavior (antecedent) produces a specific responsive behavior (consequent) in the learner. The behavior by the learner, in turn, produces a new behavior from the teacher or other learners (thus the behavior is antecedent, but also a result of the previous antecedent-consequent behavioral chain). In turn, the teacher or the other learners react in one way or another to the learner's behavior (consequent). And so it goes. Each antecedent behavior, whether it be by teacher or learner, produces a consequent behavior in the other person, a behavior which gives rise to a new antecedent behavior in that other individual. Each reciprocal behavior is linked to and dependent not only upon the previous behavior but also to the whole flow of all the previous chain of behavior which occurred. All through the continual dynamic flow of this behavioral linking, the teacher is constantly attending both to the appropriateness of the learner's consequent responses to the teacher's antecedent behaviors and to the appropriateness of those learner antecedent behaviors which proceed from the learner's just-completed consequent behavior. The teacher always adjusts her antecedent behaviors according to the way in which the learner has responded to her pedagogical behaviors.[68]

It is essential to remember that the teacher's antecedent behavior toward the learner's behavior is always enacted within an overall pedagogical structure in which the four major variables are present. To be optimally effective, therefore, the teacher's pedagogical behavior toward the learner must bring into play, as is instructionally appropriate to the attainment of the desired learning outcome, all four major variables involved in the teaching act. In this regard, the relevant empirical re-

---

68. Frederick Erickson (1979, pp. 99-126) gives the name reflexivity to the process of reciprocal influence through which people analyze each other's behaviors and adjust their own behaviors based on the messages received. I myself eschew the term reflexivity because it possibly connotes a mechanical process which excludes the appropriate involvement of the teacher's conscious and deliberative activity.

search suggests that specific teaching methods and techniques in themselves exert little or no effect on particular learner achievements. Rather, effective instruction occurs when the teacher deploys specific teaching procedures within the interactive ecology of the four major variables present in the lesson (Doyle, 1977, pp. 179-192).

This short section on teaching as antecedent-consequent behavior linking shows that the preschool religious educator should place her attention not so much on the deployment of specific pedagogical procedures in themselves but rather on the whole antecedent-consequent process in which each specific teaching procedure is existentially shaped.

Specific Procedure

Specific procedure refers to those concrete and particular teacher behaviors which are used to attain one or another desired learning outcome. Unlike general procedure, one or another concrete specific procedure is not present in all instructional activity; on the contrary, a certain concrete specific procedure is present only in those circumstances in which that particular procedure is concretely enacted by the teacher.

Elsewhere (Lee, 1973, pp. 33-35) I have shown that specific teaching procedures can be taxonomically arranged from the broadest procedure to the most particular. At the broadest level is style (such as learner-centered teaching). Then comes, in descending order from most broad to most particular, strategy (such as the discovery strategy), method (such as affective teaching), technique (such as simulation games), and finally step (such as verbal praise). Successful teaching requires that the specific procedure used at one taxonomic level be congruent with the specific procedures used at all the other taxonomic levels. For example, a teacher style which is learner-centered is not congruent with either the transmission strategy or with the technique of telling.

Procedurology. To be effective, the early childhood religious educator must realize that more than anything else she is a procedurologist, namely, a person who specializes in the enactment of teaching procedures. The preschool religious educator may know a great deal of cognitive content, be deeply aware of a wide range of affective content, and have a good command of lifestyle content, but if she lacks teaching skills she will be an ineffective teacher. Teaching is the deliberative facilitation of desired learning outcomes in another person. To the extent to which the teacher facilitates these outcomes, to that extent does the teacher teach. Facilitation is done through facilitational procedures; in the case of preschool religious education, through teaching procedures primarily. There is no escaping the truth of this hard fact. As Iris Cully (1965, pp. 7-9) observes, everything a teacher does during the lesson involves pedagogical procedures. Put differently, procedure is everything a teacher does to teach and through which a person learns. Communication and facilitation are accomplished through pedagogical procedures.

Preschool religious educators would do well to avoid two common mistakes frequently made about teaching procedures. The first of these mistakes is to assume that teaching procedures are less important than content. The second mistake is to assume that teaching procedures are different from content. Let me briefly discuss each of these in turn, reinforcing and expanding on what I wrote at the beginning of the chapter.

Teaching procedures are not less important than content because these procedures more often than not teach content directly.[69] Over and over again we can see from real-life instructional situations that the way in which a teacher teaches produces a more significant and a more long-lasting learning outcome than does the supposed content of the lesson. For example, when a teacher is teaching the Bible in a strict, juridical, and impersonal manner to young children, these learners tend to learn that the Bible is strict, juridical, and impersonal precisely because the instructional procedures used by the teacher were strict, juridical, and impersonal. As Sophia Lyon Fahs (1952, p. 15) once wrote, the ways through which the learner acquires religious content exert a more profound influence on that individual than the content itself. Instructional procedures in and of themselves directly teach values, attitudes, understandings, lifestyle orientations, and so on.

Teaching procedures are not essentially different or separate from content because pedagogical procedures are themselves content. Instructional procedures are not just ways to content; they are content. Unless teaching procedures were themselves content, they could not have the power to produce content. *Ex nihilo nihil fit.* Consequently, in my writings I have repeatedly called attention to the fact that teaching procedures are themselves content by giving the name structural content to teaching procedures and by giving the name substantive content to that which we typically call content.

I should again emphasize that the religion which the early childhood religious educator is teaching is not religious content in and of itself, but rather religious content as it flows through and is significantly altered by

---

69. This happens at more than one level. For example, there is a "hidden curriculum" in religious education that may be unintended and even unconscious to the teacher.

the entire pedagogical dynamic, a dynamic in which the substantive content of religion and the structural content of the pedagogical procedure interact to form a new developmental entity. It is this new entity, namely the religious instruction act, which produces the shape, form, contours, and thrust of the religious outcomes acquired in the lesson.[70]

Procedural Flexibility. It is imperative that the early childhood religious educator be highly flexible in the specific pedagogical procedures she uses. There is no one right teaching strategy which is universally superior to others. There is no one teaching method which always works. There is no one teaching technique which can be used in all instructional situations.[71]

Procedural flexibility is necessary for at least three principal reasons: 1) the nature and structure of each of the four major variables present in the pedagogical situation; 2) the variety of ways in which the four major variables interact concretely with one another; and 3) the nature of the desired learning outcome.

The nature and structure of each of the four main variables require procedural flexibility. First, the teacher, precisely because she is a teacher, inhabits the role of being primarily a successful facilitator of desired learning outcomes. In philosophical and theological terms, this means that the teacher is a person-for-others. In social-scientific terms, the teacher is pure function, a person whose personhood is mobilized and directed toward the function of successfully facilitating desired outcomes in learners.[72] Furthermore, as Iris Cully (1979, p. 134) notes, the teacher should become the kind of person who can accept changes and interferences positively, who can take in stride all the surprises which flow in and through the teaching/learning dynamic.[73]

If the definition of a teacher is that of effective facilitator of learning

---

70. For a further development of the points made in this paragraph, see Lee, 1973, pp. 165-174.
71. The point I am making in this paragraph is commonly recognized, not only in the empirical research on teaching, but also by every grassroots educator. Thus it is astounding that Thomas Groome actually advocates one single teaching procedure (an empirically unverified one at that) as the sole correct pedagogical procedure, a procedure which he claims works better than any other procedure at all times and in all situations and with all learners (Groome, 1980, pp. 184-232). What is even more astounding is that so many religious educationists seem to agree with his position that there is only one right teaching procedure which is universally optimum.
72. For a more detailed treatment of the religious educator as pure function, see Lee, 1973, pp. 225-229.
73. It is interesting to find that of the sixty-one footnotes in the entire Cully book only one deals with the theory of teaching and only two explicitly treat teaching procedures per se.

outcomes in a situation characterized by a wide diversity of learner personalities, by a wide diversity of subject-matter contents, and by a wide diversity of psychosocial and physical environments, then obviously the teacher must be one who is procedurally flexible. Second, learners are continuously shifting in terms of needs, interests, attention, patterns of interaction, physical condition, and so forth. Possibly at no age is this fact more salient than early childhood. The constantly changing contours of young children shout out for procedural flexibility on the part of the early childhood religious educator. Third, the substantive content of religious instruction is religion. Unlike theology which is a relatively stable cognitive verbal content (at least from hour to hour), religion is a constantly interactive and changing affair. It is interactive because religion is a cluster of a wide variety of different disciplines and sciences and perspectives each of which assumes existential priority according to the concrete experiences and conditions of the human being.[74] It is a constantly changing affair because religion is human; it exists only in human form. Because human beings such as learners and teachers are always changing in one respect or another, religion is always changing to a certain degree. Finally, the environment of learning is constantly in flux. The psychosocial environment is ever moving, and the physical environment is always undergoing modification—not just with respect to holding the lesson once in the church building and once in a classroom and once on the playground and once in the gymnasium and once in the community and once on a field trip, but also with respect to the ever changing configurations in which learning is being enacted: now in a group setting, now with learners playing individually, now with little children interacting with toys or number games, now in a learner associating with one child and shortly thereafter with another child, and so on.

The second principal reason requiring procedural flexibility on the part of the early childhood religious educator consists of the variety of ways in which the four major variables involved in all teaching interact with one another in the concrete instructional dynamic.[75] The teacher is

---

74. To an extent, theology is also interactive. However, in theology, all the realities with which it interacts are always subordinate to theological reality and to theological procedure.

75. The phenomenon known as "school culture" is one way of expressing the concrete cohesive pattern formed through the dynamic interaction among these four molar variables. Discerning parents often choose one preschool program over another on the basis of the character and thrust of the particular preschool culture. One important task of every teacher in a preschool religious education program is to work to conserve or renew or recast the culture of the preschool. For one helpful treatment of school culture, see Heckman, 1987, pp. 63-78.

constantly changing as she adjusts and readjusts her pedagogical behavior as a result of the interaction she undergoes with learners, subject-matter content, and the here-and-now instructional environment. Learners are always changing during the course of their interaction with the teacher and the subject-matter content and the environment: they ask questions, shove other children, giggle, throw toys, express like or dislike for the religion materials they encounter, sing songs, and so forth. The subject-matter is constantly undergoing modification as it is adjusted by the teacher, as it is personally interpreted and felt and lived by each child, and as it resonates or clashes with the environment. The environment is always in flux as it expands and contracts psychosocially in the course of its interaction with teachers and learners and subject-matter, as it is physically changed intentionally by teachers and learners, and so forth.

The third principal reason requiring procedural flexibility on the part of the early childhood religious educator consists in the nature of the desired learning outcome. Differential learning outcomes require differential pedagogical procedures for their attainment. Globally speaking, there are four major domains of learning outcomes (including religious outcomes). These four are psychomotor, cognitive, affective, and life-style. Each of these major domains is organically and progressively linked to a particular class of specific pedagogical procedure. Thus, for example, a cognitive pedagogical process cannot directly yield an affective outcome. To be a successful early childhood religious educator the teacher must select that kind of specific pedagogical procedure whose overall nature, axis, and thrust lies in the same domain as the desired learning outcome. Additionally, the preschool religious educator should choose from among all the methods and techniques within that domain the one which is the most closely aligned with the desired learning outcome. Perhaps an example will illustrate this point. Let us say that the teacher wishes to teach four-year-olds how to pray in an affective fashion. She chooses this objective because she is aware of the empirical research that affect is the dominant psychological process in preschool children. Her selection is also made because of the centuries-old testimony of theologians, religious novelists, and persons who have had intense religious experiences that affective prayer is superior religiously to cognitive prayer. From among the very many affective pedagogical procedures she chooses that of imaging because affective image prayer seems to have proved a successful way for young children to pray.[76] Since image prayer in young children combines the psychomotor do-

---

76. Indeed, affective image prayer appears to be effective for persons of all ages. On this point, see Kelsey, 1977, pp. 28-38.

main with the affective domain, the early childhood religious educator intertwines psychomotor activities with affective processes. The teacher holds a little party for her four-year-old children in the pastor's residence next to the church. After a few minutes in which the children express their positive feelings about the residence, the pastor enters and gives each little boy and girl a cupcake with nice gooey icing on top. After they have eaten and shouted "yummy, yummy," they play and sing happy songs. Then the teacher tells the young children to remember that the pastor is their spiritual father or mother. After this, the children draw pictures of their own parents giving them good things. When this activity is completed, the young learners close their eyes and sensorily imagine God as their parent giving them good things. They then share these sensory images by drawing, acting out, or if necessary telling the other little boys and girls how they felt toward God during their imaging activity. The lesson concludes with a happy song about God as our warm parent and a little affective prayer: "With all my heart, with all my heart, I love you God."

Some Specific Procedures. The preschool religious educator has at her disposal an enormous range of possible specific teaching procedures from which to choose. As I emphasized in the preceding paragraph, the selection of a specific pedagogical procedure and the concrete way the teacher deploys that procedure should be heavily influenced by the nature and domain of the desired learning outcome. It is, of course, manifestly impossible for the early childhood religious educator to have an active and successful instructional repertoire which includes each and every specific teaching procedure. Nonetheless, the preschool religious educator should be proficient in a minimum number of instructional procedures relevant for each of the four major domains of human learning. Before she is allowed to teach in a preschool religious education program, the prospective teacher should have demonstrated mastery of at least four major instructional procedures in each of the four major domains (the 4-4 standard for entrance into the preschool religious education profession). During each year of professional service, the early childhood religious educator should demonstrate mastery of two additional specific procedures so that her active pedagogical repertoire will grow gradually with each passing year.

Table I provides a very brief and incomplete list of some of the more important pedagogical strategies which have proven successful for young children. Each specific procedure is listed under the domain for which it is appropriate.

A careful examination of Table I reveals that in some cases a specific instructional procedure can overlap domains. For example, the imaging

TABLE I—LIST OF SOME SPECIFIC TEACHING PROCEDURES GROUPED BY APPROPRIATE LEARNING DOMAINS

PSYCHOMOTOR	COGNITIVE	AFFECTIVE	LIFESTYLE
nonverbal activities	word games	songs	free play
show-and-tell	lecture/telling	art work	project
mime	number games	sharing feelings	drama
dance	discovery thinking	role playing	field trip
fitness activities	questions	imaging	worship activities
woodworking	group discussion	storytelling	simulation games
playing musical	problem solving	trust walk	sharing activities
instrument/s	reflection	dream sharing	

technique can be enacted in such a way that it partakes primarily of either the cognitive domain or the affective domain. Or again, storytelling contains a great many cognitive as well as affective elements. The choice of the particular domain into which to insert a specific teaching procedure is made principally on two bases, namely the domain into which that procedure normally fits in preschool religious education and the way in which the early childhood religious educator tends to enact that procedure. Two examples might serve to illustrate this point. While imaging can and often does belong to both the cognitive and the affective domains, nonetheless in preschool religious education the imaging technique is usually more a part of the affective domain than the cognitive domain. The same holds true for storytelling. Furthermore, the way in which preschool religious educators deploy the imaging and the storytelling techniques tends to proceed more often along an affective axis than along a cognitive axis, though the two domains, of course, are present and interactive in both the enactment of the imaging and the storytelling techniques. Thus, the issue of proper domain placement for various teaching procedures is not one of either/or but rather both/and, or perhaps more specifically, one-more-than-the-other.

The Flow of Specific Procedure. The specific teaching procedures listed in Table I can and have been successfully used with learners of all ages, abilities, religious affiliations, and social classes. However, effective deployment of any of these and other specific instructional procedures is contingent upon broadly adapting and fine tuning the procedure so that it flows in congruent harmony with the four major variables necessarily involved in a particular teaching/learning situation. Thus, for example, a preschool religious educator will tell a biblical story far differently to her learners than will a religious educator working with adults. Both the preschool religious educator and the adult religious

educator have broad goals and specific objectives for the learners. However, the structure and contours of these goals and objectives will vary
significantly, depending on the differing ages of the learners. The substantive content will also vary according to the type of learner being told
the biblical story, such as being more concrete for young children than
for adults, more fanciful for young children than for adults, less symbolic for children than for adults, and so on. The highly specific pedagogical steps[77] which the religious educator uses in the course of telling the
Bible story will also vary according to the existential condition of the
learners (more nonverbal for young children than for adults, more deliberately incorporative of spontaneous learner inputs in the case of young
children as contrasted to adults, and so on).

The key point in the preceding paragraph is that specific teaching
procedures are necessarily fluid, melding their density and flow and
shift in concert with the four major variables involved in every instructional act. No specific teaching procedure works automatically or in
isolation from the four major variables. Every specific teaching procedure works only to the extent that it is meshed with the four major
variables.[78]

---

77. In the taxonomy of pedagogical procedure which I have developed, step is
the most specific element. The other elements, going from more specific to
more general, are technique, method, strategy, style, and approach. For a
discussion of this taxonomy of pedagogical procedure, together with its
usefulness in religion teaching, see Lee, 1973, pp. 31-38.

78. David Elkind does not seem to understand the pedagogical foundation of
this point. Elkind claims that "the focus on a specific learning task, as
demanded by formal instruction, is at variance with the natural mode of
learning of the young child. From the viewpoint of formal instruction, the
multiple learning potential of the young child is seen as evidence of distractability or in the currently more fashionable phase, attention deficit." In
response to Elkind, it may first of all be said that there is no such thing as
formal instruction. The same principles of teaching are operative in all
forms of instruction. There is instruction in formal settings or informal
settings, but not formal instruction. What Elkind probably means by formal
instruction is a complex of highly structured, tightly organized teaching
procedures like didactic teaching or programed instruction. (The Munich
Method of teaching religion, so popular in the first half of this century in
the German-speaking world, exemplifies didactic teaching.) Second, instruction, if it is to be effective, must be fashioned in congruence with the
four molar variables. Thus, the multiple learning potential of the young
child cannot be legitimately compared to an older-child or adult learning
standards (the distractability issue). To be sure, multiple learning potential
necessarily becomes one of the components which the preschool religious
educator incorporates in both the planning and the enactment of specific
pedagogical procedures. (Elkind, 1986, p. 694).

Improving the Practice of Teaching

The improvement of the practice of teaching all across the board, including preschool religious instructions, revolves around two principal axis: 1) why teaching works (theory) and 2) how teaching works (practice). At every stage of a program for the improvement of effective teaching skills, theory and practice must actively interface.

Earlier in this chapter it was shown that teaching is a set of specific procedures deliberatively enacted through and in an ongoing general framework of antecedent-consequent behavioral linking. Therefore, any effort directed toward the improvement of preschool teaching practice must be based on this central fact.

Every workable model of improving the instructional capability of preservice and inservice religious educators must first analyze and then control both general teaching procedure and specific teaching procedure. To be successful, this analysis and control must necessarily center on the concrete pedagogical behaviors of the teacher. Furthermore, this analysis and control must be primarily based on objective data on what is occurring in the concrete here-and-now teaching act rather than primarily on subjective impressions or perceptions of what is occurring.

Behavioral analysis of instructional practice is that process in which the teacher's concrete here-and-now enactment of general and specific pedagogical procedure is carefully examined in terms of each of its singular components in itself and also in terms of the overall flow of these singular components taken as a whole.

Behavioral control of instructional practice is that process in which the teacher concretely enacts one or more general and/or specific pedagogical procedures in such a manner as to lead to the demonstrated improvement of the general and/or specific pedagogical procedure.

Behavioral analysis precedes and accompanies behavioral control because behavioral analysis reveals how and in what manner a concrete general or specific pedagogical procedure is working or not.

Theory precedes and accompanies both behavioral analysis and behavioral control because theory explains why a certain general or specific pedagogical procedure is working or not. Furthermore, theory predicts which general or specific pedagogical procedure will work in a given circumstance and setting.

To be truly successful, there should be constant feedback among instructional theory, behavioral analysis, and behavioral control. (Feedback is the process in which each part of a system interacts with the other parts in such a way as to change the other parts and to be changed by them. A thermostat is a representative example of the feedback process.) This feedback should be built into the organic structure of any program for instructional improvement. The more systemic and closed-loop is the program for instructional improvement, the more feedback will be successful.[79]

Elsewhere (Lee, 1973, pp. 279-284) I propose a model which incorporates pedagogical theory, pedagogical analysis, and pedagogical control into an organic system with built-in feedback. This model is represented in Table II.

TABLE II—MODEL FOR IMPROVING INSTRUCTIONAL PRACTICE

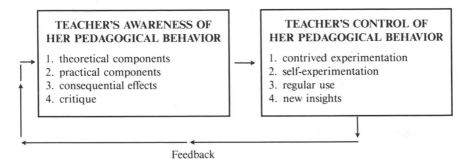

TEACHER'S AWARENESS OF HER PEDAGOGICAL BEHAVIOR	TEACHER'S CONTROL OF HER PEDAGOGICAL BEHAVIOR
1. theoretical components 2. practical components 3. consequential effects 4. critique	1. contrived experimentation 2. self-experimentation 3. regular use 4. new insights

Feedback

The left panel in the model centers around enhancing the preschool religious educator's behavioral analysis of the pedagogical act while the right panel deals with heightening the teacher's pedagogical skill (control of her teaching behaviors). The model plainly shows the flow of activities necessary to enable the teacher to optimally control her own instructional behaviors for the purpose of facilitating desired learning outcomes. This model is of particular importance because it specifies how the religious educator can effectively close the gap between her intention to be effective and her actual effectiveness as a teacher.

Enhancing Interaction Analysis. The procedure known as interaction analysis can be quite useful in helping the religious educator significantly improve her ability to analyze behaviorally the lesson(s) she is teaching. Interaction analysis examines the actual antecedent-consequent behaviors which occur in the overall context of the four molar variables, as these variables unfold in the concrete pedagogical act. Interaction analysis is a technique for capturing the quantitative and qualitative dimen-

---

79. On the role of systems and systems theory in the improvement of religious instruction, and for the place of feedback in an overall system, see Lines, 1987.

sions of observable instructional behaviors and for ascertaining broader patterns into which these behaviors fall.

A major advantage of interaction analysis is that it enables the religious educator to gain a more objective view of her teaching behaviors rather than having to rely on subjective and often distorted perceptions of what is actually happening in the pedagogical act itself. To be sure, a very important goal of all preservice and inservice teacher preparation is to help the preschool religious educator become a more conscious and a more acute observer of her instructional behavior—a nonimpressionistic and data-based observer of what is really and truly occurring in the course of her teaching performance (Hobar & Sullivan, 1984, pp. 26-34). And because interaction analysis is by its nature nonjudgmental, it is basically nonthreatening—something of great importance in working with preservice and inservice religious educators.

The most widely used of all interaction analysis systems is that developed by Ned Flanders (1966). There are ten behavioral categories in the Flanders Interaction Analysis System: 1) accepts feeling; 2) praises or encourages; 3) accepts or uses ideas of students; 4) asks questions; 5) lecturing; 6) giving directions; 7) criticizing or justifying authority; 8) student talk: response; 9) student talk: initiation; 10) silence or confusion.[80] It should be noted that no scale or value rating is implied by these category numbers. Each category number is classificatory, that is, it designates a particular kind of communication behavior or interaction. Furthermore, the categories are defined behaviorally, not judgmentally or impressionistically.

The first seven categories in the Flanders Interaction Analysis System deal with teacher talk while categories 8 and 9 center on student talk. In the area of teacher talk, the Flanders instrument distinguishes between talk of an indirect influence kind (categories 1, 2, 3, 4) and talk of a direct influence type (categories 5, 6, and 7). In this way the incidence and kind of teacher influence on the learner's behavior can be assessed.

The Flanders Interaction Analysis System has been successfully used to improve the behavioral awareness of religion teachers and subsequently to improve their actual pedagogical performance. In one of the rare empirical studies of religion teaching, Raymond Whiteman (1971) found that the use of the Flanders system combined with effective supervisory feedback produced more effective pedagogical behavior patterns both for religion teachers and for teachers of other subject areas. Eugene Hemrick used the Flanders Interaction Analysis System with a broad variety of religion teachers in the Midwest and found that it

---

80. The tenth category is coded Ø when used with computers.

significantly improved their competencies in behavioral analysis, competencies which in turn led to the enhancement of their pedagogical performance.[81]

In addition to the Flanders Interaction Analysis System, other preservice and inservice analytic training procedures have been empirically found to be effective in enhancing teachers' observations of their behavioral processes while they were engaged in the instructional act. These other procedures include Teacher Citation of Observation Variables, B. Othanel Smith's Analysis of the Logic of Teaching, and Content Analysis (Anderson, 1984, pp. 16-48).

Besides interaction analysis, there are other effective procedures which can help the preservice or inservice preschool religious educator improve the analysis of her pedagogical behaviors. However, interaction analysis has proven itself an especially fruitful way for the successful examination of teaching practice.

Enhancing Pedagogical Control. The procedure known as microteaching can be quite useful in helping the preservice and inservice religious educator to significantly enhance her pedagogical behaviors in such a way as to improve teaching effectiveness. Microteaching is a teacher training technique in which an individual practices a specified focused pedagogical skill in an instructional setting where all the normal pedagogical variables are telescoped into one small teaching unit. The teacher teaches a real mini-lesson in which the number of learners, the scope of the subject-matter content, and the time are all reduced. In a microteaching session, for example, the teacher teaches a bite-sized lesson to five learners in a fifteen minute time frame. Microteaching focuses on the accomplishment of a particular pedagogical skill which behavioral analysis or other sources have revealed the preschool religious educator needs to acquire or perfect. Microteaching concentrates on the teacher's here-and-now practice of a specific instructional skill until she has mastered that skill. Such pedagogical skills include reinforcement of learner participation, recognition of attending behaviors, nonverbal teaching behaviors, and so forth.[82]

---

81. Whiteman and Hemrick both received their doctorates in the graduate religious education program at the University of Notre Dame. This was at the time the only university-based graduate religious education program which used the most up-to-date and sophisticated instructional training devices and research to improve the quality of religion teaching. Despite its many successes, it was unilaterally disbanded by the subsequently deposed provost, James Tunstead Burtchaell, for reasons which remain unclear to this day.

82. Microteaching was developed by a Stanford University team of instructional procedurologists including Dwight Allen. His book remains one of the most important volumes on microteaching (Allen and Ryan, 1969).

A major advantage of microteaching is that it enables the religious educator undergoing preservice or inservice training to improve her teaching activity by controlling her instructional skills through practicing and perfecting teaching behaviors. Teaching consists in a wide repertoire of diverse specific instructional skills which the preschool religious educator offers to learners on the basis of what skill will most effectively facilitate the desired learning outcome. The greater number of instructional skills the preschool religious educator has perfected, the more effective will be her teaching activity.

Microteaching as a training device normally consists in a series of nine steps. *First,* a particular pedagogical skill is identified as being needed by the religious educator, or as constituting a necessary skill for the teacher to have in order to facilitate a desired outcome in learners. *Second,* the religious educator is shown videotapes of a master teacher using the specific instructional skill either in a microteaching situation or in a normal instructional setting. This videotape presentation is accompanied by a commentary drawing attention to the specific instances in which the master teacher used the particular pedagogical skill. *Third,* the religious educator plans a short lesson in which she can enact the particular pedagogical skill. *Fourth,* the religious educator teaches the short lesson to a small group of learners in an abbreviated time frame. This microlesson is videotaped. *Fifth,* the videotape of this lesson is replayed to the preschool religious educator. With the help of a supervisor, she analyzes it, using instruments such as interaction analysis. The supervisor makes reinforcing comments about instances in which the religious educator effectively used the particular pedagogical skill. The supervisor also draws attention to other situations in which the particular pedagogical skill was not enacted successfully by the religious educator. *Sixth,* in light of the videotape feedback and the supervisor's comments, the preschool religious educator replans the original mini-lesson in such a way as to deploy the pedagogical skill with greater and more consistent effectiveness. *Seventh,* the religious educator teaches the revised lesson to a different but comparable group of learners. This lesson is videotaped. *Eighth,* the videotape of the "reteach" lesson is replayed and analyzed with the help of the supervisor. *Ninth,* the "teach-reteach" cycle is repeated as often as necessary for the religious educator to master the particular pedagogical skill.

Microteaching can be approached from a wide variety of vantage points such as job-and-task activities. From this vantage point, the teaching skill to be learned is broken down even further into the many highly specific behaviors (steps) which go to make up a particular teaching skill. Each of these component skills are then practiced in such a way that they contribute to a harmonious enactment of the particular teaching skill (Merrill, 1987, pp. 141-173).

Microteaching has been successfully used to improve the behavioral control of teachers in preservice and inservice contexts (Allen & Ryan, 1969, pp. iii-viii). Also of interest is a research study which found that teachers in preservice training were generally pleased with microteaching because they found it helpful to them (McIntyre & Duthie, 1977, pp. 23-32). Microteaching experiences tend to be translated directly into subsequent real-life instructional situations and can serve as an engine for ongoing professional improvement. Thus, one study found that through microteaching activities teachers can be taught to become personally committed to changing their pedagogical behavior and to actually implement what they learned from their microteaching experience into their regular teaching situations (Devlin-Sherer, 1985, pp. 31-37).

Besides microteaching, there are other effective procedures which can help the preservice or inservice preschool religious educator improve the control over her pedagogical behaviors. However, microteaching has proven itself an especially fruitful way to enhance pedagogical skills.

Practicum. It should come as no surprise to preschool religious educators that the relevant empirical research suggests that broader teaching processes and specific teaching procedures do indeed make a significant difference with respect to facilitating learning outcomes (Weil & Murphy, 1982, pp. 912-913). Both the empirical research and experience in university-based teacher-training programs have revealed that the actual interface in a practical performance situation of theory, behavioral analysis, and behavioral control constitutes a necessary feature of genuine instructional improvement. Theory explains and predicts instructional performance but is itself not instructional performance. Behavioral analysis improves awareness of instructional performance but in itself does not directly improve that performance. Behavioral control without theory and without behavioral analysis is blind and will likely never be channeled into targeted or optimum performance (Brown, 1975, pp. 7-10). In order to significantly and optimally improve teaching practice, it is necessary to create an *integrated performance structure* in which theory, behavioral analysis, and behavioral control can be brought together in a situation in which the religious educator has to actually perform teaching activities in a preservice and inservice context. This integrated performance structure is called a practicum.

A practicum is a laboratory situation in which pedagogical theory and pedagogical practice are fused into a series of continuous, integrated, practical instructional tasks which are performed, clinically analyzed, related to pedagogical theory, and then performed again until mastery is achieved. A practicum is a purposively and deliberatively contrived experience which enables the teacher to perceive, experience, and control the antecedent-consequent links of her instructional behavior. A practicum revolves around the theory, behavioral analysis, behavioral control cycle, and recycling indicated in the previous paragraph. A practicum is generally located in a social laboratory setting in which all the instructional variables can be arranged and structured with optimum ease.

In the typical practicum situation, the following sequential steps typically occur: 1) identification of the pedagogical process or procedure to be performed; 2) examination of teaching theory in general and aspects of this theory which apply to the practice situation at hand; 3) establishment of the practice situation; 4) specification into interrelated parts of the pedagogical behavior to be practiced; 5) examination of videotapes in which a master teacher is using the designated pedagogical skill, accompanied by a commentary from an expert instructional proceduro-logist as to the specific instances in which the master teacher uses the designated pedagogical behavior; 6) planning and subsequent performance of the designated pedagogical behavior in a microteaching or other kinds of instructional settings; 7) feedback about the performance by videotape using various kinds of behavioral analysis and also by bringing teaching theory to bear upon the performance; 8) modification and correction of the performance in the light of either behavioral analysis in microteaching or other kinds of behavioral control situations; 9) repetition of appropriate portions of this whole cycle until mastery of the desired pedagogical skill is achieved.

To encourage the preschool religious educator to enroll, persevere, and succeed in a preservice or inservice practicum, there should be built into the system a meaningful consequence for the attainment of the pedagogical skill performed in the practicum situation. Participation as well as success in the practicum is very frequently contingent upon how much the practicum experience matters to the religious educator—that it matters in a way that fits into her personal and professional value system (Mager & Pipe, 1970, pp. 71-77).

Teacher Performance Center. The teacher performance center is a concrete pedagogical laboratory in which 1) any aspect of pedagogical behavior can be recorded and analyzed through the use of currently available devices, and 2) the teacher can sharpen the control of this instructional behavior. The teacher performance center refers to the concrete setting in which the practicum or any other kind of systematic scientifically based improvement of pedagogical skills occurs. In a teacher performance center, the religious educator can at any time use

any available videotape or any analytical instruments to clinically examine her pedagogical skills and work on their improvement. She can
do this alone or with the help of an accomplished instructional procedurologist if she so desires.

It is safe to say that establishing and maintaining a well-equipped
teacher performance center probably represents the most effective single
concrete provision which a parish, diocese, or other kind of ecclesiastical
jurisdiction can make to enhance the quality of religious instruction in
the locality under its auspices. If at all possible, each parish should
establish its own teacher performance center. If this is not possible, then
several adjoining parishes should combine efforts and establish an interparish teacher performance center. With the healthy ecumenical movement in place, such interparish teacher performance centers need not to
be among parishes of the same denomination but be interdenomina-
tional as well.

Media in Teaching

The use of media in preschool religious instruction is extremely important for three reasons. First, religion is essentially communication,
and media constitute an extremely powerful way of effective and long-
lasting communication (Sarno, 1987).[83] Second, all during their preschool days, young children are exposed to an enormous amount of
media exposure, exposure which exerts a significant degree of influence
on the young child culturally, morally, and religiously (Christenson,
1983, pp. 242-259; 1986, pp. 463-479). Third, media alter the structure
and the substance of persons and institutions. Just as Gutenberg's print
media fundamentally transformed the consciousness of individuals and
societies into a linear and intellectual and reflective way of dealing with
reality, the contemporary electronic media are fundamentally transforming the consciousness of individuals and societies into a lateral and
sensate and rapid-fire way of dealing with reality.

All media, print and nonprint alike, basically change both religion
and the way we teach religion.

As used in both general society and in religious instruction, media is a
term which refers to all forms or channels of communication other than
direct nonmediated human verbal or nonverbal communication. Media
are mediated forms of communication; human communication takes
place not directly face-to-face but through some indirect entity or medium.

Media are generally classified as print and nonprint. Print media

---

83. This is an extremely important book.

include books, newspapers, cartoons, and so forth. Examples of electronic media include motion pictures, television, computer games, radio, audio recordings, simulations, models, still photographs, and all sorts of teacher-made nonprint materials.

The early childhood teacher's macrotheory of religious instruction will determine the extent to which she makes media an organic part of her lesson. The preschool teacher who consciously or unconsciously adheres to the theological macrotheory of religious instruction will typically use media in an ancillary capacity, as nothing more than just another procedure to get across the real message she is endeavoring to convey. In this approach, media are always outside the real content of the lesson, namely theology. At best, media constitute a way of putting the content across to the learners. In sharp contrast, the preschool teacher who adheres to the social-science macrotheory of religious instruction will typically use media as an important structural content in its own right. In this approach, media are not outside content but *are* content. The medium itself is the message (McLuhan, 1964, pp. 7-21). Thus, media are not extrinsic or ancillary to the message but are an integral and inextricable part of the message. As structural content, media combine with substantive content to produce that kind of actual religious learning which is distinctly different from substantive content in and of itself (Lee, 1982a, pp. 165-174). Consequently, if a particular substantive content is conjoined to a structural content consisting of a cool medium such as a cartoon, the taught/learned message will be significantly different from the same substantive content conjoined to a structural content comprising a hot medium such as a photograph (McLuhan, 1964, pp. 22-32). Furthermore, media teaches learners a certain form of consciousness. This consciousness is an organic part of the way learners construe and interact with reality. Hence, media are in no way outside or even ancillary to religious instruction content, but are an integral part of this content.[84]

There are two principal ways in which the preschool religious educator works with media to significantly enhance her instructional effectiveness. The first of these is teaching in media while the second is teaching media.

Teaching in media refers to the use of media as the structural content of teaching. The phrase "teaching in media" is preferable to words like

---

84. For a superb examination of the great differential effects which the theological macrotheory of religious instruction and the social-science approach to religious instruction have upon the organicity of media use in religion teaching, see Sarno, 1987, pp. 3-40, 84-166.

"teaching by media" because the former connotes the fact that media is structural content while the latter suggests an ancillary role for media in the instructional act.

The available empirical research indicates that there is no one universal best medium, no super medium, for teaching (Schramm, 1977, pp. 25-63). The medium which the early childhood religious educator chooses should be based on its pedagogical approriateness to each of the four molar variables involved in every teaching act. For example, the nature of the subject matter-content will help determine which medium should be used. A subject matter which has affective content as its context and outcome will necessarily require encasement in a different medium than subject matters whose context and outcomes are psychomotor or cognitive or lifestyle (Gerlach, Ely, & Melnick, 1980, pp. 96-172).

Media have proven very effective in lessons which combine religious instruction and worship and in lessons which bring to salience the religious instruction co-nature of liturgy. Thus, W. A. Engstrom (1973, p. 8) notes that the environment of worship can be effectively changed by altering the patterns of sight and sound.

While most preschool religious educators tend to regard media as electronic and complicated, in actuality a great many media are simple. Teacher-made audiovisual materials are often extremely effective precisely because they are simple, immediate, and familiar. And not all electronic media are complicated.[85] The preschool religious educator can exert a significant instructional impact upon young children by using easy but effective electronic media such as taking still photographs or videorecordings of the children playing, praying, and so forth (Kemp, 1980, pp. 77-117, 262-273).

The second major way in which the early childhood religious educator can work with media to significantly enhance her instructional effectiveness is to teach media. Teaching media is a term which means that the educator is teaching the learner how to properly understand and appreciate media, as well as how to interact with and relate to media. Ronald Sarno, the nation's foremost authority on media in religious instruction, states that it is imperative for every person in the modern world to develop media-literacy. Thus, Sarno (1987, p. 235) writes: "Media-literacy is a skill by which one recognizes how one is being directly or indirectly influenced to think, act, or feel in a determined

---

85. For a simple book giving ways to use various electronic and nonelectronic media in religious instruction, see Getz, 1972, pp. 16-22.

way. Media-literacy includes the ability to accept or reject this media-effect in the light of a Judeo-Christian value system which transcends socio-media co-determinism." Though preschoolers, especially the younger among them, cannot develop a refined sense of media-literacy because of their very young age, nonetheless the early childhood religious educator can help little children to begin to separate media reality from the wilder sort of media fantasy, and to be able to discriminate, if only a very little bit, from among the substantive contents in the media message, such as violence in video animated cartoons, love in video Bible stories, and the like.

THE PRESCHOOL RELIGIOUS EDUCATOR AS COUNSELOR

Because she is a teacher, the preschool religious educator is also a counselor. There are two basic reasons underlying this fact. First, counseling is a form of education (Lee, 1971, p. 8). In some ways, counseling is a more personal educational activity than teaching because counseling deals almost exclusively with the self-actualization of the learner as a person whereas teaching deals both with the self-actualization of the learner as a person and with equipping the learner for tasks which are not as manifestly connected to his personal self-actualization. Second, the fulsome discharge of her instructional duties almost necessarily requires the teacher to engage in some kind of counseling with the learner inside or outside the classroom setting.

The importance of the teacher's role as counselor was clearly recognized in the 1950s when educational leaders proposed that the educator's title be not simply teacher but rather teacher-counselor. Many leaders in general education of that era urged teachers to take at least one preservice or inservice course in counseling so that they could fulfill their total educational function with heightened effectiveness. When a more highly and a more tightly cognitive emphasis began to wash over the nation's schools—and preschools as well—beginning with the mid-1970s, the professional idea of the teacher-counselor was shelved. Though educational leaders might have shelved the ideal of the teacher-counselor, nonetheless many teachers, especially the conscientious teachers, have kept the ideal alive in their own educational work. To be sure, it is difficult to imagine how any teacher, and especially any religious educator, can be genuinely effective if she does not engage in a significant amount of guidance and counseling with learners (and with their parents).

Importance of Guidance and Counseling
in Preschool Religious Education

Guidance and counseling are important not just in religious instruction for persons over six years of age. These two educational services are also singularly important in preschool religious education as well. It is almost impossible to think of a full-fledged preschool religious education program in which the teacher is not engaged in guidance and counseling with the learners under her care.

It is a fallacy of major proportions to claim that young children do not have problems and/or developmental concerns because they are so young. Some persons have big problems, and many more individuals have little problems—but all persons (including young children) have developmental concerns. In the latter connection, it should be noted that neither guidance nor counseling is exclusively or even primarily disease-oriented; these two educational services deal not only with problems but with developmental concerns such as establishing one's own personal identity, becoming progressively independent of parents, acquiring a sense of trust and confidence, and so forth. Furthermore, when dealing with a person's problems, guidance and counseling try to establish an environment in which these problems will not occur rather than just treat the problem after it has arisen.

It is axiomatic in psychotherapeutic practice and literature that the root of many adult psychoses, neuroses, major problems, and persistent developmental concerns of consequence stem directly or indirectly from the conditions of early childhood rearing, early childhood schooling, and early childhood experience which the infant and young child had from birth to six years of age.

There are certain problems and developmental concerns which are common to most young children, such as loneliness and anxiety. Over and over again the empirical research has shown that virtually all young children experience loneliness from infancy onward.[86] Young children almost universally experience loneliness when they first attend preschool. Deprived of their parents, siblings, and close neighborhood playmates, young children in the first months of preschool feel alone, and terribly alone at that. This loneliness breeds unhappiness and shyness. Another almost universal developmental difficulty for young children is anxiety. Like loneliness, much of the anxiety in young children stems from being separated from parental care and familiar surroundings. Separation anxiety and the first few months of preschool education go

---

86. For a fine summary of the pertinent empirical research on this point, see Natale, 1986, pp. 47-70.

hand-in-hand, especially in day care and the first year of nursery school. As one social scientist (Herbert, 1975, p. 133) has written, during the preschool class day, there is no appeal to the mother's special protection and loving comfort; the mantle of authority, nurturance, and affective sustenance has been handed over to strangers.

Developmental difficulties and full-fledged problems are especially prevalent in certain types of children attending preschool programs. Notable in this connection are young children from single-parent homes in which the parent is either divorced or never-married, from some kinds of step-families, and from homes in which the children are not accorded supreme or very high value. An example of the latter are certain types of "yuppie" households in which both parents are employed outside the home and have little time or high priority for their children. There are empirical research data which indicate that mothers in these categories often have guilt feelings about sending their young offspring to day care institutions or to early nursery schools. These data hold true regardless of the socioeconomic status of the parents or the necessity/non-necessity of sending their children to preschool programs. These research findings jibe with psychoanalytic theory and evidence on the deleterious effect of mother-absence in young children (Richardson & Johnson, 1984, pp. 842-844).[87] Such mothers then consciously or unconsciously transfer their guilt feelings in one way or another to their young children, thus causing psychological problems in the preschooler.

Regardless of whether the developmental difficulties and/or problems which the young child faces are run-of-the-mill, such as establishing autonomy or coping with loneliness, or more acute, such as severe aggressiveness and lack of emotional attachment due to feeling rejected by his parents whom he perceives as shipping him off to day care or early nursery school, the preschool religious educator must deal with the difficulties and problems of the children under her care. To effectively deal with children's problems and concerns, the preschool religious educator must not only teach well but counsel well.

---

87. While many feminists such as Richardson and Johnson maintain that guilt feelings of this kind stem from what they believe to be an outmoded philosophy which holds that the parent rather than society is the primary and natural child care-giver, nonetheless almost all mothers whether feminist or not seem to harbor such guilt feelings, even though the feminist mothers believe that they ought not to entertain these feelings. What must concern the preschool religious educator as counselor is not so much the philosophy or even the ideology of the mother but rather the fact that the mother is indeed experiencing guilt feelings in sending her offspring to day care or to nursery school.

Some Procedures for Effective Guidance and Counseling
of Preschool Children

Of the many successful procedures for effective guidance and counseling of preschool children, the following twelve are especially worthy
of mention.

First, *know each student as a person.* Effective guidance and counseling cannot operate out of an ignorance of the needs and developmental
pattern unique to each preschool child. The early childhood religious
educator should speak to the learner's parents and former preschool
teachers (if any) to learn more about the young child. The preschool
religious educator who has some background in counseling and psychology might wish to give the young child some projective activities, such
as a fantasy exercise to act out or even draw. These fantasy exercises
often reveal much about the young child's present psychological pattern,
a pattern which otherwise might not manifest itself (Ferreira, 1973, pp.
96-115). Even the psychologically untrained preschool religious educator can come to know a great deal about the child as a person by
watching him at play. Young children reveal much of their real selves in
play. After all, play is one of the very few authentic metiers of the young
child. Thus, Erik Erikson (1963, p. 209) can write that play constitutes
the royal road to the understanding of the infantile ego's efforts of
synthesis. Another depth psychologist, Haim Ginott (1961, p. 51) states
that "the child's play is his talk and the toys are his words." The preschool religious educator would do well to structure the playroom or
play area in such a way that, among other things, it encourages the free
expression and revelation of the young child's personality.

Second, *understand each learner.* Understanding is different from
knowledge in that knowledge can be gained indirectly by studying or
observation while understanding can be gained only through personal
experience (Aquinas, II-II,q8,a.b; q45, a.2). Therefore, understanding is
a higher order of cognition than is knowledge (Aquinas, II-II, q68, a.4;
John of St. Thomas, 1951, pp. 97-98). Consequently, virtually every
psychologist, every teacher, and every person-in-the-street avers that it is
more important to understand a person than simply know that individual. The preschool religious educator is an adult and, therefore, is
unable to experience the young child's world as the young child existentially experiences it. But what the teacher can do is to experience the
young child's world vicariously, especially through empathy.[88] The pre-

---

88. Empathy refers to the process in which a person imaginatively projects self
    into the concrete existential self of another so that the empathizer as far as
    possible experiences psychologically the world as the other individual ex-

school religious educator would do well to develop and then enhance her empathic skills so that she can more fully and deeply understand the young child.

Third, *accept each young child completely* as a person. In counseling language, this means to have unconditional positive regard for each learner as a person (Rogers, 1942, pp. 126-128). The preschool religious educator should verbally and nonverbally communicate to the child that though she condemns and even at times punishes those behaviors of the child which are morally or socially unacceptable, nonetheless, she does not condemn the child as a person and still values him unconditionally. It is not only good guidance practice, but also good Christian practice, to condemn the wrong but love the wrongdoer.

Fourth, *establish and maintain a personal relationship* with the young child. There is a large sense in which all significant guidance, like all significant teaching, is a matter of the educator and the learner being in a personal relationship (Rogers, 1969, pp. 221-237). Every educator should treat the learner as an end and not as a means. To use Martin Buber's term, the teacher should treat the learner as an I (person-to-person relationship) rather than as an it (person-to-object relationship) (Buber, 1958). More than any other age group, young children experience and interpret the world from the primary perspective of the personal relationship they either have or perceive they have with significant others.

Fifth, *care* about the young child. Teacher care is vitally important, not only for those children whose parents do not care or do not care enough for their offsprings, but for all the children in the preschool program. Tellingly, the etymology of the English words care and cure is the same Latin root, *cura.* To care is to play a major role in bringing about a cure for the young child's developmental difficulties and problems. It is not enough, however, that the preschool religious educator care for the young child. She must successfully communicate this caring

---

periences it. In empathy, a person psychologically jumps into the other individual's skin, as it were, while still retaining self-identity. "I experience the world as the other person does" is the way the empathizer might phrase it. Sympathy, on the other hand, refers to the process in which a person shares the experiential world of another individual. In sympathy, a person psychologically participates as fully as possible in the experiences of the other individual but all the while remains external to that individual. "I share the other person's experience of the world alongside the other person and in resonance with the other person" is the way the sympathizer might phrase it. Etymologically, the word empathy comes from the Greek via the Latin, and means to suffer in. The word sympathy is derived from a word originally meaning to suffer with.

to the learner so that he is aware that the teacher is caring not only *for* him but *about* him.

Sixth, *listen* to the young child. From the guidance point of view, listening consists in far more than simply hearing the cognitive content of the young child's verbal utterances. Listening is also being perceptive to what the child is really saying affectively and existentially. This means that the preschool religious educator should listen to the child with "the third ear," as it were (Reik, 1948). To listen perceptively, to listen with the third ear, means that the preschool religious educator has to attend to the child's nonverbal as well as verbal communications. Listening also tends to be therapeutic (promotive of cure or solution) in two ways. It enables the speaker to carthartically release his affects (at least symbolically). And it shows the speaker that someone cares about him enough and values him enough to listen to his concerns and problems (Combs, Avila, & Purkey, 1978, pp. 136-137).

Seventh, *be warm* to each learner. As a teacher-counselor, the preschool religious educator can show warmth to learners in two principal ways. She can exhibit personal warmth through the voice tone she uses, through nonverbal behaviors such as hugging learners and patting them on the back, by being acceptant of them as persons, and so forth. She can also exhibit environmental warmth by creating a warm socioemotional climate in the setting in which learning takes place, a climate which, among other things, will reinforce and expand the personal warmth she shows to each learner.

Eighth, *use a variety of nonverbal behaviors* in dealing with learners and, in turn, be sensitive to the nonverbal behaviors which the learner uses as he communicates to the educator and to other learners (Beaty, 1984, pp. 161-163). The empirical research clearly suggests that nonverbal behavior reveals the affective dimensions of one's personality more fully and more validly than does verbal behavior (Burgoon, 1985, pp. 344-345). Nonverbal behavior is especially important with young children because nonverbal behavior, more than any form of human communication entails self-disclosure and personal communication (Lee, 1985a, pp. 395-397)—two central axes of existence and communication in young children. Facial expression (especially smiles), posture, hand and arm movements, personal space and distance, head nodding—these and other nonverbal behaviors are more primary than speech as modes of significant communication to young children.

Ninth, *encourage the development of self-discipline* which will help the young child learn and develop as a person. The preschool religious educator should come to realize that self-control and self-discipline are not the same. Self-control is power, specifically that kind of power brought about by regulation of one's impulses, needs, desires, and wishes. Discipline, on the other hand is purposeful learning, namely marshaling one's resources to learn something in the finest and fullest manner possible. Self-control is a dimension of discipline, but is not identical to discipline (Lee, 1982b, pp. 208-210). Authentic discipline is necessarily positive because it is the way in which a person purposively learns. If self-discipline is inherently positive by its very nature, then the manner in which the preschool religious educator orchestrates classroom management should likewise be positive. For example, punishment in and of itself does not encourage self-discipline because punishment merely tells the learner to stop his present behavior. To be positive, punishment (when necessary) should always be combined with concrete ways in which the young child can redirect undesirable behavior toward desirable behavior. True discipline is inextricably bound up with guidance and teaching. Guidance helps the young child utilize his needs for productive personal purposes. Teaching helps the young child learn how to harness his abilities and energies to attain a desired outcome (Walsh & Cowles, 1982, pp. 27-50).

Tenth, *provide reassurance and support* to the young child when appropriate. A young child is in the first stages in the lifelong process of becoming a person. Individuals in the early phases of any endeavor need encouragement. Life—its meanings and its feelings, its essence and its tasks—is just beginning to open up to young learners. When the little child is fearful, he can be assured that things will turn out well if he tries hard and places his trust in God. When a little child tried hard but does not succeed, he should be reassured that he is not worthless and should be encouraged to try better and possibly harder. Reassurance and support should be given educationally, that is not indiscriminate but is appropriate to furthering the learner's own growth and development. Lavish, indiscriminate, undeserved, and poorly timed reassurance and support can undercut the highly beneficial results which accrue to encouragement properly given (Kennedy, 1977, pp. 37-38).

Eleventh, *provide relaxation activities and exercises* for the young child. Contemporary industrialized society is a frantic and stressful one, and it is easy for the young child who has not yet built up adequate psychological defenses to be caught up in the frenzy and strain. While most American children are products of this frenzied culture, some little children tend to be more engulfed in stress and strain than others. For example, children of always-on-the-go "yuppie" parents, and children of working single parents often grow up in home environments which are quite stressful. Physical relaxation exercises and nonphysical relaxation activities can often help alleviate the stress and strain with which uptight little children are burdened (Keat, 1974, pp. 67-68).

Twelfth, *be alert to guidance and counseling openings* throughout the preschool day (Lee & Pallone, 1966, pp. 141-142). The day care student who frequently walks around the room with a blanket over his head, the nursery school student who is extremely aggressive, the child in a four-year-old kindergarten class who never participates in group activities, the little girl who never smiles—all these young children have problems or developmental concerns which cry out for guidance attention from the preschool religious educator. For example, during a lesson on dolphins, the guidance-minded teacher can note that maybe dolphins seem to smile frequently because they enjoy what they are doing and are playing happily with the other dolphins. "What are the happy dolphins telling us?" the teacher can inquire, thus opening up an affective-oriented discussion of happiness and peer play. The preschool religious educator who approaches her work with, among other things, a guidance point of view will very likely be the one who most successfully capitalizes on the numerous guidance and counseling openings which manifest themselves throughout the preschool day.

WHAT SHOULD THE PRESCHOOL BE TEACHING?

In 1837 Friedrich Froebel in Germany established the first formal preschool in the modern era. He called this preschool the kindergarten. Unlike the twentieth-century American kindergarten which is part of the school system and which occurs for one full year immediately prior to the first grade, the Froebel-type kindergarten in Germany lasted two or more years and was not part of the school system. The chief purpose of Froebel's kindergarten was not to prepare children for later schooling, but rather to be a place where little children could grow in a natural way, develop holistically as human beings, and expand their contacts and horizons beyond their family confines. Kindergarten for Froebel and his followers meant exactly what the German word denotes, namely, the children's garden.[89]

In many European countries, notably in the German-speaking world, the Froebelian idea of the kindergarten remains more or less intact. Since 1970 in the United States, however, the situation has changed dramatically. After that time, not just kindergartens, but also a great many nursery schools (and indeed in some large northern cities, even day care) have switched from providing socio-emotional development to striving primarily for cognitive academic achievement (Nurss & Hodges, 1982, p. 507). Religiously oriented preschool programs have

---

89. One of the most important books on Froebel remains Bowen, 1882.

not been exempt from this trend towad intellectual academic achievement. Indeed, in some localities, young children wishing to enter a church-related five-year-old kindergarten must take reading and arithmetic tests to ascertain whether these applicants have acquired sufficient academic skills during nursery school to be able to do the harder cognitive academic work demanded in the kindergarten program.

Advocates of the switch in preschool programs from personal/social development to cognitive academic achievement argue that the young child, even as early as two and one-half or three years of age, is intellectually ready to master cognitive academic content and hence should be taught this kind of material. Opponents of this shift in emphasis maintain that cognitive and academic preschool programs prevent children from developing holistically in an optimal manner, are largely responsible for creating undue stress and a blasé attitude in children, and in the end rob children of their most precious gift, namely their childhood.

One of the foremost opponents of the switch in preschool education from personal/social development to cognitive academic achievement is child psychologist David Elkind. In his celebrated book *The Hurried Child* (1981), Elkind argues persuasively that there is enormous pressure on young children, especially in the middle-middle and upper-middle classes, to grow up much too fast. This relentless pressure begins in early childhood and manifests itself in many ways, most notably in the pressure for early cognitive academic attainment (Elkind, 1981, p. 6). Elkind writes that all too often adult society places excessive demands on children to achieve, to succeed, to please. In the final analysis, this undue pressure on young children—academic pressure, social pressure, and so forth—amounts to pressure to leave childhood as soon as possible and grow up. Quoting Elkind, "hurried children grow up too fast, pushed in their early years toward many different types of achievement and are exposed to experiences that tax their adaptive capacities" (p. xii). Contemporary pressures for young children to hurry up and become adults quickly include not only preschool cognitive academic achievement, but also competitive sports beginning in the preschool years, and children's dress (designer clothing, jewelry, and so on). The deleterious results of heavy adult pressure on children to hurry up and become adults include stress (the onset in some cases of peptic ulcers in four-year-old children), crime at an earlier age, and illicit sex at a younger age (pp. 3-22, Elkind, 1986, pp. 634-636). In Elkind's words, the hurried child becomes "all grown up and no place to go" (Elkind, 1981, p. 26).

Elkind states that one of the first venues and principal agents of the hurried child is the preschool program, due in large measure to parental pressure. In Elkind's view, parents try to hurry their children in preschool and elsewhere because of four factors: 1) parents today are more fearful than previously (such as being fearful of increased crime in the streets); 2) parents today are more alone, due to such factors as separation and divorce; 3) parents today are more professionally insecure, brooding over such factors as possible job loss due to technological advances; and 4) parents today are more self-centered. In the last-mentioned area, Elkind (1981, pp. 26-28) states that parents tend to hurry their children because their own stress induces them to place their own needs ahead of the needs of their children.

Combining the views of child psychologists like Elkind with the present writer's professional views gained from visiting preschool programs and from listening to the testimony of a wide variety of preschool teachers in both religious and civil settings, there is strong evidence to suggest that the phenomenon of the hurried child is one which is deleterious to the child, to the parents, to society, and to the church.[90] Children robbed of their childhood are robbed of their most precious possession, a possession which can never be recovered. One can only wonder whether some contemporary parents, especially "yuppie" parents and those parents who gained relatively easy entry into careers which were previously closed to them because of gender and racial considerations, are perhaps very insecure professionally and personally. This insecurity possibly stems from deep-seated doubts about whether they truly attained their jobs on the basis of merit and whether they are sufficiently skilled to keep their easily acquired professional positions in the face of increased competition in the job market. Some parents possibly fear that their child might not "have what it takes" to be successful in later life because they themselves really might not have what it takes. Yet it is axiomatic that no matter how much intense and demanding cognitive academic work the preschool child is exposed to, he will never finish first over the long haul if he lacks the requisite native ability. The young child who possesses great native ability will very likely be the winner over the long haul if he is given stimulus-rich experiences of a holistic nature appropriate to his state as a child rather than high-power, stressful, cognitive academic content in the preschool years.

Play

More than any other curricular process and outcome, the preschool religious education program should be teaching the children to play in

---

90. There is also some evidence that certain academic problems, particularly reading disorders, may at times be attributed to pressure to read or perform advanced cognitive tasks during the preschool years (Moore & Moore, 1979).

the most personalistical manner possible. Play is the activity par excellence in which young children fulfill their childhood. Play is also the activity par excellence in which little children acquire that basic grounding in reality which serves as a major foundation, axis, and engine for the rest of their lives.

Intertwined with the play curriculum should be appropriate levels and emphases on psychomotor content, cognitive content, affective content, and lifestyle content. But these substantive contents ought to be inserted into the overall context of play, and not vice versa. Put differently, the play curriculum should not be regarded or enacted as a prelude to the acquisition of cognitive academic content but rather as the preeminent curriculum material and as the preeminent curriculum goal in its own right. As Johan Huizinga pointed out years ago in his classic book, the element of play constitutes a necessary and permanent dimension of the human person as person. As Huizinga (1970) put it, the human being by virtue of being a human being is not just a social person but is also a playing person *(homo ludens)*.

Barbara Biber, a seasoned psychologist-educator of young children, argues on the basis of much empirical research as well as from her own professional experience with young children that play is essentially a holistic growth experience for the little child. Furthermore, "if the young child can have a really full, wholesome experience with play, he will be having the most wholesome kind of fun a child can have. For a child to have fun is basic to his future happiness. His early childhood play may become the basic substance out of which he lays down one of his life patterns, namely, that one cannot only have fun but can create fun. Most of us adults enjoy only watered-down fun—going to the movies, shopping, listening to a concert. It is the second-handedness of fun, often occasioned by the lack of direct and fully experiential play, which might well account for many adults feeling basically insecure" (Biber, 1984, p. 189).

It is a small wonder, then, that a key element in Froebel's vision and reality of the kindergarten was play. Froebel viewed play "not merely as recreation, but as the most important phase in the spontaneous development of the child, because it allows him to exercise harmoniously all his physical, emotional, and intellectual qualities" (Downs, 1978, p. 46). It is also helpful for the preschool religious educator to recall that for Froebel, the kindergarten had a spiritual objective as well—an objective ideally suited to play.

The positive correlation of play with intellectual development is especially worth underscoring in the contemporary American mentality in which many middle-middle and upper-middle class parents are pressuring preschoolers to substitute heavy doses of cognitive academic content for the traditional play curriculum. It must be emphasized that play in and of itself promotes cognitive growth. Thus, a review of the relevant empirical research on play in young children reveals that there is a definite positive correlation between language development and play. Play can and often does stimulate young children to develop innovative verbal language, to clarify new words and concepts, to increase language use and practice, to gain metalinguistic awareness, and to think verbally (Levy, 1984, pp. 49-61).

Nor is play devoid of cognitive content. It is the task of the preschool religious educator to heighten and bring into sharper focus the cognitive content inherently present in play. It is also the task of the preschool religious educator to introduce into play those cognitive contents, including religious cognitive contents, which are amenable to insertion into the play context at a level appropriate to the young child's present developmental state. Thus, the holistic preschool curriculum is not a matter of either/or, namely, either play or cognitive content. Rather, the holistic preschool curriculum is a matter of cognitive content being inserted, as appropriate, into the play dynamic according to the mode of that dynamic.

Lest the preschool religious educator (or the parent of the young child) think that emphasizing play in the early childhood program will lead to an unduly soft or "Mickey Mouse" cognitive curriculum, it is well to remember that the empirical research suggests that all the special cognitive gains made by young children as a result of intense cognitive academic curriculum in preschool or elsewhere usually disappear by the third or fourth grade. This research finding holds true for children spanning the entire spectrum of parental income level from rich to poor.[91] (And besides, Mickey Mouse was created for children and probably has been a more significant influence on children over both the immediate and the long term than have high-powered intense preschool curricula stressing the acquisition of cognitive academic content.)

CONCLUSION

Christianity is first and foremost a lifestyle, a concrete pattern of actual here-and-now living. It is not an abstract set of cognitive doctrinal propositions, however lofty these propositions might seem. Hence, Christianity at any level cannot be taught primarily as a set of cognitive doctrinal propositions. In the case of young children, this point should

---

91. See, for example, Stallings and Stipek, 1986, p. 728.

be palpably obvious. Little children do not learn and indeed cannot truly learn cognitive doctrinal propositions. Young children can only truly learn lifestyle, love, and attitudes, together with very small bits of minimal cognitive content relevant to here-and-now lifestyle, love, and attitudes. When the preschool religious educator attempts to teach little children primarily at the cognitive and academic level, these educators are actually diluting and reducing the authentic religious content of the lesson.

The context or situation for learning in the preschool religious education program should be decidedly and unabashedly Christian. This does not mean that the curriculum is insular, narrowly parochial, or fundamentalist (in the generic and negative sense of that term). Rather, a deeply Christian curriculum necessarily is one in which the added Christian dimension permeates and adds on to that which is taught in the finest holistic preschool programs available in general education. For example, in a Christian learning context, the preschool religious educator ought to accord heightened attention to such Christian concerns as love, redemption, forgiveness, suffering, compassion, purpose in life, and so forth (Fritz, 1964, pp. 24-26).

Christianity is a religion of solitariness and socialness. Christianity is a solitary religion in that the person often meets God most deeply and most existentially in the solitariness of one's own existence. But this solitariness takes place in the broader context of socialness or corporateness. Sometimes this corporateness is remote, at other times it is immediate—but it is always there. This socialness or corporateness is what we call the church, the ecclesia, the body of Christ. Hence, the preschool religious educator who wishes to teach authentic Christianity should teach in such a way that the solitariness and the corporateness, which impinge in one way or another on the young child's religious life, are developed and made salient. One extremely effective way of doing this is to bond the class into an existential Christian community. When the young children in the class become a flesh-and-blood community united with themselves, with the community of saints past and present, and with Jesus, then the preschool religious educator has taught the learners one of the most valuable lifestyle contents of all. As John Westerhoff, the tractarian, remarks, Christian liturgies of initiation all stress the corporateness and communal character of the Christian religion because that into which the person is being initiated is essentially a corporate entity, namely, the body of Christ (Westerhoff & Willimon, 1980, p. 13). The view of Westerhoff, a liberal Protestant religious educationist, is shared by Mary LeBar (1964, p. 138), an evangelical Protestant religious education specialist who writes that real community or belonging lies at the very heart of *koinonia* of the new testament church. From the Eastern Orthodox perspective, Sophie Koulomzin states that the experience of being part of a body belongs to the essence of religious growth, just like the interaction of the arm with the body is necessary for the physical growth of the arm. A young child deprived of the experience of belonging to a close organic family unit is tremendously disadvantaged. Thus, the most effective pedagogical procedures in a preschool religious education program are those which provide activities in which children can be together as a group, can play together, and work together on learning tasks as appropriate. This community context stimulates both individual creativity and a sense of belonging. The finest religious preschool program is one which is an integral part of the community or parish, and which joins parents and teachers and children in a close relationship. Liturgical worship in the church is most authentically liturgical when it is an experience of gathering together as a whole church, of praying together, of singing together, and of doing things together (Koulomzin, 1975, pp. 23-24). Perhaps more than any other group, Catholics have classically placed the most stress on the church as community and hence, by implication, on the church-related school as a religious community. Most Catholic religious educationists and educators are insistent that any restructuring and rebuilding of religious education necessarily involves a restructuring and rebuilding of community in the classroom (Piveteau & Dillon, 1977, pp. 161-163) and indeed at the ecclesiastical level (Moran, 1974).

The effective and authentic early childhood religious educator is one who teaches competently and who, in the course of her teaching, builds up the body of Christ in the learners—the body of Christ as incarnated in each learner, and the body of Christ as the living corporate legacy which Jesus gave us all as the church.

REFERENCES

Allen, D., & Ryan, K. (1969). *Microteaching*. Reading, MA: Addison-Wesley.

Anderson, S. L. (1984). Teacher training techniques from four observational perspectives. *Journal of Classroom Interaction, 20*,16-28.

Aquinas, T. (1982). *Summa theologica*. II-II, q.8, a.6; q.45, a.2; q.68, a.4.

Aries, P. (1962). *Centuries of childhood* (R. Baldick, Trans.). New York: Vintage.

Armstrong, A. O. (1971). Christian mysticism in the classroom? In G. Devine (Ed.), *New dimensions in religious experience*. Staten Island, NY: Alba.

Aspy, D. N. (1969). The effect of teacher inferred self-concept upon student achievement. Paper presented at the annual convention of the American Educational Research Association.

Barber, L. W. (1978). *Celebrating the second year of life*. Birmingham, AL: Religious Education Press.

Barber, L. W. (1981). *The religious education of preschool children.* Birmingham, AL: Religious Education Press.

Barber, L. W. (1984). *Teaching Christian values.* Birmingham, AL: Religious Education Press.

Beaty, J. J. (1984). *Skills for preschool teachers* (2nd ed.). Boston: Allyn & Bacon.

Beechick, R. (1979). *Teaching preschoolers.* Denver, CO: Accent.

Benson, W. (1988). Seeking a biblical base: An Evangelical Protestant perspective. In M. Mayr (Ed.), *Does the church really want religious education?.* Birmingham, Al: Religious Education Press.

Biber, B. (1984). *Early education and psychological development.* New Haven, CT: Yale University Press.

Bickimer, D. A. (1983). *Christ the placenta.* Birmingham, AL: Religious Education Press.

Bills, R. E. (1981). *Self-concept and schooling.* West Lafayette, IN: Kappa Delta Pi.

Bowen, H. C. (1882). *Froebel and education through self-activity.* New York: Scribner's.

Bowman, L. E. (1986). Analysis and assessment. The general Protestant Sunday school. In D. C. Wyckoff (Ed.), *Renewing the Sunday school and the CCD.* Birmingham, AL: Religious Education Press.

Brophy, J. E., Good, T. L., & Needler, S. E. (1975). *Teaching in preschool.* New York: Harper and Row.

Brown, G. (1975). *Microteaching.* London: Methuen.

Brusselmans, C., & Wakin, E. (1977). *Religion for little children.* Huntington, IN: Our Sunday Visitor.

Buber, M. (1958). *I and Thou* (2nd ed., R. G. Smith, Trans.). New York: Scribner's.

Burgess, H. W. (1983). In quest for the connection: Toward a synapse of theory and practice. In M. Mayr (Ed.), *Modern masters of religious education.* Birmingham, AL: Religious Education Press.

Burgoon, J. K. (1985). Nonverbal signals. In M. L. Knapp & G. R. Miller (Eds.), *Handbook of interpersonal communication.* Beverly Hills, CA: Sage.

Bushnell, H. (1916). *Christian nurture.* New Haven, CT: Yale University Press.

Caputi, N. (1984). *Guide to the unconscious.* Birmingham, AL: Religious Education Press.

Carkhuff, R. R. et al. (1981). *The skilled teacher: A systems approach to teaching skills.* Amherst, MA: Human Resource Development Press.

Cartwright, C. A., & Peters, D. L. (1982). Early childhood development. In H. E. Mitzell (Ed.), *Encyclopedia of educational research* (5th ed., Vol. 1). New York: Free Press.

Chaplin, D. P. (1948). *Children and religion.* New York: Scribner's.

Christenson, P. G. (1983). How children read television. In M. S. Mander (Ed.), *Communications in transition.* New York: Praeger.

Christenson, P. G. (1986). Children's perceptions of moral themes in television drama. In M. L. McLaughlin (Ed.), *Communication yearbook* (Vol. 9). Beverly Hills, CA: Sage.

Clark-Stewart, K. A. [with N. Apfel] (1978). Evaluating parental effects on child development. In L. S. Shulman (Ed.), *Review of research in education* (Vol. 6). Itasca, IL: Peacock.

Coe, G. A. (1929). *What Is Christian education?*. New York: Scribner's.

Combs, A. W., Avila, D. L., & Purkey, W. W. (1978). *Helping relationships* (2nd ed.). Boston: Allyn & Bacon.

Coopersmith, S. (1967). *The antecedent of self-esteem*. San Francisco, CA: Freeman.

Cully, I. V. (1965). *Ways to teach children*. Philadelphia: Fortress.

Cully, I. V. (1979). *Christian child development*. San Francisco, CA: Harper & Row.

Darcy-Berube, F. (1978). The challenge ahead of us. In P. O'Hare (Ed.), *Foundations of religious education*. New York: Paulist.

Devlin-Sherer, R. [et al.] (1985). The effects of developing teacher commitment to behavioral change. *Journal of Classroom Instruction, 21,* 31-37.

Dodrill, C. B. (1976). Brain functions of Christians and non-Christians. *Journal of Psychology and Christianity, 4,* 280-285.

Downs, R. D. (1978). *Friedrich Froebel*. Boston: Twayne.

Doyle, W. (1977). The use of nonverbal behaviors: Toward an ecological model of classrooms. *Merrill-Palmer Quarterly, 23,* 179, 192.

Doyle, W. (1979). Making managerial decisions in classrooms. In National society for the study of education: *Classroom management* (78th ed., part 2). Chicago: University of Chicago Press.

Elkind, D. (1964). The child's conception of his religious identity. *Lumen Vitae, 19,* 635-646.

Elkind, D. (1981). *The hurried child*. Reading, MA: Addison-Wesley.

Elkind, D. (1986). Formal education and early childhood education: An essential difference. In *Kappan, 67, 694.*

Engstrom, W. A. (1973). *Multi-media in the church*. Richmond, VA: Knox.

Erikson, E. H. (1963). *Childhood and society*. New York: Norton.

Erikson, F. (1979). Talking down: Some cultural sources of miscommunication in interracial interviews. In A. Wolfgang (Ed.), *Nonverbal behavior: Applications and cultural implications*. New York: Academic Press.

Fahs, S. L. (1952). *Today's children and yesterday's heritage*. Boston: Beacon.

Felker, D. W. (1974). *Building positive self-concepts*. Minneapolis, MN: Burgess.

Ferreira, L. (1973). Dance: An adjunct to group counseling. In M. M. Ohlsen (Ed.), *Counseling children in groups*. New York: Holt, Rinehart & Winston.

Flanders, N. A. (1966). *Interaction analysis in the classroom: A manual for observers* (rev. ed.). Ann Arbor, MI: School of Education, University of Michigan.

Frankl, V. (1975). *The unconscious God*. New York: Simon and Schuster.

Freud, S. (1953). *The interpretation of dreams* (J. Strachey, Trans.). New York: Avond Discus.

Frey, K. S., & Ruble, D. N. (1985). What children say when the teacher is not around: Conflicting goals in social comparison and performance assessment in the classroom. *Journal of Personality and Social Psychology, 48,* 550-562.

Fritz, D. B. (1964). *Christian teaching of kindergarten children*. Richmond, VA: CLC Press.

Furnish, D. J. et al. (1979). *Living the Bible with children*. Nashville, TN: Abingdon.

Gage, N. L. (1978). *The scientific base of the art of teaching*. New York: Teachers College Press.

Gerlach, V. S., Ely, D. P., & Melnick, R. (1980). *Teaching and media* (2nd ed.). Englewood Cliffs, NJ: Prentice Hall.

Getz, G. A. (1972). *Audio-visual media in Christian education.* Chicago: Moody.

Ginott, H. G. (1961). *Group psychotherapy with children.* New York: McGraw-Hill.

Godin, A. (1985). *The psychological dynamics of religious experience* (M. Turton, Trans.). Birmingham, AL: Religious Education Press.

Goldbrunner, J. (1961). Catechetical method as handmaid of kerygma. In J. Hofinger (Ed.), *Teaching all nations* (Revised, C. Howell, partly Trans.). Freiburg-im-Bresgau, Deutschland: Herder.

Goldman, R. (1964). *Religious thinking from childhood to adolescence.* London: Routledge & Kegan Paul.

Gooding, C. T. (1969). The perceptual organization of effective teachers. In A. W. Combs (Ed.), *Florida studies in the helping professions.* Gainesville, FL: University of Florida Press.

Green, D., & Lepper, M. R. (1974). How to turn play into work. *Psychology Today,* Sept., 49-54.

Griffin, E. F. (1982). *Island of childhood.* New York: Teachers College Press.

Groome, T. H. (1980). *Christian religious education.* San Francisco, CA: Harper & Row.

Haas, J. E. (1976). Some myths about children's liturgies. In S. M. O'Fahey & M. P. Ryan (Eds.), *The Pace reader.* Winona, MN: St. Mary's College Press.

Hall, E., Lamb, M., & Perlmutter, M. (1986). *Child psychology today* (2nd. ed.). New York: Random House.

Harter, S. (1983). Developmental perspectives on the self-system. In P. H. Mussen (Ed.), *Handbook of child psychology* (Vol. 4, 4th ed.). New York: Wiley.

Heckman, P. (1987). Understanding school culture. In National Society for the Study of Education, *The ecology of school renewal* (86th yearbook, part 1). Chicago: University of Chicago Press.

Hemrick, E. F. (1983). Visions and realities. In M. Mayr (Ed.), *Modern masters of religious education.* Birmingham, AL: Religious Education Press.

Herbert, M. (1975). *Problems of children.* London: Pan.

Hess, R. D., & Croft, D. J. (1975). *Teachers of young children.* Boston: Houghton Mifflin.

Hobar, N., & Sullivan, D. K. (1984). Systematic observation of instruction: Genesis, research, practice and potential. *Journal of Classroom Interaction, 19,* 26-34.

Hofinger, J. (1962). *The art of teaching Christian doctrine* (rev. ed.). Notre Dame, IN: University of Notre Dame Press.

Huizinga, J. (1970). *Homo ludens.* Boston: Beacon.

Hyman, R. T. (1968). The emotional climate. In R. T. Hyman (Ed.), *Teaching: Vantage points for study.* Philadelphia: Lippincott.

John of St. Thomas (1951). *The gifts of the Holy Spirit* (D. Hughes, Trans.). New York: Sheed and Ward.

Joyce, B. R., Wald, R., & Weil, M. (1981). Can teachers learn repertoires of models of teaching. In B. R. Joyce, C. C. Brown, & L. Peck (Eds.), *Flexibility in teaching.* New York: Longman.

Jung, C. G. (1954). The development of personality. In C. G. Jung (Ed.), *Collected works* (Vol. 17), (R. F. C. Hull, Trans.). Princeton, NJ: Princeton University Press.

Keat, D. B. (1974). *Fundamentals of child counseling.* Boston: Houghton Mifflin.

Kelsey, M. T. (1968). *Dreams: The dark speech of the spirit.* Garden City, NY: Doubleday.

Kelsey, M. T. (1971). The place of affect in religious education: Psychodynamics of affectivity and emotion. *Lumen Vitae, 26,* 71.

Kelsey, M. T. (1977). *Can Christians be educated?.* Birmingham, AL: Religious Education Press.

Kemp, J. E. (1980). *Planning and producing audiovisual materials* (4th ed.). New York: Harper & Row.

Kennedy, E. (1977). *On becoming a counselor: A basic guide for non-professional counselors.* New York: Crossroad.

Khan, S. B., & Weiss, J. (1973). The teaching of affective responses. In R. M. W. Travers (Ed.), *Second handbook of research on teaching.* Chicago: Rand McNally.

Koulomzin, S. (1975). *Our church and our children.* Crestwood, NJ: St. Vladimir's Seminary Press.

LeBar, M. E. (1964). Teaching preschool children. In J. E. Hakes (Ed.), *An introduction to evangelical Christian education.* Chicago: Moody.

Lee, J. M. (1971). *The shape of religious instruction.* Birmingham, AL: Religious Education Press.

Lee, J. M. (1973). *The flow of religious instruction.* Birmingham, AL: Religious Education Press.

Lee, J. M. (1977). Toward a new era: A blueprint for positive action. In J. M. Lee (Ed.), *The religious education we need.* Birmingham, AL: Religious Education Press.

Lee, J. M. (1982a). The authentic source of religious instruction. In N. H. Thompson (Ed.), *Religious education and theology.* Birmingham, AL: Religious Education Press.

Lee, J. M. (1982b). Discipline in a moral and religious key. In K. Walsh and M. Cowles (Eds.), *Developmental discipline.* Birmingham, AL: Religious Education Press.

Lee, J. M. (1983). Religious education and the Bible: A religious educationist's view. In J. S. Marino (Ed.), *Biblical themes in religious education.* Birmingham, AL: Religious Education Press.

Lee, J. M. (1985a). *The content of religious instruction.* Birmingham, AL: Religious Education Press.

Lee, J. M. (1985b). Lifework spirituality and the religious educator. In J. M. Lee (Ed.), *The spirituality of the religious educator.* Birmingham, AL: Religious Education Press.

Lee, J. M., & Pallone, N. J. (1966). *Guidance and counseling in schools: Foundations and processes.* New York: McGraw-Hill.

Levy, A. K. (1984). The language of play: The role of play in language development: A review of the literature. *Early Child Development and Care, 17,* 49-61.

Linam, G. (1978). The minister of preschool education. In J. T. Sizemore (Ed.), *The ministry of religious education.* Nashville, TN: Broadman.

Lines, T. A. (1987). *Systematic religious education.* Birmingham, AL: Religious Education Press.

Lowell, J. R. On the death of a friend's child.

Lynn, R. W., & Wright, E. (1980). *The big little school* (2nd ed.). Birmingham, AL: Religious Education Press.

Mager, R. F. (1962). *Preparing instructional objectives.* Palo Alto, CA: Fearon.

Mager, R. F., & Pipe, P. (1970). *Analyzing performance problems.* Belmont, CA: Fearon.

Markus, H., & Nurius, P. (1986). Possible selves. *American Psychologist, 41,* 954-969.

Markus, H. & Wurf, E. (1987). The dynamic self-concept: A social psychological perspective. In M. R. Rosenzweig & L. W. Porter (Eds.), *Annual review of psychology* (Vol. 38). Palo Alto, CA: Annual Reviews.

May, R. (1969). *Love and will.* New York: Norton.

McCarthy, M. A., & Houston, J. P. (1980). *Fundamentals of early childhood education.* Cambridge, MA: Winthrop.

McDaniel, E. [with L. O. Richards] (1973). *You and your children.* Chicago: Moody.

McDonald, K. (1980). Components of the self-concept. In T. D. Yawkey (Ed.), *The self-concept of the young child.* Provo, UT: Brigham Young University Press.

McGuire, W. J. (1984). Self for the self: Going beyond self-esteem and the reactive self. In R. A. Zucker, J. Aronoff, & A. I. Radin (Eds.) *Personality and the prediction of behavior.* Orlando, FL: Academic Press.

McIntyre, D., & Duthie, J. (1977). Students' reaction to microteaching. In D. McIntyre, G. MacLeon & R. Griffiths (Eds.), *Investigations of microteaching.* London: Croom Helm.

McKenzie, L. (1982). *The religious education of adults.* Birmingham, AL: Religious Education Press.

McLuhan, M. (1964). *Understanding media.* New York: McGraw-Hill.

Merrill, P. F. (1987). Job and task analysis. In R. M. Gagne (Ed.), *Instructional technology.* Hillsdale, NJ: Erlbaum.

Miller, R. C. (1980). *The theory of Christian education practice.* Birmingham, AL: Religious Education Press.

Moore, R., & Moore, D. (1979). *School can wait.* Provo, UT: Brigham Young University Press.

Moran, G. (1974). *Religious body.* New York: Seabury.

Moran, G. (1982). From obstacle to modest contributor: Theology in religious education. In N. H. Thompson (Ed.), *Religious education and theology.* Birmingham, AL: Religious Education Press.

Myers, D. G. (1986). *Psychology.* New York: Worth.

Natale, S. M. (1986). *Loneliness and spiritual growth.* Birmingham, AL: Religious Education Press.

Neville, G. K. & Westerhoff, J. H. (1978). *Learning through liturgy.* New York: Seabury.

Nurss, J. F., & Hodges, W. L. (1982). Early childhood education. In H. E. Mitzell (Ed.), *Encyclopedia of educational research* (Vol. I, 5th ed.). New York: Free Press.

Paloutzian, R. F. (1983). *Invitation to the psychology of religion.* Glenview, IL: Scott, Foresman.

Piveteau, D. J., & Dillon, J. T. (1977). *Resurgence of religious instruction.* Birmingham, AL: Religious Education Press.

Reik, T. (1948). *Listening with the third ear.* New York: Farrar, Straus & Cudahy.

Richardson, M. S., & Johnson, M. (1984). Counseling women. In S. D. Brown & R. W. Lent (Eds.), *Handbook of counseling psychology.* New York: Wiley.

Ringness, T. A. (1975). *The affective domain in education.* Boston: Little, Brown.

Rogers, C. R. (1942). *Counseling and psychotherapy.* Boston: Houghton Mifflin.

Rogers, C. R. (1951). *Client-centered therapy.* Boston: Houghton Mifflin.

Rogers, C. R. (1969). *Freedom to learn.* Columbus, OH: Merrill.

Samuels, S. C. (1977). *Enhancing self-concept in early childhood.* New York: Human Sciences Press.

Sanner, A. E., & Harper, A. F. (1978). The theological and philosophical bases of Christian education. In A. E. Sanner and A. F. Harper (Eds.), *Exploring Christian education.* Kansas City, MO: Beacon Hill.

Saracho, O. N. (1980). The role of the teacher in enhancing the child's self-concept. In T. D. Yawkey (Ed.), *The self-concept of the young child.* Provo, UT: Brigham Young University Press.

Sarno, R. A. (1987). *Using media in religious education.* Birmingham, AL: Religious Education Press.

Schickendanz, J. A., et al. (1983). *Strategies for teaching young children* (2nd ed.). Englewood Cliffs, NJ: Prentice-Hall.

Schramm, W. (1977). *Big media little media: Tools and technologies for instruction.* Beverly Hills, CA: Sage.

Schickendanz, J. A., et al. (1983). *Strategies for teaching young children* (2nd ed.). Englewood Cliffs, NJ: Prentice-Hall.

Smart, J. D. (1954). *The teaching ministry of the church.* Philadelphia: Westminster.

Spaulding, R. L. (1964). Achievement, creativity and self-concept correlates of teacher-pupil transactions in elementary schools. In C. B. Stendler (Ed.), *Reading in child behavior and development* (2nd ed.). New York: Harcourt, Brace and World.

Stallings, J. A., & Stipek, D. (1986). Research on early childhood and elementary teaching programs. In M. C. Whittrock (Ed.), *Handbook of research on teaching* (3rd ed.). New York: Macmillan.

Terry, J. D. (1978). The theological foundation of religious education. In J. Sisemore (Ed.), *The ministry of religious education.* Nashville, TN: Broadman.

Walsh, K., & Cowles, M. (1982). *Developmental discipline.* Birmingham, AL: Religious Education Press.

Weil, M. L., & Murphy, J. (1982). Instruction process. In H. E. Mitzell (Ed.), *Encyclopedia of educational research* (Vol. II, 5th ed.). New York: Free Press.

Westerhoff, J. H. III. (1980). *Bringing up children in the Christian faith.* Minneapolis, MN: Winston.

Westerhoff, J. H. III. (1981). Framing an alternative future for catechesis. In J. H. Westerhoff & O. C. Edwards (Eds.), *A faithful church.* Wilton, CN: Morehouse-Barlow.

Westerhoff, J. H. III, & Willimon, W. H. (1980). *Liturgy and learning through the life cycle.* New York: Seabury.

Whiteman, R. G. (1971). The differing patterns of behavior as observed in teachers of religion and teachers of mathematics and social studies. Unpublished seminar project, Graduate Program in Religious Education, University of Notre Dame.

Wicklund, R. A., & P. M. Gollwitzer (1982). *Symbolic self-concept.* Hillsdale, NJ: Erlbaum.

Wise, F. F. (1978). Christian education of preschool children. In A. E. Sanner & A. F. Harper (Eds.), *Exploring Christian education.* Kansas City, MO: Beacon Hill.

Wong, T. M. (1984). One brain's response: A reaction to Ashbrook's "Juxtaposing the brain and belief." *Journal of Psychology and Theology, 12,* 208-210.

Wyckoff, D. C. (1961). *Theory and design of Christian education curriculum.* Philadelphia: Westminster.

Yoder, G. (1966). *The church and infants and toddlers.* Elgin, IL.: Brethren Press.

Zajonc, R. B. (1980). Feeling and thinking: Preferences need no inferences. *American Psychologist, 35,* 151-175.

Chapter Eight:

Creativity and Teaching Concepts of God

E. PAUL AND J. PANSY TORRANCE

There are many alternative ways of describing how children learn. While there is much that is useful in the predominant theories of learning for teaching Bible truths, we believe that they are inadequate for this purpose. Most of them have been and still are dominated by mechanistic concepts which assume determinism in human learning. Some of them state that the same laws that govern animal learning also determine human learning. Most of them make the teacher/learner relationship a matter of stimulus and response. Our primary objection to current learning theories is that they rarely consider the infinite God. As we interpret them, these theories are not in harmony with the biblical teachings concerning the nature of man as being creative, made in the image and likeness of God. Being born in the image and likeness of God, as we see it, makes people wonderfully complex. In fact, it gives humans a touch of the infinite in terms of the way they learn and in what they are able to learn. Most learning theories tend to oversimplify the learning process and to deal with mankind in finite ways.

In our opinion, the weight of present evidence (Torrance, 1975) suggests that individuals fundamentally prefer to learn in creative ways. Teachers at all levels of education, both religious and secular, have generally insisted that it is more economical to learn by authority. It seems now that many things, though not all, can be learned more effectively in creative ways rather than by authority. It also appears that some persons have especially strong preferences for learning creatively, learn a great deal if permitted to learn in creative ways, and make little progress when we insist that they learn solely by authority.

It seems rather certain that the needs and abilities underlying creative ways of learning are universal enough to make this powerful way of learning available to all children. This does not, however, exclude other methods, as human nature requires that we have anchors, that we have structure in our environment, and that we have authorities upon whom we can depend for at least a minimum of anchoring. Just as persons differ in the extent to which they prefer to learn creatively, they also differ in the extent to which they require authorities. Although we can observe differences in these preferences in infants, even from birth, these preferences seem to emerge and become stronger or weaker as a result of the way a child's search for the truth is treated by the environment.

Learning by authority and learning in creative ways are not mutually exclusive and may in fact supplement one another. Let us examine how these two processes may operate in the acquisition of beliefs and Bible truths. It is well known that a little child will believe in the existence of fairyland, Santa Claus, and the big bad wolf, if he or she is told stories about them. Christian beliefs can be taught in the same way. This might be caused by the child's submission to the authority of the storyteller. These beliefs will not become enduring ones, however, unless impulses other than submission to authority are at work.

Childhood beliefs taught by authority alone endure only for a few years. These beliefs may be corrected, abandoned, or reinforced and confirmed. Identification with an authority hostile to the concept believed might break down the belief, or, if friendly, confirm it for a while. Confirmation by authority will not endure unless the belief is tested by experience. It is the impulse of curiosity or search for truth that leads to this kind of learning. Adults have many ways of discouraging this kind of searching, such as ridicule of the child's questions. In Sunday school, the child soon learns that there are certain kinds of questions—frequently the ones most vital to the Christian belief—that a person just does not ask. Soon he or she is afraid to ask any real questions and the teacher has lost the most powerful force for motivation.

Most preschool teachers we have observed rely upon the verbal modality entirely too much. Children three, four, and five years old have recently acquired language and few of them have begun to read. Some verbal instruction is necessary, but it is not yet a reliable mode of learning for them. Their verbal skills have not been practiced much. They have been moving and seeing all of their lives, so the movement and visual modes are more available. These modes easily augment creative learning.

THE NATURE OF CREATIVE LEARNING SKILLS
OF PRESCHOOLERS

Children in the nursery and preschool years are experts in creative ways of learning. They have not yet abandoned creative ways of learning by questioning, inquiring, searching, manipulating, experimenting, and playing; in their own way they are always trying to find out the truth. If they sense that something is wrong or missing or that there is something that they do not understand, they are uncomfortable until they do something about it. So they start asking questions, making guesses, testing, revising, and retesting. When they discover something and come upon some new (to them) truth, they want to tell somebody about it. It is such a natural process. At times, it is lightning quick, automatic and spontaneous. At other times, we must wait patiently—and then it may quickly surface. Ann taught us how it could be lightning quick and Ollie taught us that there are times when it is best to wait.

Ann and her kindergarten classmates were busy with the Circles Test. She had been given a page of thirty-five circles and asked to sketch as many objects as possible from these circles in ten minutes. She had been instructed to sketch as many *different* objects as possible, to make each one tell as complete a story as possible and to try to think of objects that others would not think of. After about eight minutes, she was told, "We now have about two more minutes before our time is up." Ann lacked about two lines of circles. Immediately, she drew a girl blowing bubbles and the unused circles were bubbles already blown by the girl.

Ollie taught us a lesson about interrupting children's thinking while taking the Picture Construction Test (Torrance, 1966). In administering this test, Paul (the examiner) had shown how to use a triangular piece of colored paper as the roof of a birdhouse with all of the trimmings. Paul then said, "Now, don't draw a birdhouse. This is just an example. Think of something different." All but two of these thirty-three kindergartners could hardly wait to start. One began in about a minute, so he did not concern us much. Ollie bothered us greatly as he just sat there. We wanted to go to him and find out why he was not working. Perhaps he did not understand what was wanted. We waited, however, and in about four minutes Ollie began drawing with great intensity. We discovered that he had been sitting and thinking about how a birdhouse would look on the inside and he was trying to draw this. Have you ever tried to imagine how a birdhouse would look on the inside? Ollie would not have been able to do this if we had interrupted him.

It is interesting to note (Singer, 1961) that highly creative children have greater ability to sit still than their less creative peers. Under the guise of administering a test to identify future space men, it was found that highly imaginative children would sit still for longer periods of time than their less imaginative classmates.

Interest Span

When we began including preschool children in studies of creative thinking, advisers cautioned us that we could not conduct an experiment that would last longer than ten or fifteen minutes. We respected expert opinion, but we were not altogether willing to accept this advice, because earlier work with four- and five-year-olds in religious education had convinced us that young children can become deeply absorbed in a task for thirty minutes or longer. Thus we dared go ahead with an experiment that extended from kindergarten through sixth grade and lasted about sixty minutes. Of course, there was considerable variety in the activities included: pasting, drawing, discussing, looking at one another's work, and even a brief "candy break" after thirty minutes. Usually the kindergarten children were so absorbed in their tasks that they kept working through the candy break. Some even put the candy aside until later or ate it as they worked (Torrance, 1965).

Severe problems may actually arise from a kindergarten or first-grade teacher's insistence that children move promptly from one activity to another. Chess and Thomas (1964) cite an interesting case of this type. Billy had shown no symptoms of disturbance at home or in nursery school. His first tantrum in school apparently occurred when the teacher shifted activities while Billy wished to continue what he was doing at the time. Billy's temperamental pattern from birth had been characterized by persistence; he would become absorbed with his toys in his playpen, playing in his bath, or whatever he was doing. He would want to go on and on with an activity. The family learned not to let Billy get involved in any activity if he would have to be pulled away in less than an hour. His real trouble began when the curriculum called for many shifts in activity during the day. In a new school Billy was permitted to spend a good part of one morning reading and a portion of another morning doing arithmetic. He was not interrupted as long as he completed his required work and did not interfere with the other children's schedule. His classmates respected his scholastic performance and accepted the fact that they did not always do the same things that he did.

We find it difficult to believe that it is natural for young children to quickly change from one activity to another. I am willing to admit that it may not be natural for an *entire* group of young children to sustain interest in the *same* activity, but in almost any creative activity there are likely to be some who want to continue. Our mistaken idea that the curriculum must be the same for all of the children in a class makes it difficult to respect and make constructive use of this absorption in an activity. This point is illustrated in the following incident described by one of Paul's university students when he asked the class to describe an incident in which they had encouraged or permitted a child to learn in creative ways and it had made a difference in subsequent behavior and achievement (Torrance and Myers, 1970):

> A three-year old on a walk with the class was shown a snail. Completely fascinated, he spent the remaining school time (one and one-half hours) observing and touching the snail, rather to my annoyance, but I left him alone while the rest of us went on with crafts. The child consequently became so interested in nature's small creatures that at age five he is quite an authority on small creatures. He approaches them stealthily and while looking for lizards practically looked a rattlesnake in the eyes. He immediately recognized it and retreated just as quietly and was unharmed.

Ability to Organize

Young children are grossly underrated regarding ability to organize their behavior. This is one of the surprising discoveries of Maria Montessori (Standing, 1962). She recognized that children wanted things to be organized but at first thought that adults must organize them. She soon discovered that children of preschool age had a real interest and talent for organizing things themselves. The following report of a preschool teacher illustrates how opportunities present themselves for permitting children to organize their behavior.

This teacher's class of twenty-eight preschoolers was presented with the problem of planting bulbs in containers and cleaning up within a thirty-minute period. Some of the children rushed to get their containers and several quickly said, "We won't get it done that way." Spontaneously some of the children recognized that they must act in a more organized manner in order to accomplish the task. One child suggested that they do the planting by rows, each taking a turn without rushing or pushing. After the class organized the groups to come to the back of the room, the planting was accomplished in an orderly fashion without accidents, spilled soil, or spoiled bulbs. Each one planted a bulb, learned which side of the bulb had to be up, watered the planted bulb, and set it in the dark. All were finished before the allotted time. One child remarked, "It sure pays to think."

Looking at Things Differently

A number of the ways for increasing creative output makes use of the technique of looking at something in a different way. Synectics (Gordon, 1961), for example, stresses the principle of making strange things familiar, or familiar things strange. One idea was sparked when a member of the team tried to imagine himself as a drop of paint struggling to get some kind of hold on a wall that had been painted and had not been scraped or cleaned before repainting. Children use the techniques of Synectics and brainstorming naturally.

Children's skills in looking at things in a different way will be sharpened if they have a chance to investigate and explore the detailed nature of objects and situations and to perceive them from many different angles and perspectives. Studies of perception show that the meaning and grasp of an object changes as we shift the point of observation. Details previously missed altogether may become important. By changing purposes, obtaining different information, or the like, the meaning of objects and experiences also change.

Children can make excellent use of opportunities for repeatedly investigating things as we learned in reading books to this age-group. Frequently when one of us would read a book to the group, they would ask immediately that we read it again. At first we thought that we would have to go through the book rapidly each time, lest they become inattentive and bored. We soon discovered that they wanted just the opposite. Now that they had seen and heard the book, the urgent tension to get through had been satisfied, and they were prepared to examine it more thoroughly. They were not bored and did not want to be hurried. They could now savor the experience to the fullest, elaborate upon it, and think more deeply about it.

Postponement of Learning by Authority

There are times when the teacher of young children might as well accept the fact that children prefer to learn creatively and postpone for a while learning by authority. An example of such a time is when young children are first given rhythm band instruments. Most teachers are almost driven to distraction on this day. They want to tell the children about the instruments, but they usually fail to gain attention for more than a moment. The alert and experienced teacher will realize that on this day the children must be permitted to encounter their instruments creatively and find out what the instruments will do. They want to feel the instruments, smell them, look at them, tap them, and sense them in every way possible. After this, children are ready to learn in other ways. They will listen and watch.

Here, as in many other situations, the learning process is thrown off course when the teacher tries to hurry and push the children to do what the teacher wants to tell them to do—namely, how to use the instruments properly. It happens almost any time we try to prepare children through verbal or authoritarian orientations.

Periods of Silence and Hesitation

Work with young children has taught us to be tolerant of moments of silence and hesitation. In administering tests of creative thinking, it was apparent that it does not pay to hurry, urge, or push children to give responses when they are hesitant. Many of the hesitant children become quite responsive when told that "it is just for fun." When they discover that the examiner is really listening and taking down whatever they tell him, they tend to become quite productive. It is better to make no evaluative remarks and only record what children dictate than to give disruptive remarks of approval and encouragement.

In discussing what he calls the "slow gifted child" who is culturally deprived, Reissman (1962) cautions against misinterpreting periods of hesitation and points out that many of these children are better at doing and seeing than at talking and hearing. They often appear to achieve better on performance tests than on verbal ones. They like to draw, role-play, and the like. They appear to think in spatial terms rather than temporal and often have poor time perspectives. Reissman also recommends the games format for use with the "slow gifted child."

Children may seem hesitant and slow because adults do not give them time to respond. This difficulty is illustrated dramatically in the story of one mother (Miller, 1961) who was shocked when her five-year-old daughter asked to eat in her room when Mrs. Green came for lunch. When asked to explain, the child said, "Oh, you know. She talks to me in a baby voice—and keeps asking me things and never lets me answer."

Then the mother recalled that every remark Mrs. Green made to the child was some little question she obviously did not expect answered. "Where did you get that pretty dress? What have you been doing today? What makes Julie grow so fast?"

As a result, the child refused to respond. Then, Mrs. Green made matters worse by adding, "My, Julie is a shy one, isn't she? Are you bashful, honey? She doesn't talk much does she?"

Taking a Closer Look

With young children, nothing can take the place of personal observation. They enjoy using a magnifying glass to get a closer look. The young child will be satisfied to watch from a distance at first, but this does not satisfy his or her curiosity. Creative thinking and learning is driven off course when children have no opportunities for a closer look, when they are forbidden to touch, when there is no real chance for creative encounter.

We place many restrictions on the child's curiosity, discouraging interest by saying that "curiosity killed the cat." If we were honest we would admit that curiosity makes a good cat and that cats are extremely skilled in testing the limits and determining what is safe and what is dangerous. Apparently, children as well as cats have an irresistible tendency to manipulate and explore objects and this very tendency seems to be the basis for the curiosity and inventiveness of adults. Even in testing situations, children who do the most manipulating of objects produce the most ideas and the largest number of original ideas.

Learning Through Fantasy

Fantasy is one of the young child's most valuable tools for learning, and should be kept alive (Torrance, 1979), developed, and guided. Many teachers and parents try to eliminate fantasy by the time children enter school. They do this because they believe that fantasy is unhealthy, failing to recognize that fantasy can be useful even to adults. Imaginative role-playing, telling fantastic stories, making unusual drawings, and the like, are normal aspects of a child's thinking and a part of his or her way of experimenting and problem solving.

Both children and adults need time for absorbed thinking and dreaming. When we are absorbed in thinking about a problem, we may be "good for little else" at the time. It might be helpful to leave a part of the young child's day unscheduled with activities in which he has to appear busy. We are of course interested in developing a sound type of creative problem solving and decision making. Fantasy must be kept alive until children achieve the intellectual development that makes this type of thinking possible. For some time, it is through fantasy that children must do much of their experimenting and exploring, and fantasy should perhaps never be completely discontinued as a way of exploring possibilities.

Griffiths (1945), who studied imagination in early childhood, maintains that fantasy or imagination provides the normal means for the solution of developmental problems in early childhood. Through fantasy the child indirectly attacks problems that are often disguised by symbolism. The child is only vaguely aware of the goal toward which he is struggling. The problem develops through a series of successively imagined solutions that constitute a gradual resolution of the problem. As a result, the child acquires information, makes changes in attitude, and becomes more socialized and objective.

Chukovsky (1963), the Russian child psychologist, also defends fantasy among both young children and adults. He believes that fantasy is "the most valuable attribute of the human mind and should be diligently nurtured from earliest childhood" (p. 116). He insists that we not interfere with its natural development. He sees the reading of fairy tales as very important for young children and supports his contention by referring to the use of fantasy by such eminent men as Darwin and a number of eminent Russian physicists and mathematicians. He asserts, "Without imaginative fantasy, there would be complete stagnation in both physics and chemistry, because the formulation of new hypotheses, the invention of new implements, the discovery of new methods of experimental research, the conjecturing of new chemical fusions—all these are products of imagination and fantasy" (Chukovsky, 1963). Thus Chukovsky posits the need for continuity between childhood fantasy and adult creative achievement.

Storytelling and Songmaking

Children are natural storytellers and can compose charmingly and excitingly, if encouraged to do so. Furthermore, this tendency can be used as a bridge to the acquisition of information and important educational skills. Seldom are children's compositions appreciated and given adequate treatment in publication. We would like to call attention to a few notable exceptions. One of these is an exciting little book by Susan Nichols Pulsifer (1963). In this book, Mrs. Pulsifer joins me in asserting that the drop in creative behavior that occurs at about age five is not a natural developmental change. Instead she believes that it is due to the influences of other children, group activities, the imposition of correct techniques and facts, and rules and regulations. She believes, as we do, that with wisdom the home and the school can do much to reduce this discontinuity in development and lessen this serious loss of creativity.

Another exception is the work of Kathleen Wrenn with her son Bobby (1949). When her son was about two years old, Mrs. Wrenn discovered that he was responding much more readily to suggestions that were sung to him than he did when the same requests were spoken. Soon, she discovered that he was responding by singing, rapidly developed a sense of rhythm and a singing scale. When Bobby was about four years old, the idea of making a book of songs began taking shape. These were simple songs about everyday happenings—songs about the fireman, the milkman, the zoo, balloons, traffic signals, and the church bell.

With new experiences, Bobby would think of ideas for songs and work them out. On one occasion, his mother asked him to put some leaves over the tulips planted in the yard so that they would not freeze. He came back with the following idea for a song:

> Here come the flowers out of the ground.
> Spreading happiness all around,
> Daffodils, hyacinths, tulips gay,
> Oh, how I wish you were here to stay.

His mother suggested the "hyacinth" was a very difficult word for little children to sing and why not say "daisies" instead. His reply was, "I'm a little child, aren't I, and it's my word." (Yes, children dislike for others to tamper with their compositions, and their reasons may be well-founded.)

Some people have commented that it was only because Mrs. Wrenn was musically talented that this procedure was successful. Another mother (Hargrove, 1964), avowedly untalented musically, made similar discoveries quite independently of Mrs. Wrenn. This mother maintains that "all children have heard the angels sing." Her advice to parents and teachers is simple: "How do you begin? Follow the leader—your child. Children often make music as they play. Sometimes they hum wordless tunes. At other times, they break into words and music. You can listen and join in. Don't make the mistake, however, that I once did. Sing *with* them not *to* them. Otherwise, you may hear something like this: 'Go away and sing *your* song. This is *my* song.' " This mother also found that singing her instructions as she assigns various duties gives work a flavor of creativity and enjoyment. My wife and I have begun experimenting with this technique with our four- and five-year-olds in church. We find that some children who never talk otherwise, will communicate through this kind of songmaking.

It is our belief that children will indeed learn more Bible truths whenever we respect the learning skills that they bring with them and are willing to graft religious education onto these skills. This involves learning how to respond to the child rather than expecting the child to respond to you all of the time.

CONCEPTS OF GOD

In our opinion, the most basic, the most fundamental thing that can be taught to preschool children is the concept of God. It seems that it is wasteful to teach them about the Bible, baptism, the Lord's supper, or anything else, before they have any conceptualization of God. Therefore, we limited ourselves to the goal of teaching them in a meaningful way three of the most fundamental concepts of God. We developed and executed a curriculum designed to do this. We taught it several times and we believe our objectives were accomplished to a considerable degree.

We called this curriculum "Ideas About God." It was intended to explore the limits to which preschool children can be taught concepts about God that will move them along the path toward a mature concept of God and will not interfere later with acceptance of truly mature concepts of God and becoming effective Christians.

An attempt was made to base these materials upon the nature and development of preschool children and the psychology of learning and teaching. We must admit that we do not believe that it is possible to teach preschool children a complete and mature set of concepts about God. However, we do believe that it is possible to help them to achieve some true, accurate concepts that will move them toward such an achievement. We cannot project how far they can move and we know that there will be tremendous individual differences: Some five-year-olds have concepts that are as mature as an average eight-year-old, while others have concepts that are no more mature than the average three-year-old. We also believe that four- and five-year-olds can be taught concepts about God that will not interfere with their later acceptance of mature concepts.

The following definition of a mature concept of God was supplied by Southern Baptist theologians and was used as a guide in preparing our curriculum:

> God is creator, sovereign, and sustainer of the universe; perfect in all his attributes. God is eternal; infinite in knowledge, power, righteousness, and mercy. God is spirit of truth, of believer, of power, and of life. God is everlasting love; he is to be loved and trusted, to be obeyed and served. God is one but he reveals himself to men as Father, Son, and Holy Spirit. As the Heavenly Father, he loves all persons with everlasting love. He justifies all who come to him through Christ by the Holy Spirit. He is indwelling in all things, seeking ever to transform them according to his own will and to bring them to the goal of his Kingdom.

Three aspects of this definition were selected for focus in our program: 1) Love, 2) Infinity, and 3) Spirit. These three aspects were chosen because we believe that children can be taught some true and useful things about these three aspects of God and that these aspects of God are fundamental to the acquisition of a mature concept of God, as well as other concepts of Christian theology.

A special attempt was made to evaluate the books, songs, and stories suggested in each unit, not only for their contribution to the concepts of God as Love, Infinity, and Spirit, but also in terms of whether or not they will be confusing. There is no doubt but that some of the songs we have children sing in Sunday school, Bible school, and so on, are confusing and interfere with the later development of mature concepts. What happens when we have preschool children sing, "We are little Christian children"? Later, they may be confused when they discover that they have not always been "Christian children" and are urged "to be born again" and "become Christian." What happens when they sing, "I believe in God; in Jesus Christ, his Son, who died that he might save me and take me to his home"? What does this mean to a preschool child? What does it mean to her when she sings, "We thank you for sending Christ, the Savior, to take our sins away"?

Three commonly used song books have been used in considering appropriate songs. For each unit, two songs have been chosen from each of these three books. Some children may already know some of these songs and may help teach other children. Both the words and the melody have been considered in making choices.

It is strongly recommended that some musical instrument be used as a guide for teaching the tune, unless the teacher is accomplished in music or in teaching new songs without an instrument. Even the small "xylophone on wheels" gives some direction to the child for making the appropriate musical sounds.

We would encourage teachers to experiment with a variety of teaching methods. Some of the methods being used in public school education—teaching by inquiring, exploring ways of thinking and doing—are a challenge to religious educators. We have noticed in the past the concrete thinking of preschoolers. For example, a rural Georgia boy protested to his Sunday school teacher, "I know one thing you can't do and pray at the same time. You can't build a fire in the fireplace and pray too." Everyone who works with children this age has had such experiences.

How much can a preschool child understand? How much do we ourselves understand about God as Love, Infinity, and Spirit? Can we teach preschool children so that concepts are clearly understood rather than being vague or misunderstood? Can we provide them experiences that will engender deeper and more expansive emotions, feelings, or thoughts than usual?

We feel that we have the best chance for meeting this challenge successfully if we involve children totally in actions that explore "Love, Infinity, and Spirit." This does not mean that every minute must be filled with noisy activity. Silence too is of great value in teaching children—not the demanded silence of the leader saying, "Let us pray" while the children are folding hands, opening eyes, wriggling, looking around the room gently kicking the chair as they repeat, correctly or incorrectly, the words of the leader. What we have in mind is the silence that comes from an absorbed interest in one of the marvels of the world—an open flower, a colorful leaf, a newly discovered bug—the silence of wonder and awe which may be overlooked when the teacher or leader overemphasizes staying "on schedule."

Silence and words are both needed. For many children ten to sixty seconds is a long time for silence. But during the fifth year we know that many of them can become absorbed in exploration and discovery for over an hour.

Efforts need to be made to help the child make sense out of Sunday school and other religious activities. Both teachers and parents may have excellent motives regarding the child's participation, but unless the child sees a need for coming—an interest aroused, a place to find out something new, rather than a place to show off new clothes and receive a stick of gum—they will fail to take those initial steps toward discovering *for themselves* the wonder of God and his universe. In helping children discover how all life is intertwined, how their actions affect others and the actions of others affect them, a natural way of living together is taught. By teaching at their concrete level a realistic and sensitive way of dealing with immediate problems, you can lead young children to a more imaginative handling of their own life problems and help them achieve concepts in the direction of more mature ideas about God.

For each session, we suggested several appropriate songs, Bible verses, a prayer, activities for an outdoor time, and several child experience stories and suggestions for using them. We shall not include these and the suggestions for using them, due to lack of space. We shall say a few words about their use and give descriptions of the creative games and activities.

IDEAS ABOUT GOD: GOD IS LOVE

Many special games, Bible and child experience stories, Bible verses, and books have been chosen to give teachers a number of sources. Some of the activities are recommended to be used more than once, as they can be built onto and elaborated with repeated use. Often, preschool children are anxious to hurry through a book, game, or the like, the first time, and they fail to get the intended message. After this, however, they are ready to go into it more deeply and will frequently ask that a book, story, game, or activity be repeated a second or third time. When they do this, they are usually asking to dig into it more deeply, to ask questions about the pictures, the words, and the characters; to relate it to their own experiences, and so on.

This section presents a variety of ways to develop the concept of love. Choose those which seem to you to be the best for your particular group for the initial sessions, although you may wish to return to this section at a later date. More than can be used in such a limited time are included to give you easy access to additional activities should the first ones chosen not be as successful as anticipated.

Doing Loving Things in Play

If you have a house-like area in your room, this would be a good time to encourage children to use it for role-playing loving things members of a family can do for one another. If dress-up clothes are available for those who play mother, father, grandmother, and so on, this will make the pretending more real. If there is available a variety of furniture, boxes, and so on, this will make more possibilities for creating situations in which family members can do loving things.

After the initial encouragement, interfere as little as possible with their activities, let them think of and initiate their own activities. They will be more deeply involved and interested longer. Afterwards, they can discuss what there was about the things that they did that showed love. This session can be used to show how God's love is similar to the love of parents for their children.

The Colors, Sounds, and Feel of Love

In the development of concepts and in their religious experiences, preschool children are greatly influenced by touch. Even in adults, a beautiful painting, piece of music, or texture may evoke strong inner responses. We are moved to respond to a gesture of the hand or to the touch of a hand on the shoulder. In trying to develop the concept of "God is Love," it is suggested that preschool children be provided with a variety of experiences in which they can experiment with making the sounds, colors, gestures, and movements of love.

It is not necessary to use books as guides for these experiences, but there are books that may be very useful in creating a reverent and warmly moving atmosphere. One such book *What Color Is Love?* by Joan Walsh Anglund (1966) can be used as the basis for the color and sight of love. After reading *What Color Is Love?*, ask the children to experiment at their easels to paint the color of love, as they feel love. You can emphasize the point of the book that we cannot use words to say the color of love; we have to "see it with our hearts."

In exploring the sounds, gestures, and movements of love, the music for one of the great songs about God's love might be used. "Love Divine, All Loves Excelling" would be one excellent possibility. If you do not have a piano in the room or cannot play a piano or organ, you might have someone record a piano or organ rendition of this or some other great song of love. Make no attempt to sing the song or study the words. Tell the children that the song is about God's love and ask them to make gestures and movements of love suggested by the music.

In exploring the feel or touch of love, pets may be brought into the group. Usually kittens, puppies, and rabbits are most appealing to pre-schoolers, but a duck, turtle, parakeet, or other pets may be used, depending upon availability and appeal to the particular children in your group. Emphasize "the feel of love" as the children handle the pet and how the pet responds to "the feel of love" differently than other handling. Show them how a squeeze may be gentle, as many children are so ecstatic in their handling of a pet that they are actually rough and hurt the pet. Even if no pet is available, the children may take turns acting as kittens or other pets while other children pet them with the "feel of love." One may also make clay pets to be loved, or use stuffed toy animals.

Pantomime Loving Things To Do

Preschoolers are very good at pantomiming. Even though they may not be able to discuss loving things they can do or that others do, they can enact these things and can guess what the others are doing.

If the children in your group have not had experience in pantomime, it might be a good idea to start them off with the Fruit Basket Act. Bring in an imaginary basket of fruit. Pick up an imaginary banana and peel it and eat it. Almost all of the children will be able to guess what you are eating. Then, in turn, mimic eating other fruits common to them. As they warm up, pass some of the fruit to them. For example, pick up a bunch of grapes, eat one or two, and then pass the bunch among the children so that each of them may have a few grapes. Then, let them take their favorite fruit from the basket, eat it, and have others guess what fruit they chose.

Even if the children know the Fruit Basket Act, repeating it might warm them up to pantomiming "loving things" to do by having them first do a round with the fruit basket or a similar exercise. Let someone volunteer to act out something loving that someone has done for them or that they can do for a friend, parent, brother, or sister. Other children can guess what the child is doing. Give everyone a chance who wants one. Permit them to talk about these loving acts as readiness develops. Try to make the conversation emphasize what there is about the behavior that makes it loving.

Doing Loving Things for People Who Are Sick

One way that Jesus did loving things for people was to visit the sick and to make them well. What are some of the loving things that you can do today for the sick?

Children may think first of doctors, nurses, and other hospital workers. If so, let them play being doctor, nurses, or others doing loving things for people. Then return to the subject of doing loving things for sick people. Find out if any of the absent children or any of the members of their family are sick. If so, have them discuss things that they could do for this person or these persons and plan something specific and helpful that they can do. If there are no such persons known to the children, find out from your pastor or church secretary some bedridden or lonely person who might be cheered by notes from the children, a visit with songs by the children, or some other loving thing that the children might do.

Making Something for a Person I Love

Preschoolers enjoy making things for the people they love. It is not necessary to wait for special days like Christmas, Mother's Day, and Father's Day. Any time is a good time for children to share their work with someone they love. Here are a few simple suggestions for things that preschoolers can make for their parents, neighbors, shut-ins, and others they love:

Make Cards. Provide pictures, crayons, construction paper, and paste. Let the children design their own cards and dictate messages to an adult worker who can write them on the inside of the cards.

Draw Pictures. This may be done with tempera paint or crayons. After the picture dries, roll it up and tie a ribbon around it.

Another type of picture can be designed by pasting various cutout shapes on a colored sheet of construction paper. The shapes may be circles, squares, rectangles, or other shapes.

Make a Simple Wastebasket. One can be made from an ice-cream carton or a cardboard paint bucket. Let each child select suitable pictures to paste on the sides of his basket. Or, the wastebasket can be covered with a solid color and decorated with a design created by the child. Perhaps even more beautiful would be wastebaskets covered with tempera paintings by the child.

Make a Paperweight. An excellent paperweight may be designed by using a small, beautiful rock which is heavy enough to hold paper. Paste a piece of felt onto the bottom of the rock. Polish the top of the rock to make it shiny and more colorful. A design could also be painted on it.

Fruit Plate. Paper plates may be decorated with crayons, paint, or pasted pictures; then filled with fruit and covered with cellophane or plastic wrap.

Pencil Holder. Small tin cans with a smoothly cut top may be decorated with adhesive paper such as "Contact." Such cans make very practical pencil holders. Children may also print or make drawings on a plain or light design of adhesive paper before it is applied to the tin can.

Friend Games

Teach the Bible verse, "A friend loveth at all times" (Proverbs 17:17). Then, play some of the following friend games, stressing love and the meaning of love throughout the games. Try to develop the idea that friendliness is something more than pretended politeness and smiling. Place the emphasis on "really being" rather than appearing to be.

To play "I See a Friend," the leader describes a child in the group, giving the color of hair, eyes, shoes, and other characteristics. The children guess the name of the child they hear described. That child then changes places with the leader and describes another friend in the group. If the child does not want to describe a friend, the leader may offer to do it or choose another child to have a turn.

In "Drawing Friends" two children must work together. (Older children will enjoy it more than younger ones.) Provide a 24″ x 48″ strip of paper for each child. One child lies on her paper while another child draws the outline of her body. The child may finish the picture herself by drawing and coloring hair, features, and clothing. This child in turn draws the outline of her friend.

IDEAS ABOUT GOD: GOD IS SPIRIT

Outdoor Activities

Binoculars may be used to help the children find "signs and wonders" of God, the Spirit, outdoors. If conditions are favorable and if any kind of telescope can be obtained, interest can develop concerning the sky. Even without a telescope, this might be a good time to encourage children to see more in the sky, to become aware of its limitlessness, to sense its "signs and wonders" of God's spirit, and to enhance the children's sense of awe and wonder.

Free Activity Time

Books and Pictures: As the children examine books and pictures, help the children to become aware of the "signs and wonders" of both God's spirit and man's spirit. Ask the children to identify the feelings of the pictured characters about one another and God. Show them some of the books and pictures dealing with worship and prayer and get the children to discuss their interpretations of the pictures.

Nature Activity: If magnifying apparatus and binoculars are available, encourage exploration in depth of nature objects. Acquaint them with the binoculars but reserve this mostly for the outdoor activity.

Building and Blocks Activity: Encourage the children to build a prayer place or a worship place. Get them to express their ideas about what a prayer or worship place should be like.

Art Activity: Encourage the children to draw or paint some "signs and wonders" of God's spirit.

Invisible Me

Ask children to just suppose they could become invisible. Explain what is meant by "invisible" or obtain from them their understanding of the word. Get as many responses as possible in about five or six minutes. As an art activity, they might be asked to paint or draw a picture of something they would like to do if they could become invisible.

Conversation About Activities and Songs

The story time may be replaced by a conversation with the children about the realities of things that are visible and invisible or answer some of the children's questions, such as:

> Why does the minister always say, "God is spirit?"
> How can God be everywhere at the same time?
> What do people mean when they say, "God is inside of us?"

A session might go something as follows: It might be started as a kind of game in which the leader names some things and the children have to say whether it is something they can see or cannot see, something visible or invisible. The leader lists very slowly such words as trees, telephone pole, wind, desk, love, electric light, electricity, fear, bravery, a thought, and so on. Another way of doing the questioning would be to ask if there could be a basketful of it.

After this game, go back and talk about the invisible things. Are they real? How do you know?

After this, move on to another game. Select one child in the group, and ask (if the child's name is Mary), "Mary, where are you?" Mary will likely say, "Here I am." The leader can continue, "But I cannot quite see you." This will probably puzzle the children and they will express their puzzlement and curiosity. The leader can continue, "Even though I am looking at Mary, I find it difficult to see *her.* I can see her blue sweater, her blue eyes (etc.) but I cannot really see *her.*" By then some of the children may be trying to guess the riddle and may begin to make some guesses about what there is about Mary that cannot be seen—her thoughts, what is going on in her mind, her feelings, what she is praying about, whom she loves, and so on. Raise the question, "Are these things real?" and try to show that they are quite real and have consequences.

Conclude with the idea that it is these things that comprise the real self. People call these invisible parts our *spirits.* God is spirit, and we, too, are spirit.

More Home-Living Activities

Add to the home-living corner items that give evidence of forces that cannot be seen, such as electrical appliances, radio, telephone, television, flashlight, and so on. Use these to reinforce the idea that there are many things that are very powerful and very real that we cannot see, but that we can see their "signs and wonders."

More Nature Activities

Add materials that might be used to emphasize the "signs and wonders" of God, the Spirit. You could have seeds, large sea shells, leaves, and any "strange and wonderful" things that you may have available. There are many very powerful and wonderful forces that we cannot see, but we can see the signs and wonders that come from them. The nature corner also offers many very special opportunities to teach this lesson.

For this first session on "God is Spirit" it is also suggested that the experiments on "Unseen Forces of Magnets" be conducted. Then, in later activities, stories, and songs, reference can be made to the power of unseen forces and to the power of God's spirit. The following suggestions are given for the experiments on "Unseen Forces of Magnets."

Experiments with magnets are good for this purpose. If possible use a fairly strong magnet. One experiment with magnets that children enjoy is seeing how many paper clips a single magnet can pick up by letting one paper clip attach itself to another. Demonstrate that before the paper clip touches the magnet, it cannot attract or hold another paper clip. After it has been magnetized by the magnet, it will hold another paper clip. This experiment is preparatory to understanding the power of God's spirit. If we stay in contact with God through prayer, praise, and worship, we can attract and support others. Without this contact, we lack this power.

Another experiment with the magnet and paper clips involves making two magnets out of one paper clip. Straighten a paper clip so it is just a wire. Rub the wire with one end of the magnet about twenty times, always going the same way. Do not go back and forth. You can then show that the wire is a magnet by picking up metal filings, steel wool, etc. You can then cut your wire magnet and each piece becomes a magnet which will pick up bits of steel wool or metal filings.

You can also make magnetic puppets. You can use a shoe box for a stage. Puppets can be cut from paper and paper clips can be fastened to their feet so that they will stand on the stage. To move a puppet, place the magnet in the shoe box, under the stage.

A variety of such experiments can be found in almost any science book for children. One with material appropriate for preschoolers is *"Prove It!"* by Rose Wyler and Gerald Ames (1963).

IDEAS ABOUT GOD: GOD IS INFINITE

The purpose of these sessions is to develop the concept of infinity in a general sense and introduce the child to the more specific concept that "God is infinite." The sessions are planned with the assumption that the foundation for the concept of God as infinite is the idea that the universe is infinite and that we shall never exhaust any important aspect of its truth. Also basic is the infinity principle which holds that in the search for truth there are no final answers, that insights are only stepping stones to greater insights, that all things on the earth (including people) are continually undergoing creative change.

We do not know how far we can go in developing an accurate concept of infinity among preschool children. It seems certain, however, that foundations can be laid and that even here the infinity principle operates. The more a child learns about something, the more rapidly, easily, and accurately he or she can learn further information and skills in the area. Furthermore, even the most mature and imaginative adults are continually expanding their concept of infinity. The most important value of an insight is the problems it opens up, rather than the problems it solves.

The central theme of this unit on "God is Infinite" is the truth that "God is infinite (boundless, limitless, everlasting, without end, etc.) and that God is good."

Where Is the End?

A number of objects can be used in an active way to demonstrate the concept of infinity. Some of the simplest would be circles, hula hoops, rings, or the like. Have the children trace over and over the circle trying to find the end. The same can be done with the hula hoop using the child's finger or hand or the ring using the finger. Just as there is no end to the circle or the hoop, there is no end to God's love, goodness, and power.

The symbol for infinity (∞) can be used in a similar manner. With an incomplete picture, it can be demonstrated that there is no limit to the number of ways that it can be completed to tell a story. A good art activity would be to give the children sheets of paper containing incomplete figures or drawings and have them complete the figures in such a way as to make a picture. Encourage them to draw a picture that they think of and usually every picture will indeed be different, which in turn can be used to further the development of the concept of infinity. The following are examples of some incomplete figures that you can use.

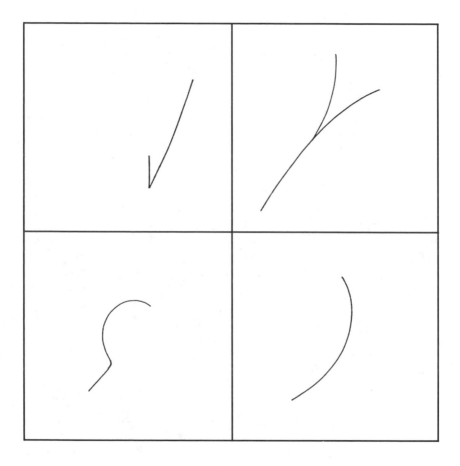

Can You Empty a Box?

Another way of helping to develop the concept of infinity is to use a demonstration trying to empty a box or other container. An empty milk carton or some kind of plastic container that can be squeezed can be used for this purpose.

Show the children that the box looks empty and tell them that it is full of air and that neither you nor they can empty it. There are a number of ways of doing this:

1) Hold the container open near a child's face. Squeeze it and let it blow on the child's face or even blow the hair.

2) Put small bits of paper on a table. Hold the carton near them. Squeeze the carton and see what happens. The air will blow the paper away.

Repeat both of these demonstrations and let the children try them also to show that no matter how many times we try, we cannot empty the carton of its air.

Jars and Shells Full of Noise

Another illustration of infinity would be to use the sounds in an empty jar or large sea shell. Have the child hold the jar near his ear. Let him listen to the roar. Tell him that this noise is from the little sounds in the air all around us and that the sounds make the air in the jar vibrate and that we hear them. Then water can be poured into the jar and no such sounds can be heard. Then empty the jar and listen again. The sounds are heard again. The same procedure can be used with a large sea shell.

CONCLUSION

We have considered the ways by which preschool children learn, the nature of their creativity, three basic concepts about God, and how these concepts about God can be learned. Concepts about God can best be learned creatively rather than by authority and content learned through creative instruction is more likely to be retained by the preschool child.

REFERENCES

Anglund, J. W. (1966). *What color is love?* New York: Harcourt, Brace and World.

Chess, S., & Thomas, A. (1964). Are parents responsible for everything? *Parents' Magazine, 39*(11), 48-49f.

Chukovsky, K. (1963). *From two to five.* Berkeley, CA: University of California Press.

Gordon, W. J. J. (1961). *Synectics: The development of creative capacity.* New York: Harper & Row.

Griffiths, R. (1945). *A study of imagination in early childhood.* London: Routlege & Kegan Paul.

Hargrove, K. C. (1964). Let the angels sing. *Living with children, 8*(4), 10-11.

Miller, I. E. (1961). How to talk to children. *Home Life, 15*(11), 13.

Pulsifer, S. N. (1963) *Children are poets.* Cambridge, MA: Chapman & Grimes.

Reissman, F. (1962). *The culturally deprived child.* New York: Harper & Row.

Singer, J. L. (1961). Imagination and waiting ability in young children. *Personality, 29,* 396-413.

Standing, E. M. (1962). *Maria Montessori: Her life and work.* New York: Mentor Books.

Torrance, E. P. (1965). *Rewarding creative behavior.* Englewood Cliffs, NJ: Prentice-Hall.

Torrance, E. P. (1966). *The Torrance Tests of Creative Thinking.* Bensenville, IL: Scholastic Testing Service.

Torrance, E. P. (1975). *What research says to the teacher: Creativity in the classroom.* Washington, DC: National Education Association.

Torrance, E. P. (1979). *The search for satori and creativity.* Buffalo, NY: Bearly Limited.

Torrance, E. P., & Myers, R. E. (1970). *Creative learning and teaching.* New York: Harper & Row.

Wrenn, B., & Wrenn, K. (1949). *Fun for everybody: Songs for children.* Cincinnati, OH: Willis Music Co.

Wyler, R., & Ames, G. (1963). *Prove it.* New York: Harper & Row.

Chapter Nine:

Stories, Enactment, and Play

DONALD RATCLIFF

> The story of Moses and the Egyptian plagues was mildly interest-
> ing to the children, but Bob realized they weren't as involved as
> they should be. Interest waned as he read through the accounts of
> the locusts, lice, and other indelicacies the Egyptians suffered, and
> even Bob began to wonder whether the effort was really worth it.
>
> Then he decided to try something different. "Let's pretend we
> were there and act out what happened," he suggested, and immedi-
> ately new interest was generated. After assigning parts (including a
> couple of locusts), the children began to act out the events. Bob
> made appropriate sound effects, which the children imitated, and
> found that they were all having fun as well as learning about those
> events of long ago, learning by first-hand experience.

Most preschoolers have a love for stories, a natural inclination of
preschoolers everywhere. It seems fairly obvious that some combination
of story and play would therefore be at the heart of preschooler religious
education.

Unfortunately the literature related to play in religious education is
quite limited. While he admits that spiritual growth might be fostered
by play, Elkind (1980) illustrates his idea of "story play" by having
adolescents rewrite and act out Bible stories. A book titled *The Christian at Play* (Johnson, 1983) is almost completely about adult recreation, while another work *The Sacred Play of Children* (Postolos-Cappadora, 1983) is about liturgical worship. An otherwise excellent book
on story enactment by Miller, Snyder, and Neff (1973) recommends this
approach not be used before seventh grade!

More recently there have been indications that religious educators are
beginning to appreciate the potential in story enactment by pre-

schoolers. The new edition of *Childhood Education in the Church* (Clark, Brubaker, & Zuck, 1986) includes a chapter on "Story Playing" which contains a number of interesting ideas, but no systematic research is cited for their effectiveness. One brief study of preschoolers learning church roles (Ratcliff, 1985) is the only research of preschooler play in religious education that could be located.

In this chapter the general research of stories and play/enactment with preschoolers will be considered in detail. We will first consider how play is preparatory for learning stories, then consider story structure and content as revealed through play and enactment, and finally the evidence for learning as a result of story enactment. Applications to religious education follow each of these major topics, as well as the entire concluding section.

PLAY AS A FOUNDATION FOR STORIES

A number of abilities are developed through play that contribute to the understanding of stories. First, however, it is important to distinguish play from the enactment of stories. Play refers to the more spontaneous "replaying" of events, commonly found in preschoolers, while enactment is the acting out of an event or story in response to another person's request. The play of infants and early preschoolers prepares the child for story comprehension in later years, thus this section will concentrate upon the play of the younger preschooler.

Gardner (1982), in his report of Harvard's Project Zero, cites evidence that storytelling by preschoolers is actually an outgrowth of earlier play. During infancy babies begin to use objects in ways other than that intended (the first stage of play), while later in the preschool years dolls are used in a play sequence. Still later children substitute themselves for the dolls and are able to portray roles and themes through their own actions.

Language becomes particularly important during play by the fourth year. Earlier, objects and words were both used to outline what was going on in a play sequence, but by four years of age words alone are sufficient (Gardner, 1982).

Both stories and play require children to use other children's perspectives rather than their own. In addition, both play and stories involved the suspending of reality and the use of objects in a fictionalized manner (such as a block being a toad in play or a talking stone in a story). Research indicated that cause and effect reasoning was used by preschoolers to resolve conflicts when playing out roles, which indicates an understanding of why characters in a story act as they do (Pellegrini,

1985). Play was also found to be organized by cause and effect, as well as time sequences, both of which are foundational for story comprehension.

An important aspect of understanding stories is maintaining a distinction between the story and the child's actual situation—the story line must never be confused with the context of its telling (the schoolroom, for example). This understanding of a world independent of the real world is a result of play (Wolf & Pusch, 1985). The concept of boundaries in stories will be considered later in more detail.

Initially the ongoing play is fused with the context—when a telephone rings, the intrusion into the play is acknowledged. After about three and a half years of age a second phase develops in which the contextual interruption is absorbed into play (the telephone ringing becomes a part of the event being played out). By the late preschool years the child acknowledges explicitly how the interruption is to be viewed, usually in a lowered voice. This progression indicates a clearer distinction is being made between the actual context and the "story line" of the play or story, a phenomenon sometimes referred to as the "play frame."

Understanding Roles in Play

Early in life the child comes to understand that others are independent agents who act according to their own self-made rules. By the end of the second year of life the child understands the autonomy of others, that people have separate roles in a social situation (Wolf, 1982). The language used implies that the other person does not know or has not experienced what the preschooler has (also see Pellegrini, 1984).

Being independent agents in some ways parallels the development of roles in stories. Rubin and Wolf (1980) traced the progression in understanding roles in stories by which the story is separated from the real world and different actors are distinguished in a story.

At twelve months of age the child can play a single role; the game of peek-a-boo does not include any exchange of roles, thus the infant is not able to shift perspective to gain another's viewpoint. Between twelve and eighteen months the child comes to understand that interactions between different roles take place and that when one role is adopted the partner must play a complementary role. Roles are distinguished from actors; roles are understood to be assumed, not fixed with the person.

Between eighteen and twenty-four months speculation is added to recall in play sequences. A narrator role is added to actor roles, a precursor to the "metanarrative" in stories, to be considered later in this chapter. Characters in play become increasingly distinct. Monster themes become prominent between twenty-four and twenty-eight months of age, and roles become polarized as either victim or aggressor. Physical aggression predominates at this age, in contrast with the psychological tension of older preschoolers.

During play, conflicts are temporarily resolved by the child stepping into the story line rather than playing out resolutions through characters. Chase and escape actions recur, no extended plots are developed, and no change of character occurs, Rubin and Wolf conclude.

Differing roles are distinguished by use of a variety of vocalizations by age three (Garvey, 1984). Talking softly, whining and whispering are used to denote emotions and social context information. By four years of age these variations are expanded further to include whispering secrets and using a higher pitch to animals or babies, while the role of father is represented by a lower or more gruff voice. Different tones of voice are used for different characters at this age, possibly a modeling of bedtime story experiences.

McLoyd, Ray, and Etter-Lewis (1985) found that playing out family roles was to some extent culturally based. Four- and five-year-old African American girls used less complex speech with shorter words when enacting a big sister role in play, considered by the researchers to be an extension of the mother role.

The distinction of roles, integral to both play and story, clearly occurs in a developmental progression during the preschool years. This role distinction is a part of a framework which is further developed in what researchers call the "scripting" for stories and play.

Scripting in Play

Nelson and Seidman (1984) note that the fantasy world, present in both play and stories, must be held in common by all participants. Thus play with peers is more demanding than play with adults, since peer players must reconcile their different perspectives (adults are more likely to concede to the child's viewpoint). This agreement of perspectives is negotiated through talking, agreement is usually aided by use of "scripts" or general outlines of events.

Flavell (1985) has noted that these scripts help preschoolers structure events so that interpretation and recall are more likely. Causal relationships are implicit in scripts, indicating the patterns of events and routines (see chapter one for more on causal relationships).

Nelson and Seidman (1984) studied four-year-old children and found that scripts structured the conversation and activity of play. The number of scripts used increased between three and five years of age, and older children were more likely to use scripted play episodes.

Scripting begins as early as age two for some children (Sachs, 1980). Just prior to age two no story line could be determined in play, but within a few months dolls were attributed with animacy and having feelings by the child. While the doll became a play partner rather than play object, the child did not speak for the doll until much later (about three and a half). Sachs concluded that the parent talking about play activities during the child's play helped the child develop scripts.

French, Lucariello, Siedman, and Nelson (1985) found that scripts could be elicited from two- to four-year-olds by asking "what happens when . . ." and stating an activity. Scripts were found to be consistent between children and between varying situations for the same child. The child was able to "repair" a script which omitted one of a series of events as early as age two. The roles taken in scripted episodes were not as flexible with preschoolers as they are with older children, but they were clearly not egocentric. Scripting is fragile with preschoolers and often tied to toys that specifically relate to story content.

Applications for Religious Education

Babies and preschoolers need plenty of opportunity for free play and exploration. The more opportunity children have for practicing mental abilities, the more likely those abilities will transfer to the understanding of stories. The content of preschoolers' religious education is largely dependent upon stories, and thus preparatory skills are crucial.

The amount of time to be devoted to free play is inversely proportional to age—infants should be allowed to play most if not all of the time, although they should not be kept from hearing older children being told stories. Exploration of the environment and other activities will contribute to feeling comfortable in the religious education context, while play with other children and adults should facilitate their mental development. Introduction and reinforcement of play scripting, roles, and other slightly advanced forms of play activities may help the child to develop somewhat more rapidly. However, speed of development is not the only issue with infants—many opportunities for repetitive play activities are more likely to "consolidate" what has been learned. Speed of acquisition must be balanced with thoroughness of learning, as Piaget (1973) noted.

At the toddler stage a large amount of time is still needed for the purpose of consolidating learning. In contrast, older preschoolers may not need as much time for free play (although some is still needed). Instead listening to stories and guided enactment of those stories are more likely to enhance learning, as later evidence will bear out. The content is more likely to be explicitly religious, although the religious

educator should avoid more abstract content (see chapter one). Spontaneous play is preparatory to general story comprehension, yet guided
enactment helps in understanding a specific story.

STORY STRUCTURE AND CONTENT

Stories have a schematic structure much like play scripts, a sort of
story "grammar" (Mandler, 1983). Story schemas commonly include an
initiating event, the reaction of the protagonist usually involving a goal
(although it may not be explicitly stated), an attempt to reach that goal,
and the results of the attempt, including the consequences, responses of
participants, or the termination statement "they lived happily ever
after." Bruner (1986) simplifies this sequence to three "deep structures"
in stories: the different characters, their crises, and the underlying consciousness of their plight.

Preschoolers retell stories according to Mandler's understanding of
schemas, and sequences are least likely to be rearranged when familiar
content is used or when events have causal or enabling connections.
Mandler notes that story structures are used to infer information not
explicitly stated in the story, and that comprehension is less likely if
story events do not fit the standard schema. Story schemas develop
gradually between two and five years of age. Mandler cites research
which indicates four-year-olds may be able to infer intentions of characters in stories, although they are less sensitive to the use of deception in
those events.

Slackman and Nelson (1984) studied the development of unfamiliar
story schemes in preschoolers and older children. As might be expected,
the preschoolers recalled less, particularly after a time delay. Specific
details were more likely to be recalled immediately after a story, while
the skeletal outline or schema was more likely to be recalled after the
delay. Thus long-term memory would appear to be schematic in contrast to short-term memory which is more detailed.

Preschoolers were more likely to recall items presented first than
those presented last, and sequencing of events was similar at all ages.
The researchers concluded that story schemes were clearly evident and
that repeating stories was more likely to produce general recall even
though details were still likely to be forgotten or confused. More abstract summaries were produced when children had heard the same or
similar stories repeated several times. Curiously, preschoolers were more
likely than older children to recall stories that were not logically organized, apparently the logic of a story being more crucial with age.

McCartney and Nelson (1981) studied the effect of emphasis in stories told to kindergartners and second graders. Younger and older children did not differ in their recall of unemphasized sections of stories, but large differences were found of the emphasized content. The younger children had slightly better recall of emphasized material, while older children had much greater recall of that material.

While second graders recalled more events and details than kindergartners, later questions revealed that nearly half of the kindergartners could remember events which had not been given in their earlier reconstructions of the story; recognition exceeded recall. Children were able to suggest changes that could be made in the stories, which indicated that children may have two types of scripts: a personal script which includes preferred events, and a stereotypic script which is more schematic.

Four-, five-, and six-year-old children participated in a study by Brown and Hurtig (1983) related to factors often found in story scripts. The six-year-olds were more sensitive to time chronology than were the preschoolers, and the critical event in the story was more likely to be placed in the most logical position by the older children. When asked to reconstruct stories using pictures on cards, the four-year-olds were as likely to construct stories beginning with the last card as with the first. In contrast five-year-olds were more likely to develop stories beginning at the end, and six-year-olds were more likely to initiate story reconstruction at the beginning.

While the older children were more likely to make causal and time inferences in stories, four- and five-year-olds were able to develop events logically three-fourths of the time. The framework for the story was more general for six-year-olds, while younger children were more likely to use specific relationships in story recall. Logical conclusions were more likely to be made when stories had positive consequences, yet the narratives of children were more congruent when negative consequences resulted. When story characters intended negative consequences, children were less likely to reconstruct temporal relationships.

Boundaries Between Story and Reality

Scarlett and Wolf (1980) detail research indicating that the three-year-old is unable to separate fantasy and reality clearly; the world of the story narrative intrudes into everyday life and vice versa. The child does not enter into the story completely, yet is unable to pull away from it completely. In other words, the story events are not autonomous, the immediate wishes of the child take precedence over antecedents within the story framework. As was noted earlier, the distinction between play and context provides the foundation for maintaining story boundaries.

At age three and a half, the boundaries of stories told by children (using figurines) are permeable; the activities of the real world and those in the story are not always distinguished. For example a child's story of a lion includes a statement that he is "not bothering us," thus designating the child and possibly the adult within the story frame. Also at this age the children had difficulty resolving the story, and often the child directly intervened to end the account.

Scarlett and Wolf note that near the end of the year these children use language that goes beyond action to the description of motives and feelings. Instead of talking about characters, children speak for the props. Most of the meaning is now in the narrative rather than in the actions of the props.

Shortly after age four, more elaborations were made upon the story. Prototypical victims and villains surfaced in the stories children developed, with definite scripting. The child becomes a stage manager and the boundaries of the story are firmly maintained. The four-year-old becomes more aware of the audience's perception of the story, as evidenced by the birth of the "metanarrative," the comments on the story. Initially this takes the form of a cue to the story beginning, such as "Let's pretend." The story boundaries are maintained by the metanarrative, making the crossing and recrossing of the division between story and real world more easily accomplished. Yet it is still difficult for the child to tell stories at this age apart from gestures and props.

By age five the story world becomes even more autonomous, as the child uses components already in the story to resolve the problem, rather than imposing additional capacities or information from outside the story context. In addition these older preschoolers were able to have their characters change roles within the story (recall the development of roles in play, mentioned earlier).

Sutton-Smith (1980) had children tell stories to graduate students. More realistic stories were told to female researchers, while more imaginative ones were told to males. While two-year-olds failed to mark the beginnings and endings of stories, by age three terminal markers such as "happily ever after" and "once upon a time" were used, as well as references to context such as location, time, conditions, and participants in the story.

Sutton-Smith notes that preschoolers use repetitive actions between characters in their stories. Storytelling by these youngsters makes use of past tense and each sentence is only slightly connected to the one that follows, indicating a lack of logical connection between actions. By age four, rhymes, alliteration, and playing with words were noticed, while characters are more impersonal (the terms "he" and "she" were used rather than names). Young children used story markers to communicate the "storiness" of the presentation; for example, they set apart the story from other talk by using a different tone of voice (older children communicate this through the plot). By age five the middle of the story becomes more developed.

Because of the development of the boundary between the story and the real world, langauge takes a more prominent role in the story while props (dolls, figurines, and another toys that support the story) take a decreasing role. At first the story meaning is almost entirely carried by the child's manipulation of props, but eventually the child begins to articulate what the prop is doing. Previous and future events are referred to in the narrative although these are almost exclusively the *actions* of the prop. As a result the thoughts of characters are now included, and a distinct audience role is formulated. The way the audience construes the story being told by the child becomes an important function in the telling.

Conflict and Story Comprehension

Miller (1980) presented stories to children which involved two characters in conflict situations. When asked if both could get what they desired, the children indicated three levels of understanding conflict.

The first level, characteristic of four- and five-year-olds, involved a simple understanding of conflict. Asked if both people can get what they want, many at this age answered randomly. When justifications for their answers were requested, the children interpreted the question as "What does each character want?" The protagonist and antagonist were not clearly distinguished.

A second level surfaces among some five-year-olds and predominates among six-year-olds, where children systematically answer that both in the conflict cannot obtain what they want. The child is able to conclude the story but assumes that the story *must* conclude the same way the child intended. A general understanding of conflicts still seems to be missing in children's responses at this age, as their justifications are based almost entirely upon the conclusions they develop in their particular version of the story ending.

Later, by age seven and afterward, the child answers that both characters can get what they want in the conflict. This conclusion is based upon making assumptions other than those accepted in the real world, or by making a different interpretation of the story opening. Even if unable to invent a conclusion where both characters get what they want, these children continue to maintain that it is possible. This is an advancement over the second level in that many outcomes are understood to be possible, yet this stage lacks a realistic understanding of conflict. Eventually by age nine or ten the child concludes that both cannot get what they want, usually justifying their responses with the concept of mutual exclusion.

Ethnic Differences in Story Content and Communication

In her study of literacy in three American communities, Heath (1982, 1983) emphasized the diversity in the way different ethnic groups make sense of stories. Heath contrasted a middle-class "Maintown" community with a white working-class community she called "Roadville," and "Trackton," a black working-class milltown.

The evening "bedtime story" is an accepted context for parent-child interaction in Maintown, an event which helps prepare these children for school instruction. The mother and child participate in reading cycles in which the child is asked questions or attaches labels to objects displayed in a book, followed by a response from the mother (this process is further documented in Bruner, 1986). Through these experiences with books, the child learns to associate two-dimensional pictures and drawings with objects in the real world. By the time these children are six months old they have learned to attend to books, and the parent pays attention to the infant's vocalizations and extends them into appropriate responses.

As the child begins to talk, adults make a running commentary on book related objects or events, which aids the child in relating book material to real situations. Children are allowed to tell fictitious accounts, and talking about books is reinforced. By age three these children are no longer allowed to interact during the story but are required to take an audience role by listening and speaking only when occasionally asked a question.

In contrast, Roadville parents often ask the child to recall past experiences with objects portrayed in a book, but they are not encouraged to transfer their knowledge from books to other contexts. If the child does not make the link between the picture and real world objects, the parent does not explain the difference. Roadville children, unlike those in Maintown, do not receive a running commentary from parents on similarities and differences between what is found in a book and real life. Children are punished if they do not take the listener's role by being quiet during the story.

In Roadville, a good story is a true story; fabrications and exaggerations are considered to be lies. Only real events are allowed to be told. Specific people are designated as storytellers, and stories are used to display the weaknesses of everyone. Personal transgressions are the main source of content for stories, thus emphasizing community norms. Proverbs and summary statements from stories are used to enforce desired behavior. Few books other than Bibles can be found.

As a result, Roadville children have difficulty creating stories and are often unable to relate knowledge to contexts different from that in which the information was learned. Stories told by children are often coached by adults and cannot be initiated unless invited.

The black working-class community of Trackton contrasts markedly with both Maintown and Roadville. Adults pay little attention to the initial vocalizations of infants, considering it only to be noise, not potential words (opposite the sentence extending of Maintown). Children are rarely read to by parents and there is no ritual "bedtime story."

Analogies are required of children, rather than the "what" questions of Maintown and Roadville. The context of stories is considered an important cue to understanding, thus the children learn to describe context thoroughly in their stories. Accounts are initiated by announcing the topic; there are no formula openings and closings to stories as are found in Maintown and Roadville (e.g., "Once upon a time").

Evaluations from the audience are solicited, even when preschoolers are telling stories. Participation by the audience often takes the form of intermittent nodding, laughing, and "yeah's." Storytelling is highly competitive with the most aggressively told stories gaining the most attention. Stories are self-assertive, rather than self-demeaning as in Roadville; rivalries and ultimate victories are prominent themes. While there may be a seed of truth in a story, most of the content is fiction. Usually there is no moral to the story; it is told only for entertainment. Language is not simplified for children, and the question/answer format, so familiar to children in Maintown and Roadville, is absent in Trackton.

The distinction in story presentation in the three communities underscores the diversity of use of stories, as well as the differences in how well these prepare children for school. In addition the distinctions lay the groundwork for misunderstanding and miscommunication between these three communities—stories take on a basically different meaning for each.

Stories Cross-Culturally

Trackton had much earlier antecedents in a different culture, that of Africa with its strong oral tradition. Mitchell (1986) traces the historical linkage between the traditional forms of education in Africa, how they were acculturated during slavery, and their remaining influence in the current black experience.

The oral traditions in Africa were (and from her casual observation, still are) intensely fused with the everyday lifestyle of those in the culture. In the very intimate context of the tribe, the moral message of the oral traditions surrounded the child every day. The story was an art form which could capture the attention of listeners for days, and the tales included many important moral lessons for children. Often the stories would be sung instead of told, portrayed in dance or accompanied by drumming. Strong emotions were associated with the stories, and performers might interact with the audience during the account. (Perhaps the "yeah's" in Trackton are a holdover from this.)

Mitchell notes that small children often took part in intricate dancing in the African culture, giving preschoolers a prominent place in the proceedings. Clearly there was a unity between the cognitive content, affective dimensions, and lifestyle. Much of this same style of teaching was fused with biblical content when Africans became slaves in America, and to some extent remains within the black subculture and particularly the black church.

McCarron (1987), a university professor in Nigeria, also describes the role of folk tales in the transmitting of values within African cultures. One large and diverse group of Nigerians, the Igbo, uses folk tales as well as rituals, festivals, and songs to pass on their values. The folk tales are not only to entertain but also to educate, with moral overtones intended to instill traditional attitudes and values.

Scollon and Scollon (1981) described the personal history narratives in the Alaskan northern-Canadian region, to illustrate that stories are used to communicate the meanings and common understandings of a society. The narrative is central to communication development in the Athabaskan child, since the story is considered an art form integral to social relations as well as entertainment.

Pauses are used by Athabaskans to indicate emphasis, rather than the American approach of using intonation and loudness to punctuate sentences. Athabaskans often use two or four sequences in a story, rather than the common use of three's found in European and American stories (e.g., the three bears).

While studying the Chipewyans in Alberta, Scollon and Scollon became sensitized to the manner in which their own preschooler was being socialized, in contrast to the people they were studying. As Heath (1982, 1983) described in her study, they found themselves asking their child questions and expecting answers about the stories being told.

The Scollons described their child as being literate before she could read, due to the early experiences with stories. She was allowed and even expected to display her knowledge at storytelling, while adults listened to her. In contrast, the Chipewyans expected adults to display their storytelling while children listened.

In telling stories about herself, the Scollon's preschool child referred to herself in the third person ("the girl") indicating a decontextualizing of herself in the storytelling. She framed her storytelling by both an opening and ending, and realized an audience role (common characteristics for preschoolers, as noted earlier). In contrast a much older Chipewyan girl told a story about herself using "we" and "my," as well as more conversational intonations.

Applications for Religious Education

Much of this section has to do with what children can and cannot understand in story structure and content, as well as variations in the ability to tell stories. Age appropriateness is certainly a key application in teaching children religious content. In general, many story components are developing during the early preschool years, yet are not mature until later.

Would this suggest that we should not tell stories to younger preschoolers? Certainly we should be aware of their limitations, but early exposure to simple stories would help teach them story schematic structures. Biblical accounts would probably need to be greatly simplified, in accordance with the limitations at this age, and gradual inclusion of more complex material would tend to facilitate development to a successive level. Schachter (1985) believes that using episodes rather than complete stories is the best way to introduce the Bible to preschoolers.

A question that might be raised at this point is *what* Bible stories should be used with young children. Clearly not all biblical content is appropriate—obvious examples are Jael's murder of Sisera (Judges 4) and the rape of Tamar (II Sam. 13). Developing a comprehensive list of appropriate stories is impossible since the selection depends upon the values of the selector (should violent and sexual content be presented?), one's hermeneutical orientation, and perhaps church tradition.

However, several guidelines might be considered in choosing stories. First, the children's abilities and limitations should be considered (see chapters one, two, and three). Second, while one should avoid sanitizing biblical accounts, differential emphasis of story segments should be considered, such as concentrating upon Noah receiving instruction and protection rather than emphasizing judgment by flood (stories might be reconsidered later in childhood with other emphases via the "spiral curriculum"—see Wilhoit, 1986). Third, age association (God calling Samuel, Jesus welcoming children) and interests of children could be a factor in choosing stories. Finally, one should also consider the relation of story content to personal trauma (an abused child hearing the story of Abraham sacrificing Isaac).

The important cultural and ethnic differences are outlined in the last two studies in this section. The research to date suggests that stories not only take on a different role and function among different groups, but also that religious content will vary in its perceived importance. Heath's note that the Bible is the central book in the lower-class white community only marked the strong moralism that pervaded that group. The fusion of African oral traditions with biblical content, noted by Mitchell, indicates how important the Bible became to African slaves. Yet it is with some irony that even though both communities value a similar religious heritage, the creativity in storytelling by the lower-class blacks would be considered lying to lower-class whites. Religious educators need to consider such distinctives as they attempt to communicate religion to such groups, to promote understanding within the student's cultural context.

When one considers the stylistic variations in biblical and religious materials, there appears to be content suitable to each of the cultural and ethnic contexts described in these studies. The Christian religion is ultimately transcultural in this respect, although it also bears the marks of its cultural origins as well. Ultimately the student comes to a fuller understanding of religion and its documents through appreciation of the diversity between peoples today as well as the differences between one's culture and that of earlier eras of religious history. The cultural groups described in this chapter could have all gained a broader worldview by attempting to understand this diversity, and we can likewise gain through such understanding.

Religious education has the potential of exploring cultural understandings, even with preschoolers. While the teaching of religion is paramount in our efforts, we should not neglect the potential for greater understanding of the world through consideration of sociological distinctives. Religious education can facilitate such broader understandings by exposing children to cultural variations, thus inducing disequilibrium and less egocentric perspectives. This includes not only the different ways people act in various cultures, but also the way they understand God and religion, and the cultural context of the Bible. This could be accomplished by showing films, or better yet having ethnic minority children in the class.

Certainly we must be impressed with the fusion of cognitive content, the affective and also lifestyle aspects in the African cultures mentioned. These have more recently been underscored as components to a truly holistic approach to religious education (Lee, 1985) and thus the fusion of African oral tradition with biblical content may provide an important model to be emulated in modern religious education. While adults may be too inhibited, preschoolers can be just as involved in the telling and retelling of stories with religious content, using all of the variety suggested, including music, dance, and festivity.

DOES ENACTMENT FACILITATE STORY COMPREHENSION?

Thus far we have considered the part that play contributes to story comprehension, as well as the degree to which preschoolers understand the components of story and how those components develop. Recall of specific story content can be facilitated through the use of enactment, a pedagogical technique which will be advocated particularly for older preschoolers. Does story enactment increase understanding for stories and under what conditions with what age children?

Story Comprehension

In a key study, Pellegrini and Galda (1982) considered how well children could reconstruct stories given three different conditions. Children were read a story, after which one group enacted the story with peers and the experimenter did not participate. Another group discussed the story and answered questions with an adult. A third group was asked to draw the story. Each condition was repeated twice.

Kindergarten and first-grade children who enacted the story scored significantly higher than the others, while those who discussed did significantly better than those who drew the story. No significant difference was found between the three conditions with second graders, however. This indicates that preschoolers are more likely to profit from story enactment than older children.

Using a story retelling procedure, significantly more events were recalled by an enactment group than either a discussion or drawing group, and sequences were more accurate among the children that enacted the story. In addition, kindergartners who played roles requiring the most active involvement were the most likely to recall story content, while second graders were superior in amount, sequence, and quality of stories (Galda, 1984).

In a follow-up study, Pellegrini (1984) investigated the effect of adult-directed versus peer-directed enactment as well as how conflicts over role components were resolved. Kindergartners performed significantly better when an adult had given each child a specific role to play and had made comments about the enactment. A second group where the adult only designated roles produced better results than groups where children were only asked questions or when they only drew pictures related to the story. The last group received the poorest scores of story comprehension.

One week later the groups were again tested for story recall. The adult and peer enactment groups still had better recall than the other two groups. When asked to retell the story one week later, there were no differences between the play groups and questions group. An additional measure of story comprehension was a picture rearrangement task, in which both enactment groups were better than the group that discussed questions, and all three groups performed better than the group that drew pictures. Thus enactment of stories, with or without an adult, is an optimal strategy for increasing story comprehension until about six years of age, but other methods are equally effective with older children.

The degree to which enactment increases the understanding of a story is at least partly dependent upon the child's familiarity with the enactment process. Silvern, Williamson, and Waters (1983) studied middle- and lower-class kindergartners who heard ten stories, one each week, over a ten-week period. Each child was in one of five different conditions: the child either enacted a character in the story, used puppets to show what a character did, was shown drawings corresponding to the story, heard each sentence of the story read twice, or was told to think about a specific character. In the latter three groups the experimenter also dramatized the character's role.

Initially the highest learning occurred in the drawing condition. However, by the completion of the ten weeks the enactment group was learning significantly more than those under any of the other conditions. This would indicate that once children become familiar with the enactment approach it becomes the most effective method of teaching preschoolers.

Williamson and Silvern (1984) note that children enacting stories are more likely to benefit if they do so with other children rather than playing the roles alone, probably due to the accommodation function of conflicts (Pellegrini, 1984). They also note research indicating that while familiarity with the enactment approach aids learning from that approach, mere familiarity with the story does not influence the effectiveness of enactment. The researchers conclude that adults need to aid enactment if the story is unfamiliar to children, although the adult only needs to direct, not participate.

The context in which enactment takes place has also been found to influence a child's ability in enacting a story. Kelly-Byrne (1982) found that enacting stories within the privacy of the child's home produced less guarded and more sophisticated enactment than enactment in a public context. Even the location within the home influenced enactment, with private home situations (the child's bedroom) being superior to public home situations (the living room or kitchen).

Cognitive Advances with the Disadvantaged

In research by Saltz, Dixon, and Johnson (1977), low-income children aged three to four and a half years, heard stories and then enacted for four to six sessions. An adult initially took the key role, but later encouraged children to trade roles. It was found that children who enacted stories increased in IQ, perceived causal relationships to a greater extent, made realistic judgments and resisted temptation to a greater extent than children who were only asked questions about the story or did activities such as cutting, pasting, and looking at animal books. Previous studies by these researchers also indicated increased memory, story comprehension, and empathy as a result of enactment.

Improvement in the above areas was particularly high with children who began the study with high IQ's. It should be noted that some of these increases did not reach statistical significance at the accepted level ($p < .05$) but were easily significant at a less stringent level ($p < .10$).

Dansky (1980) conducted a somewhat similar study with preschoolers from low socioeconomic backgrounds. The five-year-olds played out roles related to a suggested theme, using props. An adult encouraged, modeled, and sometimes suggested alternative actions. These children scored significantly higher in tests of verbal comprehension and memory than did a group that investigated objects and discussed with an adult. They also performed better than a group that was allowed to play as they wished with an adult present to answer questions. In addition those in the first group were more fluent, organized, and imaginative in their verbal productions.

In her study of low-income Mexican-American five- and six-year-olds, Villarreal (1982) described the results of enactment upon a number of comprehension measures. Recall was significantly higher when stories were enacted in contrast to groups where puppets portrayed the story or children worked on puzzles and colored pictures after the story. Enactment at intervals *while* the story was being told was found to produce superior learning compared with enactment *following* the story.

Applications for Religious Education

Clearly the research indicates that enactment is a positive means of teaching stories to preschoolers, and is apparently the best way to do this up to about second grade. After that age it is still useful, although not superior to other commonly used approaches. There is also evidence that children need to have a number of experiences in story enactment before it reaches its highest potential as a teaching device, since they may be unfamiliar with the procedure.

Enactment can take place in any context, but religious education in the home, using enactment of stories, is more likely to produce greater skill performances (though the degree to which this affects learning has not been investigated). Enactment with peers produces higher learning, yet that enactment should preferably be in a familiar environment; enactment of religious stories should be done in a context where the child feels comfortable and relatively uninhibited.

Enacting religious stories should preferably be done during phases of a story, not just one long enactment. This would coincide with the limitations in cognitive processing (the slots in memory noted in chapter one). However, since familiarity with content and procedure allows for more material to be processed simultaneously, it is likely that episodes could be combined as enactment is repeated until an entire story could eventually be enacted at one time.

Adult involvement by directing and supervising the enactment is to be preferred, although the adult need not actually perform a role within the play. On the other hand, it is likely that if a key role is difficult the adult may need to model that role in the initial enactment.

There are many extra benefits from the enacting of stories other than increased story comprehension, including possible IQ and social cooperation increases. In addition it should be noted that while enactment is superior to many other more commonly used approaches, several methods could be used with enactment to give the child multiple exposures and perspectives to the story content. Other methods that religious educators could use, in order of effectiveness, include puppet enactment, discussion, and drawing. Merely repeating the story or being told to pay close attention are far less effective in aiding story recall.

STORIES, ENACTMENT, AND RELIGIOUS EDUCATION

Research on stories and enactment procedures using religious content is virtually unknown. However, since religious concepts are apparently processed much like concepts in other areas, it can be assumed that the above methodological research would be equally applicable.

I Love to Tell Stories

While there has been little research of the area, a number of writers within the Christian tradition have written on the subject of stories and their function in both religious education and the Christian framework more generally. Substantial bibliographies are to be found in two chapters related to storytelling and "story playing" in the recent revision of *Childhood Education in the Church* (Clark, Brubaker, & Zuck, 1986) as well as a book-length treatment of the subject by Lucie Barber (1981). It is unfortunate that the former is apparently based upon intuition and general theory rather than empirical research (Barber is research based).

Professionals from outside religious education have also commented on the importance of the story to Christian values and training. Educational psychologist William Kilpatrick (1983, 1986) has noted that stories speak to the heart and to one's values unlike any other mode of communication. The telling of stories has historically been the most important means of moral education, says Kilpatrick, and stories help to provide meaning and purpose for life. "The cosmic drama" of life is seen in embryo in the small child's play, he concludes.

Joy (1985) notes that Jesus often used stories (parables) to communicate truths to his audience. He also states that good storytelling is an art that the best preachers have cultivated and use effectively in their sermons. Joy identifies stories with right brain functioning and elsewhere (1986) has suggested that the distinct characteristics of the male brain are particularly amenable to the story as the method of communication. This is because men are more likely to be reached through the affective aspects of stories; people are called to discipleship through feeling, not logic, says Joy. Clearly the story, particularly when enacted, includes both the cognitive and affective realms, and even approximates the lifestyle dimension of religious experience; enacting can be similar to, and practice for, everyday life.

Other Applications of Enactment in Religious Education

In addition to enacting stories, how else might enactment be used by religious educators? The little research on enactment that exists within a religious education context relates to church *role* acquisition. Ratcliff (1985) used enactment to teach preschoolers the roles of praying, taking an offering, song leading, and preaching. One group of children enacted the church roles with the experimenter participating, while a second group enacted the roles as the experimenter commented on missing components of the roles. While both groups increased in their role performance, those with which the experimenter enacted the roles improved the most.

Religious behavior should certainly be more than just performance of roles, yet it is in such performance that children can begin to understand roles. Thus there is the potential for using enactment to teach certain activities associated with worship. Mini "worship services" could be developed in church contexts in which children could participate in such roles. Ideally these skills should be trained apart from adults, and later practiced in a joint service with adults (perhaps the first few minutes of a standard service).

Could enactment be used to teach preschoolers how to worship? While it might be possible to shape the child's behavior to conform with the socially defined physical posture for worship (e.g., raising hands, kneeling, standing with bowed head, etc.), worship involves more than outward behavior. Indeed, worship has not been a well-defined activity; descriptions tend to be vague and mystical.

Perhaps worship is primarily metaphysical and thus not subject to empirical verification and systematic training. (Wilhoit, 1986, lays the groundwork for such a position, although he does not specifically address the subject of preschooler worship.) Yet surely there are cognitive and possibly behavioral referents—is not the thinking in Christian worship distinct from that in a Hindu mantra? If evidence can be provided for children being truly able to worship, then enactment may have some value in teaching related behavior. However, there is always the danger that enacting "worship" may only be teaching outward form without attendant spiritual reality, behavior without belief. The church already has too much of this.

If enactment has dubious value for teaching worship, might it be used to teach traditions? Sociologically these forms tend to enhance the sense of community within churches and families (see Gaede, 1985) and have been an important part of the African and American black experience, as seen earlier in this chapter. Teaching rituals and traditions might be possible, as long as adults do not emphasize the abstract meanings.

Most traditions are symbolic in nature, and an adult understanding of such symbolism is not possible for the preschooler. The punitive effect of boring, incomprehensible rituals may have unfortunate long-term effects upon the attitudes a child develops about those activities specifically and religion generally, as was noted in chapter one. On the other hand, to be completely excluded from these activities may result in negative emotional reactions and an opportunity will be lost for the child to see the importance of religious traditions to the parents and other significant adults. The important social function of these events may be underscored perhaps by brief and preferably active involvement during part of such activities. Prior enactment of segments would help not only in the performance of expected behaviors but also desensitize the child to the possibly unusual context.

Another use of enactment would be developing scenarios common to human existence which children would role-play. Children would enact situations familiar to either preschoolers or older children, incorporating principles derived from religious instruction. This might be prefaced by a discussion of how principles could be applied in such contexts, as suggested by the religious educator. To some extent adult contexts could also be enacted, as long as they are consistent with the child's developmental readiness. This could be combined with moral development content, helping to bridge the broad gap that exists between moral reasoning and moral behavior.

CONCLUSION

There is considerable evidence for the utility of using play, stories, and enactment as learning methods for preschoolers. These may, in fact, be foundational to the learning of religious education at this age, since both the cognitive and affective realms are engaged with each of these. As has been noted, enactment would also simulate the lifestyle dimension, perhaps the most difficult area to address in religious education, yet certainly one of the most important goals in our endeavors.

REFERENCES

Barber, L. (1981). *When a story would help*. St. Meinrad, IN: Abbey Press.

Brown, C. J., & Hurtin, R. R. (1983). Children's discourse competence: An evaluation of the development of inferential processes. *Discourse Processes, 6*, 353-375.

Bruner, J. S. (1986). *Actual minds, possible worlds*. Cambridge, MA: Harvard University Press.

Clark, R. E., Brubaker, J., & Zuck, R. (1986). *Childhood education in the church*, (rev. ed.). Chicago: Moody Press.

Dansky, J. L. (1980). Cognitive consequences of sociodramatic play and exploration training for economically disadvantaged preschoolers. *Journal of Child Psychology and Psychiatry, 20*, 47-58.

Elkind, D. (1980). The role of play in religious education. *Religious Education, 75*, 282-293.

Flavell, J. (1985). *Cognitive development* (2nd ed.). Englewood Cliffs, NJ: Prentice-Hall.

French, L. A., Lucariello, J., Seidman, S., & Nelson, K. (1985). The influence of discourse content and context on preschoolers' use of language. In L. Galda & A. Pellegrini (Ed.), *Play, language and stories: The development of children's literate behavior*. Norwood, NJ: Ablex.

Gaede, S. D. (1985). *Belonging: Our need for community in church and family*. Grand Rapids, MI: Zondervan.

Galda, L. (1984). Narrative competence: Play, storytelling, and story comprehension. In A. Pellegrini, & T. Yawkey (Ed.), *The development of oral and written languages in social contexts*. Norwood, NJ: Ablex.

Gardner, H. (1982). The making of a storyteller. *Psychology Today*, 49-63.

Garvey, C. (1984). *Children's talk*. Cambridge, MA: Harvard University Press.

Heath, S. B. (1982). What no bedtime story means: Narrative skills at home and school. *Language in Society, 11,* 49-76.

Heath, S. B. (1983). *Ways with words.* Cambridge: Cambridge University Press.

Johnson, R. K. (1983). *The Christian at play.* Grand Rapids, MI: Wm. B. Erdmans.

Joy, D. (1985). *Bonding: Relationships in the image of God.* Waco, TX: Word.

Joy, D. (1986). Innate differences between males and females, Focus on the Family (taped radio broadcast), September 15.

Kelly-Byrne, D. (1982). *A narrative of play and intimacy: A seven year old's play and story relationship with an adult.* Ph. D. dissertation, University of Pennsylvania.

Kilpatrick, W. (1983). *Psychological seduction.* Nashville: Nelson.

Kilpatrick, W. (1986). Why secular psychology is not enough. *Imprimis, 15,* 1-6.

Lee, J. M. (1985). *The content of religious instruction.* Birmingham, AL: Religious Education Press.

Mandler, J. M. (1983). Representation. In J. Flavell & E. Markman (Ed.), *Cognitive development. Handbook of child psychology, (Vol. 3),* New York: John Wiley.

McCarron, M. M. (1987). Folktales as transmitters of values. *Religious Education, 82,* 20-29.

McCartney, K. A., & Nelson, K. (1981). Children's use of scripts in story recall. *Discourse Processes, 4 ,* 59-70.

McLoyd, V. C., Ray, S. A., & Etter-Lewis, G. (1985). Being and becoming: The interface of language and family role knowledge in the pretend play of young African American girls. In A. Pellegrini (Ed.), *Play, language and stories: The development of children's literate behavior .* Norwood, NJ: Ablex.

Miller, D. E., Snyder, G. F., & Neff, R. W. (1973). *Using biblical simulations.* Valley Forge, PA: Judson.

Miller, L. (1980). The idea of conflict: A study of the development of story understanding. In E. Winner & H. Gardner (Eds.), *New directions for child development: Fact, fiction, and fantasy in childhood.* San Francisco: Jossey-Bass.

Mitchell, E. P. (1986). Oral tradition: Legacy of faith for the black church. *Religious Education, 81,* 93-112.

Nelson, K., & Seidman, S. (1984). Playing with scripts. In E. Bretherton (Ed.), *Symbolic play: The development of social understanding.* Orlando, FL: Academic Press.

Pellegrini, A. D. (1984) Identifying causal elements in the thematic-fantasy play paradigm. *American Educational Research Journal, 21,* 691-703.

Pellegrini, A. D. (1985). Relations between preschool children's symbolic play and literate behavior. In A. Pellegrini (Ed.), *Play, language, and stories: The development of children's literate behavior.* Norwood, NJ: Ablex.

Pellegrini, A. D., & Galda, L. (1982). The effects of thematic-fantasy play training on the development of children's story comprehension. *American Educational Research Journal, 19,* 443-452.

Piaget, J. (1973). Piaget takes a teacher's look. *Learning,* Oct. 22-27.

Postolos-Cappadora, D. A. (1983). *The sacred play of children.* New York: Seabury.

Ratcliff, D. E. (1985). The use of play in Christian education. *Christian Education Journal, 6,* 26-33.

Rubin, S. & Wolf, D. (1980). The development of maybe: The evolution of social roles into narrative roles. In E. Winner & H. Gardner (Eds.), *New directions for child development: Fact, fiction, and fantasy in childhood.* San Francisco: Jossey-Bass.

Sachs, J. (1980). The role of adult-child play in language development. In K. Rubin (Ed.), *New directions for child development: Children's play.* San Francisco: Jossey-Bass.

Saltz, E., Dixon, D., & Johnson, J. (1977). Training disadvantaged preschoolers on various fantasy activities: Effects on cognitive functioning and impulse control. *Child Development, 48,* 367-380.

Scarlett, W. G., & Wolf, D. (1980). When it's only make-believe: The construction of a boundary between fantasy and reality in storytelling. In E. Winner & H. Gardner (Eds.), *New directions for child development: Fact, fiction, and fantasy in childhood.* San Francisco: Jossey-Bass.

Schachter, L. (1985). Alternative to Bible stories for young children. *Religious Education, 80,* 308-312.

Scollon, R., & Scollon, S. (1981). *Narrative, literacy and face in interethnic communication. Advances in discourse processes (Vol. 7).* Norwood, NJ: Ablex.

Silvern, S. B., Williamson, P. A., & Waters, B. (1983). Play as a mediator of comprehension: An alternative to play training. *Educational Research Quarterly, 7,* 16-21.

Slackman, E., & Nelson, K. (1984). Acquisition of an unfamiliar script in story form by young children. *Child Development, 55,* 329-340.

Sutton-Smith, B. (1980). Presentation and representation in children's fictional narrative. In E. Winner & H. Gardner (Eds.), *New directions for child development: Fact, fiction, and fantasy in childhood.* San Francisco: Jossey-Bass.

Villarreal, B. (1982). *An investigation of the effects of types of imaginative play in relation to sex and temporal proximity on vocabulary and story comprehension in young Mexican-American children.* Ph. D. dissertation, The Pennsylvania State University.

Wilhoit, J. (1986). *Christian education and the search for meaning.* Grand Rapids, MI: Baker.

Williamson, P. A., & Silvern, S. B. (1984). Creative dramatic play and language comprehension. In T. Yawkey & A. Pellegrini (Eds.), *Child's play: Developmental and applied.* Hillsdale, NJ: Lawrence Erlbaum.

Wolf, D. (1982). Understanding others: A longitudinal case study of the concept of independent agency. In G. Forman (Ed.) *Action and thought: From sensorimotor schemes to symbolic operations.* New York: Academic Press.

Wolf, D. P., & Pusch, J. (1985). The origins of autonomous texts in play boundaries. In A. Pellegrini (Ed.), *Play, language and stories: The development of children's literate behavior.* Norwood, NJ: Ablex.

Chapter Ten:

Planning, Evaluation, and Research

DAVID STARKS AND DONALD RATCLIFF

Planning and evaluation of preschooler achievement should be priorities for religious educators. Apart from systematic planning how are we to know what education is to take place? And how can methods of teaching, curriculum alternatives, and even entire preschools be compared without assessment? Religious educators need to consider evaluation and planning as foundational to their enterprise, since it is possible to expend considerable time and effort and yet fail to make a significant, lasting impact upon the child. Are we really accomplishing anything, or are we only fooling ourselves?

A corollary question is, "How can I improve my instruction so that concepts and attitudes will be more readily or more thoroughly acquired?" Thus the instructor should continually seek to improve the curriculum and his or her skills, using the evaluative process to find the most effective means of accomplishing the educational task.

When assessing the effectiveness of a set of procedures or a program, you may be attempting to answer questions such as, "Are we realizing the results we expect?" "Are the children prepared for kindergarten after one or more years in our nursery school?" and "How do the results of our program or preschool compare with the results of other programs or preschools?" These issues need to be evaluated periodically—programs can too easily be continued or new ones initiated on the basis of hunches, subjective experiences, or fads rather than actual findings based upon data.

Religious educators should cultivate an attitude of curiosity and skepticism. Daily we should ask ourselves such questions as "Are the parents satisfied with the new curriculum in our Sunday school (or preschool)?" "How helpful has it been to separate the three-year-olds from the four-year-olds?" "Why do the children apply principles from Bible stories when one teacher tells the story but not when another teacher tells it?" "If we lengthen the time the nursery school is in session, will it make a noticeable difference in learning?" "Why do some materials seem to appeal to boys more than girls?" and "What parts of our music program should we revise this year?" These are only examples, of course, of the many questions that one can generate. It is suggested that religious educators devote some time to posing such questions about their work, since each question is a potential issue for evaluation.

Nearly two decades ago David Elkind (1970) wrote a landmark chapter on the need for research and evaluation in religious education. He encouraged religious educators and researchers to measure the various effects of instructional media, students, agencies and agents of instruction (usually teachers or parents). Elkind emphasized that the large, global studies (particularly survey studies) that have been done often produce ambiguous results. He recommended that more detailed investigation of relevant variables in the educational process be conducted.

This chapter will outline the process of religious education as being composed of three phases: planning, implementation, and evaluation. Some of the components of each of these have been given consideration earlier in this handbook, particularly in chapters seven through nine. The emphasis here is upon evaluation and preparation for evaluation through planning and implementation. A final section of the chapter will briefly consider research methods and provide guidelines for interpreting and understanding research studies.

PLANNING

Basic to any religious education should be a set of general goals. Sometimes these purposes may be stated in a single broad statement of institutional mission or philosophy of education. In preschools, such a statement or set of goals may be a part of the original organizational documents, such as articles of incorporation. Sunday schools and families are perhaps less likely to have developed such components.

It is instructive to reflect upon the basic reasons for religious education. Why should we expend the effort to provide such instruction? Parents and teachers may find it helpful to consider this question before going further in their planning. It is advantageous to spend adequate time with preschool teachers, staff, parents, and others in developing written goal statements.

Objectives

A specific lesson or task for children is based upon notions (sometimes fuzzy, sometimes clear) about what one desires to achieve. Some goals are explicit while others are implicit, unstated, or even unknown. In order to study and produce useful results, desired outcomes need to be precisely defined in terms of student or learner behavior. Broad statements need to be sharpened to the extent that they represent behaviors or actions that can be observed and measured. The formulation of learning objectives can be a great asset to religious education (Ratcliff, 1982; Heck & Shelley, 1979; Lee, 1985).

For example, a broad goal would be to teach children about some of the prominent families in the Old Testament. One objective that would help accomplish this goal is describing the families and designating the characteristics of specific people in the stories.

A good objective should include four characteristics (Mager, 1962). First, objectives should be worded in terms of the learner's behavior. Some examples include: "*Children* will be able to describe one way that Miriam helped Moses when he was a tiny baby" or "*Students* will state how they can be helpful to their brothers and sisters in ways similar to those shown by Miriam."

As can be seen in the above examples, objectives should also be stated in terms of some observable or measurable behavior. Too often objectives fall short at this point—we may want children to "know" or "understand" or "appreciate," but these are impossible to objectively evaluate unless stated in terms of student behaviors. Better and more measurable descriptions include verbs that state student behavior, rather than vague notions of knowing or understanding. What is the student to *do*? Good objectives include precise verbs such as: write, recite, identify, differentiate, solve, construct, compare, and contrast (Mager, 1962). Additional examples include: express, describe, distinguish, specify, discuss, select, define, recognize, design, give examples, and give applications.

The third and fourth characteristics of a good objective are the conditions and extent of the desired behavior. Under what circumstances should the target behavior occur and to what degree is it required before the child is considered to have achieved the objective? This may involve a statement of what resource/s the child will be provided and the standard to which the child's behavior will be compared. For example, "*Given a songbook,* the child will lead the other children in singing *by waving arms, singing, standing, and facing the other children.*" In this example, being given the songbook is the condition, while waving, singing, standing, and turning in a particular direction are the standards for accomplishing the role-playing task. Should the child not exhibit all four behaviors at least once, the objective is considered not to have been met. Often the standard is stated in terms of the number of behaviors or percentage of correct responses required.

Must all objectives be *behavioral,* based upon the principles of psychological conditioning? As Barber (1981) has aptly demonstrated, behavioral pedagogy has a definite place in the teaching of preschooler values. Yet Elkind (1970) clearly prefers appealing to the child's interests rather than external rewards and punishments. However, it can be argued that these are not mutually exclusive—one can capitalize upon intrinsic interests, allow time for free play and exploration, *and* challenge the child by introducing religious content and reinforcing accomplishment. Concentrating only upon the child's present interests is likely to truncate religious education to the child's immature perspective and limited experience. Would even the most antibehavioral religious educator have us do away with praising a child's achievement because it is reinforcing?

It can be argued that objectives should always be behavioral in the sense that tangible, measurable behavior is the criterion for accomplishment. They may be but are not necessarily linked to the behavioral methodology of extrinsic reinforcement. Rather, it is quite likely that some mentalistic concepts can also be included, as long as those concepts can be specified in terms of measurable behavior. Cognitive objectives lead to behaviors assumed to be indicators of desired concepts or mental tasks. For both behavioral and cognitive objectives, some *activity* must be observed and measured to determine whether the child has accomplished the goal.

A specific objective may or may not be appropriate for an entire class of children. Differences in cognitive abilities, experience, moral reasoning, and spiritual understanding may very well call for individualization in teaching. Religious educators must individualize, but group objectives are also appropriate at times (for example, in story enactment— see chapter nine).

In recent years the strict form of behavioral objectives has been questioned by some. Lee (1985) noted that "open objectives" are alternatives to "closed objectives," the latter being characterized by Mager's outline. Some educators believe it is improper to project all learner behavior prior to teaching. There are outcomes that cannot be predicted, particularly in the realms of the affect, esthetics, and insight (Brookfield, 1986). Yet specification of most desired ends are imperative if we are to have evaluation within the cognitive and behavioral domains.

IMPLEMENTATION

Design

Several designs are available to the religious educator. Many objectives state specific criteria or standards to which children's responses are compared. These lead to criterion-based evaluations. Comparison to a standard is used when a standard is available and appropriate. For example, the goal of a teacher is that *all* children discriminate between events that came *before* and those that occurred *after* a particular event in a story. Evaluation of this objective is said to be criterion-referenced in that children are not compared to each other but to a predetermined standard.

An alternate design is the norm-referenced approach. Here the goal is to evaluate a child's performance in comparison to the behavior of others rather than a standard. Group comparisons are possible when groups are taught the same content in different ways or by different teachers. Many designs with considerably greater complexity can be developed by modifying the above designs, or by use of qualitative design (qualitative methodology will be considered under the research section).

Methodology

The choice of design is in part influenced by instructional methodology. While the selection of the specific method of teaching is beyond the scope of this chapter, it is crucial that children be adequately prepared for the content to be taught and the processes involved in that teaching.

Behavioral psychology has given us the concepts of "shaping" and "chaining" which can be used in teaching religious concepts and behaviors to preschoolers. Psychologists are able to train mentally impaired children to distinguish colors, a behavior not commonly found in this population. This is accomplished by systematically rewarding or reinforcing activities that are more and more like the desired behavior. For example, a child is first given praise when he looks toward the color red when asked, "Which circle is red?" After he is regularly looking in the correct direction, he is then reinforced only when he touches the red circle. When such movement becomes habitual he is only reinforced when he chooses red objects from an array of five colored circles. Gradually, step by step, his behavior is shaped.

The concept of "chaining" involves a *series* of behaviors being taught, each one linked to the one before. Chaining uses a procedure called "task analysis" to break down the desired behavior or attitude into specific components. The instructor then teaches them one at a time (Barber, 1981), such as teaching the proper method of building a pyramid with ten blocks. In shaping, the goal is often teaching one behavior (raising your hand to be called on) whereas in chaining a sequence of behaviors is taught (tying a shoe).

Preschooler educators may use shaping and chaining to develop certain behaviors. For example, children may need to learn to listen to a story, show consideration for others, use books without tearing or marking on them, take turns in playing with a toy, and how to use the tape recorder to play a favorite song. Every experienced teacher or parent knows that expecting perfection immediately is sure to produce frustration on the part of both the child and teacher or parent. But patiently shaping or chaining procedures over several sessions may produce gradual improvement. The instructor needs to develop a *set* of objectives in these cases, one for each step in the process. The final skill is termed a "terminal" objective while the subskills are called "instrumental" or "intermediate" objectives.

A similar procedure is needed when teaching concepts to children. Too often religious educators (and other educators as well) overlook the necessary prerequisite skills to learn the desired concept. For example, one must be able to add before one can multiply. The child could memorize the "time tables" before being able to add, but would not understand the *concept* of multiplication.

Many cognitive skills require prior environmental and academic experiences for acquisition. Learning usually builds upon prior learning and to ignore this fact is likely to produce failure and frustration for all involved.

The religious educator should carefully consider what prerequisite skills and abilities are needed for a desired behavior or mental task and be certain those skills have been acquired. Should later evaluation indicate that the intervention failed, the educator should reconsider the possibility that foundational skills were absent, as well as consider other potential sources of failure.

Measurement

In many education settings the measures of the criterion are called tests. However, this term is too restrictive for the kinds of measurement that are likely to be employed with preschool children in religious education. In a religious education setting you are more likely to employ observation, checklists, self-reports, and reports by parents rather than formal testing instruments. These measurement techniques are summarized below:

Technique	Description	Example
Self-report	A statement by a child of some learning or activity related to an objective	How did you help your mother this week?
Interview	Structured questions about a child's behavior and/or learning answered by another person (often a parent)	What songs did your child sing this week?
Observation	A guide to direct a teacher or observer summarize specific behavior/s in the class setting	In what ways did a particular child communicate with other children?
Checklist	A structured instrument designed to direct a teacher, observer or parent to record the occurrence of particular behaviors	Mark each time that a child: leaves the group, asks for help, picks up a book, cries, etc.

While the above list is not exhaustive, it shows several possible types of outcome measures that can be employed. It is a good idea to keep a file of questions that specify individual measurable behaviors, such as those in the above examples and those at the beginning of this chapter. You should add to that file as you read about, observe, and discuss children's activities. Encourage those with whom you work to develop appropriate questions.

Many of these questions will fall into one of the two categories which were considered earlier: cognitive or behavioral. Cognitive measures are those that are used to answer questions about (assess) any aspect of thinking, such as facts, knowledge, ideas, reasoning, applications, or problem-solving. Behavioral measures are those that describe actions or activities that a child does. Cognitive outcomes are used to determine if children have learned factual information, distinctions between events, specific characteristics, sequences, or applications of ideas. Behavioral measures are used for determining outcomes, such as whether children apply actions at home, whether they spontaneously offer to help after a story on helping, or whether they share toys with a sibling.

Be sure that your list includes *both* behavioral and cognitive criterion measures. After you have developed a list you should then select those that you want to use in a specific learning event. You may wish to limit yourself to a set of measures that will allow you to assess each segment of children's activities, such as one Sunday school lesson or one-half day of preschool, with two to four questions. The measures that you have developed must themselves be evaluated to help you determine whether you have an appropriate and trustworthy set (see "validity and reliability" in the next section).

EVALUATION

Subsequent to implementing the educational procedure, the religious educator needs to examine the results. This may involve an individual comparison of the child's performance with the original objective, comparison of the child with the class as a whole, or comparison of the child or group with another kind of group. Examples of the latter include a similar group taught in a different manner, other preschools in the area, or a larger regional or national sample as in norm-referenced testing.

Determining whether a difference found is a significant difference is beyond the scope of this chapter (see Hinkle, Wiersma, & Jurs, 1979, for a detailed discussion of the statistical calculations involved in determining a significant difference). Later in this chapter the concept of significant difference will be considered in relation to understanding a research report.

However, if the child has achieved the criterion (standard) stated in the objective and has failed to do so previously, improvement is obvious. Comparing one group of children to another is more difficult because the two groups of children may not have begun at an equal starting point—thus the need for pretest/posttest design.

Should the teaching moment be successful, the child may still require additional practice with the acquired skill before attempting a more advanced task. Failure to achieve the desired criteria requires a reexamination of the methodology (it may have been inappropriate), the objective (it may be unrealistic and need to be broken down into simpler components), or the prerequisite skills (one or more may have been missing and overlooked earlier). When the child has not accomplished the objective, alternate instruction is generally called for; mere repetition of the identical training is unlikely to help, unless failure was due to inadequate physical or cognitive development. In this case waiting a few months and repeating the training may improve the performance.

Validity and Reliability

The religious educator should consider the adequacy of the measuring instrument before concluding that failure is due to the child or the method of training, or that apparent success is necessarily genuine success. The first test of an instrument is whether it measures what it is intended to. If you are interested in behavioral change you need to look at behavior. If you want creative applications of ideas, then evaluate the novel applications made by the child. Likewise, examine for specific facts if factual information is desired.

Validity is the term used to describe this first test. Has the test or measure assessed what it purports to assess? For this chapter we are limiting discussion to content validity, which involves asking whether a measure samples or includes all of the essential points of an educational program. A valid criterion measure will include all of the major elements in the goals and objectives and none outside the domains of these statements. Thus, there is both an inclusive test and an exclusive test for the validity of the measure; it should include *all* that is essential and *nothing* outside of what is essential with respect to the goals. You might put your measures to the test by asking others knowledgeable in the field to read, evaluate, and help modify the items used to evaluate children.

A second attribute that your measures must have is *reliability.* They must allow you to measure content or behavior consistently so that you and others can trust the results. You would never use an elastic tape to measure how much a child is growing; neither should you try to assess an important educational outcome with an "elastic" measuring device. Reliability is measured in four ways: consistent results 1) at different points in time, 2) with different forms of the same instrument, 3) within a section of an instrument, or 4) across judgments. This last approach, sometimes referred to as interjudge reliability, is most relevant for religious education. If you are using interviews, observations, or verbal questions to collect data, you are relying on people to make judgments. They will observe or listen and report what they heard or saw.

You would like to think that this information is objective and factual so that you can use what they report to draw conclusions, but because the information is open to interpretation you will need to make sure those judging are using the same criteria. Interjudge reliability is verified by having all of your judges assess the same event independently and then comparing their descriptions to be sure that all are the same. If you find that observers or judges are operating with different standards or are interpreting rather than describing, you will need to bring the evaluators together and provide feedback to each person regarding what others are observing and reporting so that the evaluations will be consistent. You might point out that judges or observers must describe, not interpret. Interpretations should only come *after* all the observations are completed and you report the findings.

Studies of interjudge reliability often find that individuals differ because errors indicate:

1. They are looking at different parts of the same event. Some might see the beginning and others the end of an event.

2. They are weighing different parts of an event differently. Some may think that a factual error is more important than an error of interpretation. Others might not make this distinction or even assume the opposite.

3. People will use the same words to mean different things. Words do not necessarily mean the same thing to everyone. One person's idea of a clear explanation may to another be a confusing of the facts.

4. Some will interpret even though the instructions state they should describe. You will need to train judges to avoid interpretation and just give the facts.

Consistency across time, between different versions of the same test instrument and within an instrument from item-to-item or section-to-section are other common means of judging reliability. If you believe that these areas of reliability should be addressed, consult a standard reference in testing or evaluation.

Formative and Summative Evaluation

There are times when your evaluation will examine a program before it is completed and the findings will be used to modify and improve the procedures, practices, or materials before they are put into their final form. This *formative* evaluation yields helpful information that will enable you to produce a more polished product. In contrast, evaluation that is conducted with the final form of a program to assess effectiveness is termed *summative* evaluation.

Formative evaluation requires the evaluator to examine components of a program to determine the effectiveness of each section. Assume that your church has prepared a new curriculum for preschool children that involves the integration of stories, play, drama, music, and art. This twelve-week program has been carefully planned and developed over a period of months and parts have been tried out and refined.

You are now ready to implement the program but wish to collect further data prior to using it with all of the children. Based upon your goals and objectives you will need to design criterion measures that will provide information on the effectiveness of each aspect of the program. Formative evaluation provides information that will enable you to make modifications so that the program becomes more effective.

In order to use formative evaluation you must have a program that is well-developed and one to which you are willing to devote considerable effort both in evaluation and modification on the basis of evaluative data. It is essential that you detach yourself and others from the level of emotional attachment that makes it impossible or difficult to accept negative findings and make change. This type of evaluation has been found to be extremely valuable in recent years in the refinement of instructional materials.

To further illustrate formative evaluation, a unit might be planned to teach children to express their ideas and feelings about worship through a variety of means, including creative art, song, drama, dance, prayer, and original stories. The evaluator would collect data on each of the expected criterion measures and modify the instruction to produce the level of results desired. Each week the evaluator, who is not the teacher, collects the art work, uses a checklist to observe the class sessions, and phones parents with questions to determine the specific behaviors that children are demonstrating at home. She then suggests changes in the materials and activities that might lead to the desired levels of performance.

To illustrate summative evaluation, a series of classes during Advent could be directed toward teaching children the Christmas story. It is expected that they will be able to identify the principal characters by name and state how each fits into the narrative. They should be able to tell the story in the correct sequence and sing two Christmas songs. They should also be able to tell the story using figures from a manger scene provided by the teacher. A pretest may be given by both teachers and parents to identify the level of performance prior to instruction. Performance on the pretest is compared to posttest performance during the first week of January yielding a measure of effectiveness.

RESEARCH

Research can be considered an extension of the evaluative process outlined above. As in teaching, there is planning, implementation of the plans, and evaluation.

Research is not, however, identical to evaluation. Research is designed to describe relationships between methods of teaching, characteristics of learners, and teacher characteristics by the measurement of specific learning outcomes. Evaluation, in contrast, provides information about the effectiveness of programs, materials, and methods to enable you to monitor and improve the quality of your practice. Thus the preschool religious educator is most likely to be concerned with questions of evaluation when making decisions about the effectiveness of programs, practices, and materials. The precision and controls necessary to conduct rigorous empirical research are likely to be lacking while conducting programs in a local setting.

Research studies enable you to examine comparative data and ascertain whether treatments, techniques, or characteristics of individuals lead to divergent outcomes. The two primary types of research are experimental and correlational investigations. Experimental studies require that groups of learners be treated differently and the impact of the differing treatments on learning outcomes be measured. The conditions that you manipulate are termed independent variables; the results measured are dependent variables. The goal of experimental research is to discover what type of treatment will be likely to produce a given set of outcomes. Experimental research is predicated on the assumption that differences in teaching methods or other methods of treating children will produce differing outcomes. Studies of instructional methods are conducted using experimental designs.

Correlation research designs are based upon another set of assumptions and attempt to attribute differences in performance to preexistant characteristics of people. Many studies of cognitive and moral development described in this book (chapters one and four) are examples of correlational designs. These types of investigations do not allow for the determination of causal relationships; the presence of a correlational relationship merely indicates that two sets of characteristics occur with a degree of regularity and are related.

Results of correlational studies are reported in the form of *correlation-coefficients*. These coefficients vary between -1.00 and +1.00 and indicate the degree of relationship that is found between two measures. Coefficients between .70 and .99 show that two variables are highly related. Those between .00 and .30 show that two variables are unrelated. Between .30 and .70 the relationship ranges from low to moderate. A positive relationship is indicated by a positive number, sometimes prefaced with a plus (+). A negative relationship is indicated by a number prefaced with a minus (−).

Both positive and negative correlation coefficients demonstrate relationships. For example, chronological age and ability to form concepts are correlated positively (as age increases, the ability increases), but chronological age and dependence upon parental support are correlated negatively (as age increases, parental support becomes less likely). High relationships between actions and age exist in both examples even though the direction of relationship is reversed.

To illustrate correlational research in a religious education context, the teachers in a preschool department might have noticed there are variations in the amount of time that children spend in free play and in group activities. Some of the teachers believe this is related to age. A study was designed that will measure time on tasks as measured in seconds, compared to the child's age in months. A person other than the teacher will be in the room to serve as an observer. From that data, the relationship between age and attention span could be calculated and expressed as a correlation coefficient.

In contrast, experimental research in religious education would be quite different. For example, the goal of a study unit might be to discover the relationship between teaching methods and learning outcomes in a lesson about biblical families. The children in a kindergarten class were randomly assigned to one of two groups. Each was given the same instruction except that one group was told a story each week by the teacher and the other was shown a professionally produced videotape of the story each week. Criterion measures were administered during each session and at the end of the four week unit. These were given to determine the relationship between method of teaching and learning outcomes.

Overview of Statistical Tests

Below you will find a summary of several statistical tests used to determine if the findings of research are significantly different from a standard or another set of results.

STATISTICAL TESTS	PURPOSES/USES
Students t test	A test to determine if the means or averages of two groups differ beyond what would be expected from random variation.
Repeated measures student t test	A test to determine if the performances of one group of people significantly differs if the group is measured at two points in time, usually prior to instruction and after instruction.
Analysis of variance (F test)	A test to determine if the performances of individuals in several treatment groups differ. This test is used in situations where an experimenter is studying the performance of students that receive several instructional treatments.
Correlation (r test)	A test to determine if there is a relationship between performance and another measurement of the same group of individuals. Usually used to assess the relationship between two sets of characteristics of the same group of people.

Chi-square (χ^2)	A statistical test to determine if the performance of people placed into categories differs beyond that which would be expected by random variation. This is usually used when individuals are separated into high and low groups of performance, and high and low groups on other characteristics, to determine if the individuals are different in the way they fall into the four groups.

Statistical tests are used in all cases to determine if differences between and among groups of people, or differences and characteristics of the same group of people, are beyond those that one would expect by random variation. The *level of significance* (usually designated "P") is used to designate the probability that the differences that are measured would be found by chance alone. If $P < .05$, that indicates that less than 5% of the time one would expect these differences by chance alone. Thus one can be more certain if $P < .01$ than if $P < .05$, since the former indicates that less than 1% of the time the results would be due to random error. The goal of using statistical levels of significance is assuring that the observed differences are ones that can be trusted to be found in new situations and are not just due to random and unexplainable variations in the particular study being conducted. An experimenter or instructor must always be cautious of reporting observed results that appear to be significant differences but do not prove to be significant when subjected to statistical analysis.

Qualitative Research

Experimental and correlational research methods are sometimes described as "quantitative" because they involve tabulating and manipulating numbers to determine the results. In contrast to these methods is "qualitative" research which generally relies upon description rather than numbers. The most familiar example of qualitative research is ethnography, characteristically used in anthropological fieldwork. The semi-clinical interview technique used by Piaget is also an example of qualitative methodology (see Elkind, 1964, for details on how to use Piaget's approach in the study of children's religion). In recent years educational research has employed qualitative methods of study in a variety of areas.

Cook and Reichardt (1979) have summarized the generally accepted ways in which qualitative and quantitative approaches differ:

QUALITATIVE	QUANTITATIVE
phenomenological	positivistic
inductive	hypothetico-deductive

holistic	particularistic
subjective (insider oriented)	objective (outsider oriented)
focus on process	focus on outcome
anthropological world view	natural science worldview
uncontrolled	controlled
understanding behavior from actor's reference	facts and causes sought
dynamic reality assumed	static reality assumed
discovery oriented	verification oriented
explanatory	confirmatory

However, Cook and Reichardt are careful to note that this may be a false dichotomy, since there can often be overlap in concerns and characteristics. It is possible and sometimes beneficial to combine the two approaches.

One of the more concise outlines of the qualitative approach is Lofland and Lofland (1984). They describe three components to qualitative research: 1) *gathering* data, which refers to writing detailed descriptions through observation, interviews, and other methods, 2) *focusing* the data, including the development of coding units from the data which are used to organize and clarify the descriptions, and 3) *analyzing* the data by comparing, contrasting, and otherwise relating the units in the form of a summary or report.

Lofland and Lofland not only give a concise summary of qualitative methods but also provide many helpful guidelines for conducting any kind of research, such as the influence of the researcher's role upon the findings and how to gain access to closed settings. More complete summaries of how to use qualitative methodology in educational contexts can be found in Bogdan and Biklin (1982) and Goetz and LeCompte (1984).

An example of how qualitative research could be used in preschool religious education is to systematically examine overt and latent functions of Sunday school. First the researcher would need to state his or her assumptions about this area so that the researcher's eventual conclusion can be compared with his or her opinion at the beginning of the study. Then the individual would begin examining a Sunday school chosen because of some particular characteristic. Careful notes would be taken of all that occurs in each class session, including incidental activities of the teacher and students. From the initial study the researcher might branch out to other classes in different churches to discover both similarities and divergences.

As the above researcher studies Sunday schools, categories of behavior (the coding units) will emerge from the observations. Overt behaviors such as teaching religious vocabulary, listening to stories, eating a snack, unanticipated actions, and requests for going to the bathroom are likely to be noted initially. Rather than emphasizing how often these occur, the researcher would concentrate on seeing how such behaviors relate to the activities of religious education. With time, categories of more latent activities are likely to surface, such as passive noninvolvement being rewarded while active involvement is punished, or custodial care tasks taking a priority over religious content. The study would be concluded by labeling and describing the categories that are most revealing, giving specific examples of those categories, and analyzing how such categories varied according to context.

Is Research Useful in Religious Education?

While James Michael Lee presents excellent arguments for social science being a foundation for religious education (Lee, 1985 and chapter seven of this handbook), Wilhoit (1986) maintains that research does not influence religious education as much as common sense, ideology, and theology. This is in part due to the distrust of social-science findings and in part to the limitations of the scientific method. These limitations include the high cost of research, the necessary slowness in validating principles of education, the lack of definitive answers on some issues, and the non-measurability of certain religious goals.

While cautioning that religious educators should avoid an idolizing of scientific research, Wilhoit nevertheless states that research can play a crucial role in religious education. He offers six suggestions for utilizing research: 1) do not prooftext research to prove one's own viewpoint, 2) formulate theories in concrete terms so they can be made verifiable, 3) use primary rather than secondary sources of research, 4) acknowledge one's values and presuppositions, 5) realize the commonality between theological and scientific truth ("all truth is God's truth"), and 6) become a lay "scientist" in the sense of observing contexts and effects carefully; the precision of controlled laboratory research is not always required to obtain useful information.

In a similar vein, psychologist Mary VanLeeuwen (1982) has seriously questioned the natural science basis for research in the social sciences. In her opinion, the techniques developed for the "hard sciences," such as physics and chemistry, may not always be appropriate for the social sciences. Are positivistic assumptions appropriate to the study of human behavior? VanLeeuwen believes that such an approach tends to overlook the distinctives of human behavior, including the wholeness and unity of the person as opposed to the particularism so often found in social-science research. She also emphasizes human "reflexivity" as a key concern in research: the influence that knowing research is occurring has upon the behavior of subjects.

While not eliminating the predominant approach to the study of the social sciences, VanLeeuwen recommends a new paradigm that begins with Christian presuppositions and a more humanized approach to research. She particularly calls for the use of qualitative research methodologies as a necessary complement to other methods of research.

Both Wilhoit and VanLeeuwen include a place for standard social-science research in addition to other approaches. Likewise, research conducted by religious educators may prove useful even though it may fall short of the strict standards of the natural sciences, (Engel, 1977, and Gibbs, 1988). It is worthwhile to consider employing other research paradigms, including that of qualitative methodology.

CONCLUSION

The evaluation and research concepts presented in this chapter are designed to help us sharpen skills and become more systematic in assessing strengths and weaknesses in programs and activities. Only through such assessment can we build upon our strengths and turn our weaknesses into strong points. Through it all we must keep in sight that our goal is to provide learning environments for young children that will allow and encourage them to grow and flourish.

Elkind (1970), in his foundational chapter, underscored the importance of religious education, evaluation, and research for preschoolers. His words are an excellent conclusion to the present chapter as well as this entire handbook:

> We need to reexamine our approach to preschool religious instruction. . . . Perhaps waiting until the child is "ready" for religious instruction misses an opportunity for more adequate preparation during the preschool period. This is not, after all, a new idea. Both Froebel and Montessori have stressed the importance of religious preparation in the preschool child. The most adequate means for such instruction, its quantity and extent, needs to be studied systematically; but it certainly is possible that beginning religious instruction in early childhood would greatly facilitate the whole later course of religious growth. One reason that religious families routinely produce religious children is probably the fact that the child is exposed to a religious orientation and to religious practices at an early age. Indeed, it could well be that research and evaluation of religious instruction during early childhood is the most imperative need in religious instruction today.

REFERENCES

Barber, L. W. (1981). *The religious education of preschool children.* Birmingham, AL: Religious Education Press.

Bogdan, R. C., & Biklen, S. K. (1982). *Qualitative research for education.* Boston: Allyn and Bacon.

Brookfield, S. D. (1986). *Understanding and facilitating adult learning.* San Francisco: Jossey-Bass Publishing.

Cook, T. D., & Reichardt, C. S. (1979). Beyond qualitative *versus* quantitative methods. In *Qualitative and quantitative methods in evaluation research.* Beverly Hills, CA: Sage.

Elkind, D. (1964). Piaget's semi-clinical interview and the study of spontaneous religion. *Journal for the Scientific Study of Religion, 4,* 40-47.

Elkind, D. (1970). Research and evaluation in teaching religion. In J.M. Lee & P. C. Rooney, *Toward a future for religious education.* Dayton, OH: Pflaum Press.

Engel, J. (1977). *How can I get them to listen?* Grand Rapids, MI: Zondervan.

Gibbs, E. S. (1988). Practical implications of basic research in Christian education. *Christian Education Journal, 8,* 41-47.

Goetz, J. P., & LeCompte, M. D. (1984). *Ethnography and qualitative design in educational research.* Orlando, FL: Academic Press.

Heck, G., & Shelly, M. (1979). *How children learn.* Elgin, IL: David C. Cook Publishing.

Hinkle, D. E., Wiersma, W., & Jurs, S. G. (1979). *Applied statistics for the behavioral sciences.* Boston: Houghton Mifflin Company.

Lee, J. M. (1985). *The content of religious instruction.* Birmingham, AL: Religious Education Press.

Lofland, J., & Lofland, L. H. (1984). *Analyzing social settings: A guide to qualitative observation and analysis* (2nd ed.). Belmont, CA: Wadsworth Publishing Company.

Mager, R. F. (1962). *Preparing instructional objectives.* Belmont, CA: Fearon Publishers.

Ratcliff, D. (1982). Behavioral psychology in the Sunday school classroom. *Journal of the American Scientific Affiliation,* March.

VanLeeuwen, M. S. (1982). *The sorcerer's apprentice: A Christian looks at the changing face of psychology.* Downers Grove, IL: Intervarsity Press.

Wilhoit, J. (1986). *Christian education and the search for meaning.* Grand Rapids, MI: Baker.

Contributors

HENRY (KEN) P. BROCKENBROUGH has a Bachelor's degree in Special Education and Early Childhood as well as a Masters degree in Special Education, both from the University of North Carolina. A United Methodist, he is completing a Ph.D. in the Graduate Institute of Liberal Arts at Emory University and is a graduate assistant at the Center for Faith Development at Emory.

MARY ANNE FOWLKES is currently Professor of Childhood Education at the Presbyterian School of Christian Education in Richmond, Virginia. Previously she taught at the University of Louisville in the Early and Middle Childhood Education Department. Dr. Fowlkes has completed an undergraduate degree in sociology, an M.R.E. in Religious Education at Union Theological Seminary as well as a Ph.D. in early childhood education at Emory University. She has written several book chapters and articles for professional journals and authored church curriculum for kindergartners. Dr. Fowlkes primary interest is play and early social development.

JEAN-MARIE JASPARD is Head of the Department of Religious Psychology at the Universite Catholique de Louvain in Belgium. He authored a chapter titled "The Relation to God and the Moral Development of the Young Child" in the 1980 book *Toward Moral and Religious Maturity.*

JAMES MICHAEL LEE is Professor of Education at the University of Alabama at Birmingham and is also the publisher of the Religious Education Press. He completed his doctoral work at Columbia University. Dr. Lee is perhaps best known for his massive and scholarly trilogy on religious instruction, which outlines a macrotheory embracing the social-science approach as the foundation for religious education.

CLAITY P. MASSEY is Assistant Professor of Early Childhood Education, teaching at both campuses of Houghton College in New York. She has completed an M.Ed. degree at the University of North Carolina (Greensboro) and a Ph.D. at SUNY in Buffalo, both in early childhood education. She has made presentations at a number of conferences related to young children and is on the kindergarten and preschool committees for the Aldersgate Publications Association, an affiliation of nine Wesleyan-oriented denominations. Dr. Massey is also a member of the Children's Review/Preview Committee for the Wesleyan denomination.

ROMNEY M. MOSELEY is Associate Professor of Theology and Human Development and Acting Associate Dean of Candler School of Theology, Emory University. He was formerly the Associate Director of James Fowler's Center for Faith Development at Emory. An Episcopal priest, he possesses an undergraduate degree from Boston University and a Ph.D. from Harvard University. Dr. Moseley supervised a recent project involving the research of faith development with preschoolers.

DONALD RATCLIFF is Assistant Professor of Psychology and Sociology at Toccoa Falls College in Georgia. He holds an undergraduate degree from Spring Arbor College, a Masters from Michigan State University, and a Specialist in Education from the University of Georgia. He has published a number of articles in professional journals as well as several books on psychology and sociology and has conducted research on using play in preschool religious education.

PATSY SKEEN is an Associate Professor at the University of Georgia in the Department of Child and Family Development. She possesses an Ed.D. from the University of Georgia in Early Childhood Education, as well as a Masters from the University of Tennessee and a Bachelors from Radford College. Previously she held the position of Undergraduate Curriculum Coordinator in her department at UGA and has received a large number of awards and honors for her academic accomplishments and teaching ability. Her many publications include three college textbooks related to child development.

DAVID STARKS is the Director of the Office of Educational Resources in the School of Dentistry at the University of Michigan. He is Director of Counseling and an Associate Professor of Dentistry and Education and a Research Scientist with the Center for Research on Learning and Teaching at that university. He did his undergraduate work at Wheaton College in history and received a M.A. from Northern Illinois University and a Ph.D. from Purdue University, both in psychology. He has authored numerous publications and papers on topics related to teaching and learning. Dr. Starks has also directed a number of research and development projects supported by federal agencies and foundations.

KALEVI TAMMINEN is Professor of Religious Education at the

University of Helsinki in Finland. He holds both Ph.D. and Th.D. degrees. His research work has concerned the history of curricula in religious education, moral development, and the didactics of religious education. He has published a large number of books and journal articles and is the president of the Church Education Center (Lutheran) in Finland.

E. PAUL TORRANCE is considered one of the world's foremost authorities on creativity in children, perhaps best known for his Torrance Tests of Creative Thinking. He possesses an A.B. from Mercer University, an M.A. from the University of Minnesota, and a Ph.D. from the University of Michigan. While in retirement he continues as an advisor for the Torrance Center for Creative Studies at the University of Georgia and remains active in writing and holding conferences. He and his wife, Pansy, worked for several years as teachers of four- and five-year-olds in children's worship and day care contexts. He also developed a preschool curriculum for the Southern Baptist Convention titled "Ideas About God." The curriculum was extensively field tested, with very positive results. Torrance has published a number of books on creativity as well as innumerable journal articles.

J. PANSY TORRANCE possesses an A.B. and M.Ed. degrees from the University of Minnesota. She serves as an advisor for the Torrance Center for Creative Studies. She has specialized in psychiatric nursing, nursing education, and creative problem solving. She has coauthored several major books on creativity with her husband, Dr. E. Paul Torrance.

RENZO VIANELLO is Associate Professor of Developmental Psychology at the University of Padova in Italy. Born in Venice, Vianello has a degree in pedagogy and a Ph.D. in psychology. His research has primarily concentrated upon children's concepts of religion, death, magic, and handicapped children. He is the national chairman of the CNIS, an organization concerned with teaching the handicapped, and also chairs a center concerned with research of the handicapped at his university. He has published a number of books and journal articles on children's religious concepts.

CHARLOTTE WALLINGA is Assistant Professor of Child and Family Development at the University of Georgia. She is also the Child Life Coordinator at UGA. Dr. Wallinga holds B.S. and M.S. degrees in child development as well as a Ph.D. in counseling education, all from Iowa State University. She has presented a large number of papers at national and international education and family conferences, and has published many articles in scholarly journals. The recipient of four Headstart research grants, she has also received numerous awards and honors for academic accomplishments and teaching.

INDEX OF NAMES

INDEX OF SUBJECTS